# English 3–11

In line with the Primary National Strategy, this core introductory textbook provides comprehensive, up-to-date and, most importantly, *creative* guidance on teaching English in the early years and primary classroom. It includes links to the renewed Framework for Literacy and Mathematics and Communication, Language and Literacy in the Early Years Foundation Stage. Covering all of the key curriculum areas in manageable and accessible chapters, *English 3–11* contains numerous activities and practical advice which will help motivate and support teachers to achieve enjoyment, progression, breadth and balance in their teaching of effective and creative English. Key topics covered include:

- the effective teaching of early reading, including the implications of the Rose Review;
- assessment for learning;
- co-operative learning;
- multi-modal texts;
- ICT and English.

By combining subject knowledge with effective pedagogical approaches to teaching English, this book is an essential and thought-provoking one-stop resource for all busy trainee and practising teachers, encouraging reflection and debate on current teaching methods.

**David Waugh** is Head of the Centre for Educational Studies at the University of Hull and a former deputy headteacher.
**Wendy Jolliffe** is Programme Director of BA (Hons) Early Education and Care and BA (Hons) Learning and Teaching (Primary Teaching) at the University of Hull and is a former deputy headteacher.

Also available

**History 3–11**
**A guide for teachers**
Hilary Cooper
978–1–84312–459–7 Pbk

**Geography 3–11**
**A guide for teachers**
Hilary Cooper, Simon Asquith and Chris Rowley
978–1–84312–421–4 Pbk

**Physical Education and Development 3–11**
**A guide for teachers**
Jonathan Doherty and Peter Brennan
978–1–84312–456–6 Pbk

**Science 5–11**
**A guide for teachers**
Alan Howe, Dan Davies, Kendra McMahon, Lee Towler and Tonie Scott
978–1–84312–319–4 Pbk

**Modern Foreign Languages 5–11**
**A guide for teachers**
Jane Jones and Simon Coffey
978–1–84312–390–3 Pbk

# English 3–11

A guide for teachers

David Waugh and Wendy Jolliffe

Routledge
Taylor & Francis Group

LONDON AND NEW YORK

First published 2008
by Routledge
2 Park Square, Milton Park, Abingdon, Oxon, OX14 4RN

Simultaneously published in the USA and Canada
by Routledge
270 Madison Avenue, New York, NY 10016

*Routledge is an imprint of the Taylor & Francis Group, an informa business*

© 2008 David Waugh and Wendy Jolliffe

Typeset in Palatino by BC Typesetting Ltd, Bristol
Printed and bound in Great Britain by
TJ International, Padstow, Cornwall

*British Library Cataloguing in Publication Data*
A catalogue record for this book is available from the British Library

*Library of Congress Cataloging in Publication Data*
A catalog record for this book has been requested

ISBN 10: 1–84312–443–2
ISBN 13: 978–1–84312–443–6

# Contents

# Acknowledgements

The authors would like to thank the following for their contributions to this book:

Claire Head for contributing Chapter 10, 'Learning and teaching in a multilingual classroom'.
Claire is PGCE Early Years Programme Director and a lecturer in Primary English at the Institute for Learning, University of Hull.

Richard English for contributing Chapter 13, 'Using ICT to enhance the teaching of English'.
Richard is Programme Director of the Primary PGCE at the Institute for Learning, University of Hull.

Claire Hostick, a former pupil of David Waugh at Mount Pleasant Church of England Junior School, Market Weighton, for her kind permission to use samples of her writing 'The Fog'.

# Introduction

This book is written at a time when the Primary National Strategy is succeeding the National Literacy Framework, which, in turn, came to be seen by some schools as replacing the National Curriculum for English, although the latter has remained in place throughout.

Since 1990, when the National Curriculum for English was first published, it too has been rewritten and revised. Those with long memories will recall the publication of *A Language for Life* (The Bullock Report) in 1975 and the impact this had upon teaching English in primary schools, as well as reflecting upon various debates about the teaching of reading (real books, reading schemes, phonics etc.).

Teaching English for children aged 3–11 is a challenge, not only because English and an ability to read, write and speak is central to success across the curriculum, but also because, since English is such a central part of the curriculum, it is a matter for constant debate. And when this debate is informed by concerns about standards of literacy, politicians become particularly interested and seek ways to address perceived problems. Hence, the repeated modifications to the English curriculum and the regular changes in emphasis on the way in which teachers are expected to teach.

This book should be read in the context of the changes described above. It is intended to provide guidance on how to teach the curriculum as it is currently constituted, but we hope that it will also promote discussion and reflection upon practice. Anyone entering the teaching profession in the twenty-first century needs to be adaptable and flexible enough to incorporate change and to adapt teaching when the curriculum is revised. Teachers also need to be able to understand why changes come about and to ensure that they are able to justify their methods to parents and pupils, as well as to themselves. We hope that this book will provide a starting point for such reflection and that many of the activities within it will encourage teachers to think about their practice.

In Chapter 1, the pedagogy of teaching English is discussed, with key elements of knowledge, decision-making and teachers' actions explored. Chapter 2 takes the pedagological theme further by looking at classroom management, and discussing practical strategies for improving this. One of the most welcome changes to English teaching in recent years has been a return to focusing on creativity and enjoyment, and this theme is the subject of Chapter 3.

In Chapter 4, we examine communication in the early years, discussing the role of play, literacy at home and printed texts in the environment, as well as looking at early reading and writing and the development of phonological awareness. Chapter 5 examines the knowledge about language which teachers need to acquire if they are to deliver the curriculum successfully, and provides practical ideas for classroom activities to develop children's linguistic understanding.

Teachers have welcomed the higher profile given to speaking and listening in the Primary National Strategy and Chapter 6 explores the importance of developing and managing talk, and the value of drama and cooperative learning strategies. Chapter 7 focuses on the teaching and learning of reading and examines different approaches, while offering practical advice on teaching phonics and using shared and guided reading effectively.

Chapter 8, 'Fiction and poetry', not only discusses the value of literature in the classroom, but also provides examples of stories and poems which can be used both to entertain and to engage children's interest in the genres. Chapter 9 looks at non-fiction texts and at strategies for developing children's understanding of information texts.

In Chapter 10 there is a particular focus on children who have English as an Additional Language (EAL), with the strategies designed to support them having wider implications for the ways in which we help others who face the challenge of developing language and literacy skills.

The development of children's writing is the theme of Chapter 11, and here again there are many practical ideas for work in the classroom, as well as a discussion about positive approaches to writing and the development of independent writing. Spelling and strategies for learning to spell in a language which is often irregular and inconsistent phonically are the focus of Chapter 12, and there are opportunities for readers to test their own spelling understanding and develop their own spelling abilities.

Chapter 13 explores the use of information and communications technology (ICT) in teaching and learning in English, offering advice on resources and tips for how to make the most of what is available. In Chapter 14, we look at planning for English and, in particular, at planning using the renewed Primary Framework for Literacy. Chapter 15 on assessment for learning complements Chapter 14 in that it explores building assessment into curriculum planning, as well as the characteristics of assessment for learning, and involving pupils in the assessment process. It also discusses the assessment of speaking and listening, reading, and writing.

At the beginning of each chapter we set out the chapter's purpose, and we summarise key points at the end. Every chapter has one or more activities designed to encourage discussion and reflection, and you can do these independently, but you may also like to do them cooperatively with fellow students and professionals.

We hope that when you read this book you will find it thought-provoking as well as practical, and that it will lead you to reflect upon your own practice and discuss the value of different approaches to teaching English from 3 to 11.

# 1 The pedagogy of teaching English in the primary school

'This could be heaven or this could be hell'
The Eagles, *Hotel California*

## Purpose of this chapter

This chapter aims to:

- Look at the nature of pedagogy and examine what the term means.
- Explore the knowledge which teachers need to teach effectively.
- Look at teachers' decision-making and how this is informed by their knowledge.
- Examine how teachers' actions are influenced by their knowledge and by the decisions they make.
- Look at the qualities needed to teach English effectively in the primary school.

## What is pedagogy?

Pedagogy is defined by the Oxford Dictionary as 'the science of teaching'. Alexander (2000: 540) states: 'Pedagogy encompasses the performance of teaching together with the theories, beliefs, policies and controversies that inform and shape it.' However, pedagogy is not a term used by many teachers. Hayes (2000) discusses those experienced teachers who maintain that teaching is a practical activity and that the theoretical study of teaching in higher education is irrelevant once one enters the classroom. However, he counters that

> those who are charged with the difficult and demanding task of educating our children and young people must be clear about what they are doing, why they are doing it, and how they will know if it is successful.
>
> (Hayes 2000: 20)

To be effective as a teacher one needs to think about what one does and why. In this chapter, we will use the three important elements identified by Kyriacou (1991: 5) to focus discussion:

- *Knowledge:* comprising the teacher's knowledge about the subject, pupils, curriculum, teaching methods, the influence on teaching and learning of other factors, and knowledge about one's own teaching skills.
- *Decision-making:* comprising the thinking and decision-making which occurs before, during and after a lesson, concerning how best to achieve the educational outcomes intended.

- *Action:* comprising the overt behaviour by teachers undertaken to foster pupil learning.

In this chapter we see how the three key skills apply generally and then specifically in the teaching of English. We will see that knowledge is essential if decision-making is to be informed and effective, and that decisions that teachers make affect the actions they take and in turn affect the ways in which children learn.

## Knowledge needed by teachers

In this section we will look at some of the different types of knowledge teachers need to enable them to teach effectively.

### Knowledge of the curriculum

Fox (2005) uses the term *pedagogical content* knowledge to represent 'subject matter knowledge centred on classroom tasks, activities and explanations' and states that it includes knowledge of the following:

- Representation of facts, concepts and methods in the subject, using metaphors and analogies to connect with more general knowledge.
- Tasks that are productive for learning, including the relevant resources, their organization, and health and safety issues.
- Examples of key ideas, rules and problems which link the particular to the general and thus promote understanding.
- Students and their existing levels of understanding and skill in the subject, including common misconceptions and errors.
- How understanding in the subject typically advances from one level to another.
- Productive locations for out-of-school work.
- Knowledge of research that supports teaching and learning in the subject.

(Fox 2005: 257)

It is important to realise that pedagogical content knowledge is constantly changing, just as the pupils we teach change each year, leading effective and reflective teachers constantly to review their practice.

The curriculum for English in English schools has gone through several incarnations since the inception of the National Curriculum for English in 1990 (Department of Education and Science (DES) 1990). While there are many common features, there have also been changes of emphasis which have demanded that teachers examine their own subject knowledge before planning schemes of work for their pupils. For example, an increasing emphasis in government documents upon the teaching of phonics has culminated in the Primary National Strategy placing the teaching of synthetic phonics at the heart of the teaching of reading (Department for Education and Skills (DfES) 2006b). While the Primary Strategy, like the National Literacy Strategy which preceded it, is not statutory and is therefore not a compulsory part of the primary school curriculum, it would be a brave school which ignored it without being certain that an inspection by Ofsted (Office for Standards in Education, Children's Services and Skills) would not reveal any weaknesses in literacy teaching and learning which could be attributed to a school's independent approach.

The teaching of phonics is discussed in detail in Chapter 7, and so the mechanics will not be explored in depth here. However, as a teacher you need to ensure that you understand the terminology relating to phonics teaching and that you are able to teach children how to use phonic knowledge to decode unfamiliar words. Remember that not all experienced teachers received adequate training in the teaching of phonics, particularly before 1990 when some training courses virtually ignored phonics in favour of less structured approaches to reading. It is by no means certain, therefore, that you will see good practice in your school, and you may find that you have a more sophisticated understanding of phonics than some of the teachers with whom you work. For a basic knowledge of phonics teaching and learning see Jolliffe (2006a).

Another aspect of the curriculum which may challenge teachers is the growing emphasis on ICT, with the latest Primary Strategy including many activities related to film and computers, interactive whiteboards, children's writing and so on (see Chapter 13 on using ICT and English).

The levels of subject knowledge required to teach children about language are now considerably greater than many of us acquired during our secondary schooling, and even during teacher training. Chapter 5 on 'Knowledge about language' explores ways of teaching about language through meaningful activities, but many people may initially be confused by much of the terminology which appears there and in the Primary Strategy. Many students arrive at initial teacher education courses thinking that mathematics and science will be the most challenging subjects but quickly discover that English, a subject they had previously felt confident about (after all they could read, write, speak and listen), is their greatest weakness. Among student teachers' main concerns are:

- understanding the parts of speech and their functions
- understanding punctuation, especially possessive apostrophes
- understanding linguistic terminology
- understanding how to teach reading.

Fortunately, each of these areas can be taught and learned so that the overwhelming majority of primary teachers begin their first job quite confident about them. However, with several other subjects to understand, as well as class management (the major concern of most trainees), training and induction year programmes have become increasingly intensive. One would hope that by the time the children who were educated through the Literacy and Primary Strategies reach higher education, teacher trainers will need to give far less attention to explaining the first three items in the bullet list, which, on the whole, remain constant. As for the fourth item, teaching reading, this highly important part of the curriculum is a matter for constant debate and frequent changes of emphasis. Even those teachers described by Hayes (2000), who argue that teaching is a purely practical profession, must find out about the latest theories on reading and consider adapting their teaching accordingly, if only because a failure to do so might be damaging if Ofsted comes calling.

### Knowledge of pupils

Knowledge for the teacher is not restricted to the curriculum. It is vital that you know and understand your pupils and are able to differentiate your teaching to meet their needs. Also you should assess pupils' progress in informal, semi-structured and formal ways, not only because teachers need to plan for progression, but also because children, parents and colleagues will want to know how the children are progressing too. Information about children can be acquired from other teachers, but must be kept up to date and modified as children progress.

Then there are the special needs of children, which must be identified and acted upon. Good teachers will know a range of strategies for supporting pupils, and will regularly seek professional development to increase their understanding of the needs of children with English as an Additional Language (EAL), various physical disabilities, and learning difficulties such as dyslexia and dyspraxia. Where children in their classes receive external learning support, teachers will ensure that they know what the children do on these occasions and how it may be linked to how they work with the children in class.

Teachers also need to be aware of children's changing interests and that by sometimes relating teaching and learning to children's hobbies and interests, teachers may be able to engage them, hold their attention, and provide stimuli for discussion.

### Knowledge of factors which affect teaching and learning

The classroom environment will impinge upon the way in which teachers teach and children learn, and this will be discussed in relation to language in the section on decision-making. However, besides understanding the features of a language-friendly classroom, teachers also need to be aware of the impact the weather, ventilation and temperature in the classroom can have. Experienced teachers tend to be alert to the effects of the physical environment and even anticipate these and modify their teaching accordingly, especially on windy days (notorious for affecting pupil behaviour!) and days when children are kept inside all day due to bad weather. Attempting a lesson which requires lengthy periods of sitting still when children have been inactive can be very challenging, and teachers often modify tasks to make them more active and vigorous in such circumstances, perhaps using drama or debate.

### Knowledge of how to teach the curriculum

Besides understanding the content of the curriculum and the needs of their pupils, and the environmental factors which may affect their learning, teachers need to be aware of current thinking on how to teach the curriculum. We will explore this further, but at this stage we will focus on some of the knowledge teachers need to acquire. For example, it is important to keep up to date on the latest government initiatives and to be aware of key pieces of educational research. While most teachers do not have time to read academic journals and government documents, they can find concise reports and reviews in the *Times Educational Supplement* on Friday and *Guardian Education* on Tuesday. Without an understanding of what is actually being said, teachers are as susceptible as the rest of the population to tabloid press misinterpretations and may find it difficult to justify their teaching methods when questioned by parents.

### Knowledge of one's own teaching skills

Central to professional development is self-knowledge and an ability to reflect upon one's teaching and pupils' learning. Reflection and self-evaluation are key elements of teaching placements during initial teacher training programmes, with trainees usually having to write lesson evaluations or reflective diaries. Teachers are helped to reflect during training by being frequently observed and often receiving written and oral feedback, with strengths and weaknesses highlighted and targets being set.

While teaching observation is now a part of teachers' professional development, it is seldom as intense or as frequent as during training. Thus, teachers who wish to develop their teaching skills need to invite constructive criticism from respected colleagues on their teaching style, mannerisms, resources used, classroom organisa-tion and class management. This interaction should not be something to fear, but should form part of a continuing professional dialogue.

---

**Activity: Reflecting on your teaching of English**

- What do you do well?
- What could you do better?
- What do you really struggle with?
- What could you do to improve your teaching of English?

---

The way in which your knowledge affects your teaching can be compared with the way in which professional snooker players play a shot. In deciding which ball to aim for, snooker players draw upon past experience of the consequences of similar shots, an understanding of angles and where the balls are likely to end up after the shot, as well as considering the bigger picture and the next shots they will play. They also use prior knowledge to determine how to strike the ball to give it back spin or power. Experienced snooker stars make many of these decisions almost sub-consciously because their knowledge base is so great that they can sum up their next move very quickly. Skilled teachers, too, often act instinctively, making hundreds of decisions every day about resources to use, ways of conveying information, class-room organisation, responses to children's questions, and questions to ask. Most of these decisions will be made quickly and will be based upon knowledge and experience. At other times, teachers have the luxury of being able to plan indepen-dently or with colleagues, reflect upon past lessons, and observe how others work. Good teachers tend to make an increasingly high percentage of their decisions instinctively, but still take time to reflect and plan, just as good snooker players build up their knowledge by practising.

In the next section we will look at decision-making, focusing in particular upon decisions which teachers can make about the environment in which they and their pupils work.

## Decision-making

Wragg (1997: 94) stated that 'Decisions about how pupils should learn and how teachers should teach need to reflect both purpose and context.'

He went on to illustrate this point with examples:

> When teachers are telling a story to a class of 5-year-olds, it is usually best sense to read the story to the whole class, rather than individually to each of 30 or more children. By contrast, if 30 people aged from 17 to 70 want to learn to drive, then they will expect individual practice in actually driving a car, not a mass lecture on the function of the clutch. Anyone wanting to sing in a quartet will need three like-minded people. Matching what is desirable to what is feasible is part of the art of teaching effectively.
>
> (Wragg 1997: 94)

In exploring the kinds of decision-making which teachers of English engage in, we will look first at the nature of the classroom and then at planning for teaching, before examining ways in which teachers might reflect upon their teaching in order to improve and develop it.

### Creating a classroom environment for language

At the heart of good English teaching is the environment in which teaching and learning takes place. Some classrooms are rich in language and opportunities for language. Not only are walls redolent with brightly coloured displays, including pictures and objects for children to discuss, but also they are adorned with pieces of text, lists of useful words, and examples of children's writing which can be read by the class and by visitors. There may, especially for younger children, be an area in which role-play activities are focused on, say, a shop, café, house or train. There will be language games, newspapers, books, timetables and advertisements, as well as, perhaps, league tables, interesting lists, and facts about topics which interest children.

As children move through the school, they will find that the language stimuli in their classrooms change and increasingly cater for their different needs and interests. It is part of the teachers' decision-making process to ensure that they create an appropriately stimulating environment for their pupils, which conveys the idea that language, both written and spoken, is valuable and to be celebrated.

Many of the children we teach will come from clean, tidy, well-decorated homes in which there are many stimulating things with which to play. They may have video recorders, computers, music systems, iPods, DVDs and electronic games. By contrast, the classroom can appear dull and uninviting. However, the provision of an attractive and linguistically stimulating classroom does not necessarily involve the inclusion of large amounts of sophisticated electrical equipment. Nevertheless, there are times when equipment such as an interactive whiteboard can provide almost instant access to a wealth of material which could never be so readily avail-able using printed texts.

The language-friendly classroom will include a range of stimuli both written and aural and the presence of tactile displays which children are encouraged to discuss. It will also provide opportunities for children to use language and explore its possi-bilities within a secure setting. In Key Stage 1 classrooms, in particular, the presence of structured contexts for play may lead to variations on the traditional home corner. Ross (1992) suggested that such contexts should reflect some of the children's experiences outside school and asserted that children are aware of a wide range of environments and places, particularly through television, and that they will use these naturally in play. Ross (1992) suggested the following variations on the home corner, each of which may be created with a minimum of resources:

| *Shops* | *Transport* | *Health services* | *Workplaces* |
|---------|-------------|-------------------|--------------|
| supermarket | buses | surgery | bakery |
| shoe shop | station | hospital | café |
| clothes shop | trains | veterinary surgery | building site |
| post office | airport | optician | |

To this list might be added pizza restaurants, fast food shops, cars, lorries, dental surgeries, offices and factories. Within these, children might be presented with different scenarios and invited to adopt the roles of a variety of people. There might also be opportunities for reading and writing, for example using menus in a restaurant and taking customers' orders, or making tickets, writing prescriptions or recipes.

The organisation of the furniture in a classroom can affect the possibilities for language development. Tann (1991) maintained that, although in many classrooms children are seated in groups around a table or cluster of desks, research had shown that 90 per cent of teachers never used collaborative group work. However, this figure may have changed since 1991, particularly as the Primary National Strategy (DfES 2006b), with its increased emphasis on speaking and listening, becomes embedded in schools. Seating arrangements in a classroom do affect communica-tion, even if this occurs in a way which the teacher does not intend. When children sit in groups, they have eye contact with all the others in the group, which may lead to greater interaction between them. Teachers who wish to reduce the level of talk in their classrooms often introduce alternative seating arrangements such as rows and horseshoes. These, too, may promote conversation, but this may be limited to pairs and trios (see McNamara and Waugh 1993). Teachers should consider the nature of the interaction which they wish to foster when arranging the furniture in their class-rooms, and be flexible in changing. Such decision-making may well involve seeking the views of classroom assistants and the children themselves.

Teachers need to decide how they want children to enter the classroom and what they will find when they get there. There may, for example, be written guidance on what the children should do, with instructions for the first task of the day written on the board. The drawers and cupboards may be labelled so that children can find things easily without constant reference to the teacher. This should not only develop reading skills, but also encourage independence and free the teacher to concentrate on teaching rather than managing resources.

The teacher in a language-friendly classroom will take on many roles and will make almost subconscious decisions about these. The teacher may act as a writer or reader to provide a *model* for pupils, may be an *audience* for their ideas and an *arbitrator* when disputes arise in discussions. The teacher may provide *stimuli* for language activities and *initiate* and *facilitate* their development. The teacher will also be a *source of information* and direct teaching of language skills as well as being an *assessor* and *recorder* of children's progress.

The language-friendly classroom is more than an attractively adorned room filled with words and literature. It is an interactive environment in which teachers play a leading role in fostering the development of pupils' language skills through extensive use of the resources which they provide and which they encourage the children to bring to school. It is also an environment in which teachers constantly evaluate and assess what is happening and make decisions about what will happen next.

---

**Activity: Examining a classroom's features**

Think about a classroom you have worked in or are currently working in and answer the questions below:

- Are books attractively displayed and changed regularly?
- Are instructions provided in writing as well as orally?
- Is extensive use made of labelling so that children can find things independently?
- Are children encouraged to share *ownership* of the classroom?
- Are displays of writing a regular feature?
- Are displays interactive?
- Are writing and reading areas provided?
- Are words discussed with the children regularly?
- Are children's interests taken into account when reading materials are selected?
- Is teaching style and teacher's role adapted to different circumstances?
- How are adults other than teachers involved?

---

## Planning and preparation

Chapter 14 on planning gives details of how to plan effectively for English, but a chapter on pedagogy would be incomplete without highlighting the need for careful preparation and planning, which takes into account:

- the abilities of the children
- the resources available
- the environment in which the lesson is to take place
- ways of extending the most able and engaging the less able children.

Planning should be based upon realistic goals which children can reasonably achieve and which they can identify and relate to. It should also be done in conjunction with colleagues teaching the same year groups where possible, and should involve teaching assistants, who have a key role to play in classrooms and whose expertise should be recognised and drawn upon.

One aspect of lesson planning which is often neglected by inexperienced teachers, who otherwise plan in great detail, is deciding how to introduce a lesson. A lesson's opening is crucial to children's attitudes to it, and it is vital that teachers show that they are enthusiastic about the lesson and that they share this enthusiasm with their pupils. Good lessons might begin with an activity, a DVD, a piece of music, a visual aid, or a reading from a text. They will also probably include:

- reference to previous lessons
- differentiated questioning to involve everyone
- use of children's prior knowledge
- sharing of learning objectives
- involvement of pupils.

## Actions

If our knowledge helps inform our decision-making, then both will determine how we teach and how we are perceived by our pupils, their parents and our colleagues. Before we look at teachers' actions in more detail, look at the activity.

---

**Activity: Remembering your own favourite teacher**

Think back to your own schooldays, either primary or secondary.

- Who was your favourite teacher?
- What qualities did this teacher have which you appreciated?
- Did you work better and learn more with this teacher than with others?

---

When asked similar questions at interviews for teacher training courses, candidates tend to refer to strictness but fairness, enthusiasm, sense of humour, and knowledge of pupils. Some talk of lively, outgoing teachers, while others mention quiet, calm ones who never raised their voices.

There is no recipe for the perfect teacher, but without enthusiasm for subjects and children taught, teachers are unlikely to be successful or remembered fondly. Teachers' actions profoundly affect children's perceptions of subjects and of learning. We will now turn to ways in which their knowledge, decision-making and actions can impact upon the teaching of English in the primary school.

## Qualities needed to teach English effectively

The Primary National Strategy cites three pedagogic approaches – *direct, inductive* and *exploratory* – and teachers will make decisions about which is appropriate when (DfES 2006b). Let us look at these approaches in the context of English.

### Direct

The direct approach is often used when the purpose is to acquire new skills. Typically, this is the mode employed in whole-class literacy work and includes shared reading and writing and teaching and learning about word and sentence level features. This might be followed by individual or group work in which children are able to demonstrate that they have acquired the skills and knowledge taught.

### Inductive

Inductive approaches are designed to develop a concept or process and involve the teacher setting up a structured activity which has directed steps. For example, they might be given a list of words and their plurals and be asked to work out a spelling rule for making words ending with *y* plural (see Chapter 12 on spelling).

### Exploratory

The exploratory approach enables children to consolidate or refine skills and understanding and might involve children in testing a hypothesis set up by the teacher. For example, 'Sentences cannot begin with *Because*'. Children could then look for examples in texts and attempt to write their own before drawing conclusions. Because children may arrive at misconceptions, teachers should complete such activities with a plenary session in which conclusions are shared.

The cooperative learning strategies discussed in Chapter 6 'Talking to learn', underpin a pedagogic approach which provides opportunities for children to interact and learn together. Such strategies are ideal for exploratory work, and can be linked to both direct and inductive approaches.

Teachers can draw upon a knowledge of different pedagogic strategies when teaching English, but what constitutes 'good literacy teaching'? Towards the end of this chapter an activity focuses on the things effective teachers of English do and invites you to consider the extent to which you possess these qualities. However, before looking at the activity we will examine the qualities of good literacy teaching identified in the Primary National Strategy (DfES 2006b: 19). The Primary National Strategy refers to lively, engaging teaching with 'a carefully planned blend of approaches' with children being 'challenged to think'. There will be both support for children and independence when necessary. Rather than arguing for a brisk pace as its predecessor the National Literacy Strategy did, the Primary National Strategy maintains that in good literacy teaching, 'the pitch and pace of the work is sensitive to the rate at which children learn'. The increased emphasis on speaking and listening is reflected in the assertion that 'the strong interdependence between speaking, listening, reading and writing should underpin planning and provision for learning' (DfES 2006b: 19).

The final paragraph is worth quoting verbatim since it neatly sums up the themes which run through this chapter:

> Leading children's learning requires a broad repertoire of teaching and organisational approaches. There are lessons where the emphasis is on techniques and the teaching is quite directive: there are lessons where the directing is less evident and teachers use carefully chosen activities and well-directed questioning. Good literacy teaching requires a good knowledge of the subject; an understanding of the progression in the curriculum being taught and recognition that some teaching approaches are better suited to promote particular learning and outcomes.
>
> (DfES 2006b: 19)

In addition, we would argue that good teachers see a bigger picture – they make links between aspects of lessons (see Medwell et al., 1998) and they see teaching and learning in a wider context, including across the curriculum as well as within a subject. At the level of a literacy lesson this means making clear links between text, sentence and word level work, rather than treating these as discrete units. In phonics teaching, for example, the Rose Report (DfES 2006a: 39) found that the best practice 'took advantage of opportunities to reinforce aspects of phonic knowledge and skills throughout the curriculum'.

---

**Activity: Analysing effective teachers of English**

Wray and Medwell (2002) identified the following features of effective teachers of English:

- make explicit the purpose of teaching and how this contributes to making meaning
- centre much of teaching around shared texts
- teach aspects of writing and reading in systematic way
- have strong philosophies about teaching literacy
- well-developed systems for monitoring progress
- have extensive knowledge about literacy
- undergo regular in-service training

Think about yourself as a teacher of English and rate yourself on a 1 to 10 scale for each of the items above. Discuss your self-assessment with a colleague and talk about ways in which you could improve in those areas in which you scored least well.

---

## Key points

- To teach effectively, teachers need to reflect upon their practice and understand why they do what they do.
- A key element of pedagogy is knowledge, and this includes knowledge of the curriculum, pupils, factors which affect teaching and learning, how to teach the curriculum and knowledge of one's own teaching skills.
- Teachers' knowledge influences their decision-making and influences ways in which they organise their teaching and their classroom.
- The way in which teachers act affects the way in which their pupils learn and the pupils' perceptions of them.
- There are identifiable qualities in good teaching which teachers need to be aware of.

## Further reading

Lambirth, A. (2005) *Primary English Reflective Reader*. Exeter: Learning Matters.
Wray, D. (2006) *Teaching Literacy Across the Primary Curriculum*. Exeter: Learning Matters.

# 2 Classroom management for English

## Purpose of this chapter

This chapter aims to:

- Explore ideal scenarios for teaching English.
- Enable the reader to reflect on classroom management and consider the effects of different approaches.
- Examine classroom management in specific English-teaching situations, including the literacy hour, reading sessions, writing sessions and class discussions.
- Provide practical ideas for successful class management.

## Ideal scenarios for teaching English

Classroom management can be a preoccupation for both inexperienced and experienced teachers. Teachers often complain that they spend hours preparing lessons, only to have them spoilt by the behaviour of some children. W. C. Fields once said that one should 'never work with children and animals'. Both can be unpredictable and difficult to work with. However, both can also be trained and a great source of pleasure!

A Primary National Strategy training pack (DfES 2004a: 22) suggests that literacy training course participants should consider – in teaching terms – what might be an 'ideal scenario' by trying to imagine the perfect literacy lesson with their class. They should think about what they and the children would be doing and what they would see. This is a worthwhile exercise, as it focuses consideration of classroom management strategies on to a subject area with which we are all familiar, rather than upon classroom management in general. It enables us to relate class management to the activities which make up a typical literacy hour, and to consider how these can be organised so that lessons are not disrupted and are productive. As Hayes (2003: 159) has argued, 'The key to dealing with misbehaviour is to try to prevent it from happening on the first place'. This involves anticipating where problems might arise, and planning lessons so that potential troublespots are identified and strategies put in place to avoid them.

### One teacher trainee's experience

A teacher trainee was asked to write about how her literacy lesson would ideally run:

As the children came into the classroom after playtime they went to the carpet quietly and sat sensibly waiting for the lesson to begin. Some chatted quietly, and I could hear a few conversations about the story we'd been reading for the past week. As soon as I sat down and raised my hand they all stopped talking and I could see twenty-seven pairs of eyes looking at me. After praising them for being such a 'mature, sensible class' I began, 'today we're going to look at part of the next chapter of our story, but first I'm going to read a couple of pages to you. Can you remember what had just happened and what Danny was about to do?' Virtually every hand shot up, including, I was delighted to see, those of Chelsea and Luke, neither of whom could read very well, but both of whom were loving listening to *Danny the Champion of the World*. I made a point of asking Luke to respond and he gave a fairly lengthy answer in a clear voice while the rest of the class listened attentively. He is clearly beginning to understand the need to think about his audience when he speaks!

After a short discussion about the story so far, I read the next couple of pages and induced a huge groan from the class when I told them that we would have to stop, just at the point where Danny had seen a car coming towards him as he drove to the woods to rescue his father. They cheered when I told them I was going to show them the next paragraph and would read to them before we all read it together. They listened and followed open mouthed as I read the paragraph which I'd displayed on the screen and there were gasps when they realised that the approaching vehicle was a police car. When we all read together, I was really pleased with the way the children put expression into their reading and I was able to stop reading aloud myself and point to the text so that they could follow and keep together.

Before I even asked the children what they thought about the paragraph or how Roald Dahl had used punctuation to help the reader to sense the pace of events, Jade put up her hand and said, 'Miss Parkes, it's full of really short sentences.' David's hand shot up: 'Except the first one and the last one, Miss!' We looked at the text together and I asked Sam to read it aloud as we did so. The children could see that the punctuation was used skilfully to emphasise that the cars were hurtling towards each other (as Lucy put it!), with short sentences followed by a longer one just after the cars had passed. We even had a discussion about sentences beginning with 'and' as the final one does, prompted by Ben's comment that a teacher at his previous school had told he class that they should never begin sentences in that way.

We were already addressing the objectives I had set (Y5T1 SL6 and TL2) and I hadn't even shown them to the children yet! When I did they all seemed to understand them because we'd spent time talking about the punctuation in the paragraph. I explained that we would be looking at other examples from other stories in future lessons, but that today I wanted the children to write their own paragraph in the style of Roald Dahl, describing what happened next in the story. They would need to plan this first and could discuss their ideas with their writing partners, but they should use the punctuation to help their readers to know how to read the paragraph. We discussed long and short sentences and I noted on the board some of the devices they could use such as exclamation marks, question marks and putting words in italics or, as Dahl had done with '*SWISH*', in both italics and capitals.

When I told the children it was time to go to their places to begin to prepare their writing, everyone sat sensibly willing me to choose them to be first. Before playtime I had made sure that they all had a pen, pencil, paper and rubber on their desks, so they were able to get to work quickly and without fuss.

Within 30 seconds of the first child going to her place, they were all working busily and there was a lovely buzz of task-related conversation in the room. I worked with the low ability group and was thrilled to see Chelsea making notes furiously before I even began to talk with them. I made sure I could see everyone by sitting with my back to the wall, but I didn't need to remind anyone about concentrating on the task. After about ten minutes, I made a tour of the classroom and was delighted not only by the amount of work which had been produced but also by the quality. I couldn't resist reading a few examples aloud and I could tell that this was helping to give ideas to those who might be flagging a little. I wrote a few words on the board which had been misspelled by some of the children and we talked briefly about the spellings before I returned to my group.

There were a few groans when I told the children there were only three minutes left to write in, but they were pleased when I said they could continue their stories later in the day.

In order to get the children from their desks to the carpet I used a technique I'd seen another teacher use and it worked beautifully. The children had to look at me and when I caught their eyes they had to go, one at a time with their writing, to the carpet. I told them that I would choose two really sensible people to sit on the chairs in the carpeted area, and this proved an added incentive for them to behave well. Of course, I remembered to praise everyone who went to the carpet sensibly, which turned out to be all of them!

We shared some of the children's work with the whole class and I was delighted that the children seemed able to use punctuation to convey pace and tension, and that they read aloud clearly and with their audience in mind. I didn't want to disappoint those for whom there was not enough time to read, so I asked them all to take turns to read their work to two other people. This proved a little noisy, but the noise was productive and I had no trouble quietening the children when I raised my hand. They've really responded well to this signal!

We looked again at the objectives and the children were very clear that they had understood the need for punctuation as an aid to the reader, and that they had begun to achieve the text level objective by looking at how Dahl built up pace in his paragraph. I explained that we would be comparing other parts of the story and other stories in future lessons.

We finished just as the bell went, but no-one started to move because they had remembered my comments about this from yesterday. I used the eye contact technique to dismiss them and they all put away their writing materials and left their reading books on their tables ready for quiet reading after lunch.

---

**Activity: Analysing a literacy lesson**

Consider the following:

- At which stages in the lesson did potential troublespots occur?
- Which classroom management techniques did the trainee teacher deploy?
- What alternative strategies could she have used?
- What effect did the content of the lesson have upon the children's behaviour?
- The teacher did not share her objectives at the very beginning of the lesson. Is this a valid strategy sometimes?

---

What seems to be clear from the trainee teacher's description of her lesson is that she has picked up useful techniques from other teachers in order to avoid the kind of minor disruption which makes teaching and learning less enjoyable for teachers and pupils. She has also planned carefully and has prepared the children for the lesson in such a way that they anticipated it eagerly. The Elton Report (DES/WO [Welsh Office] 1989) maintained that 80 per cent of disruption in schools was directly attributable to weak organisation, planning and teaching. A little thought in advance about what might go wrong may help to avoid problems.

## Effective classroom management

Central to effective classroom management is the creation of an environment in which children and teachers feel comfortable and confident that they can work without distraction. Morris (2001: 136) maintains that 'An unkempt, untidy room sets the stage for students to develop the same kind of behaviour'. In other words, the way in which the teacher presents the classroom will influence the way in which the children behave within it. It is also important that, as Pohan (2003: 317) states, 'The general room arrangement (e.g. furniture, materials) and procedures for moving about the classroom help to achieve physical safety'.

Part of creating the right ambience for working involves the teacher in making it clear to children what they will be doing and why, and what they will learn as a result. As Pollard (2002) has argued, it is vital to:

> introduce and interest children in the planned activities, to provide them with a clear indication of the learning objectives for the session, a clear understanding of what they are expected to do, and to structure the activity in practical, organisational terms.
>
> (Pollard 2002: 246)

When teaching literacy and numeracy, teachers usually share objectives with their pupils at the beginning of lessons, and then revisit these during the plenary session. By doing this, children are able to feel a sense of achievement and can be made aware of where individual lessons fit in a wider scheme of learning. It was interesting to note that the trainee teacher whose lesson is described earlier did not introduce her objectives at the beginning of the lesson, but did so after the children had seen the text they were to study. However, she made a point of enabling the children to see what they had achieved and what they had still to achieve during the plenary.

Many of the rudiments of successful classroom management for English are the same as those for other subjects. To most experienced teachers, the use of these strategies is second nature and they deploy them without having to plan or analyse. However, inexperienced teachers should set out the strategies which will be used in some detail in lesson planning, and discuss them before and after teaching, with more experienced colleagues.

## Managing the literacy hour

Table 2.1 sets out some of the possible problem areas within a typical literacy hour and provides strategies which could be used to ensure that the lesson runs smoothly. Consider the strategies offered and try to add ideas of your own. Think about a class you teach or have taught, and decide whether the strategies would work with them, or if they would need to be modified, adapted or changed. Consider, too, which of the strategies the trainee teacher's lesson included.

The literacy hour runs to a tight schedule and demands that children are attentive and on task at all times. There is a high degree of direct teaching and discussion and it is important that time is not wasted on trivial classroom management issues. Careful planning which takes into account potential management difficulties will be rewarded.

Within the literacy hour, children are expected to work in different ways at different stages of the lesson. At the beginning, they may be listening, speaking to the whole class or to small groups, or reading aloud. They may be asked to write ideas on a mini whiteboard and share these with the class, or they may be engaged in drama or role-play or other forms of presentation. Later, they may be asked to work independently or with partners, or may be involved in guided group work with an adult. Finally, they may be asked to present their work to the class or to a group. As we are now being urged to be flexible in our approaches to the literacy

*Table 2.1* Problem areas and strategies for class management

| | |
|---|---|
| Children's entry to the classroom | • Tell them before they come in what they should do.<br>• Look for those who do the right thing and praise or reward them.<br>• Make your expectations clear.<br>• Devise routines. |
| Movement to carpeted area (if applicable) | • Provide some 'special' chairs for the most sensible children.<br>• Move a few children at a time.<br>• Praise those who are sensible.<br>• Explain what you expect.<br>• Make sure that children have everything they will need for group work ready. |

*continued on next page*

*Table 2.1* continued

| | |
|---|---|
| Beginning the lesson | • Tell the children what they will learn.<br>• Make the lesson sound as if it is going to be interesting: show your own enthusiasm for it.<br>• Use visual aids.<br>• Insist upon attentiveness from everyone.<br>• Make sure that everyone can see and hear you. |
| Shared reading | • Make sure that the text is clearly visible to everyone.<br>• Discuss the text and its presentation before reading it.<br>• Involve the children as much as possible.<br>• Use a pointer so that you do not obscure the text. |
| Word and text level work | • Children may have become restless and fidgety by this stage: ask them to stand up for a moment.<br>• Look for opportunities to bring some to the front of the class.<br>• Use visual aids. |
| Group work | • Make sure that children know what they will be doing.<br>• Send them to places a few at a time.<br>• Praise those who get on with work quickly.<br>• Make sure they know what you will be doing and know not to disturb you.<br>• Make a quick tour of the classroom to ensure that everyone is on task, before going to your group.<br>• Sit in a position which allows you to scan the whole class.<br>• Occasionally show that you are aware of what other groups are doing.<br>• Remind children of how much time they have left. |
| Plenary session | • Discuss the way in which the children have worked and praise good practice.<br>• Give children opportunities to talk about what they have achieved.<br>• Provide positive feedback on their work.<br>• Talk about the ways in which the work will be followed up.<br>• End the session calmly and dismiss the class a few at a time. |

hour, these stages may vary from day to day, according to the nature of the lessons. This may lead to class management issues, especially if children are uncertain about procedures and unsure about what is expected of them. It is important, therefore, that they feel that the teacher is in control of the structure of the lesson and has anticipated potential problems. It is vital too that the teacher's expectations are made clear and that children understand these. Cowley (2003) recommends the strategy of 'explain, repeat, explain':

> Explain: tell the class what you want them to do; repeat: choose a student and ask the child to repeat what you just said. . . . By hearing the students' interpretation, you may find out that they did not actually understand the instructions you gave; explain: repeat the instructions again in your own words, clarifying any areas of uncertainty, and then ask: 'Is there anyone who's not sure what we're going to do?'
>
> (Cowley 2003: 44)

Or, as many experienced teachers would have it: 'Tell them, then tell them what you told them, then ask them to tell you what you told them!'

In the following sections we will look more closely at key aspects of English lessons and will examine potential problems and possible solutions.

### Managing reading sessions: independent, hearing readers, shared, guided, group

A constant problem for teachers is managing to hear children read while ensuring that the rest of the class remain on task and do not become disruptive. This was especially true when teachers tended to hear children read individually frequently, but it is also a problem when conducting guided reading sessions with groups during the literacy hour. The strategies below may enable teachers to create an appropriate atmosphere to allow them to devote attention to those children with whom they are working, while making it possible for others to be gainfully occupied.

- Always sit in a position which allows you to scan the whole class from time to time.
- Occasionally make it clear that you are aware of what children are doing.
- Praise those who are getting on quietly.
- Resist the temptation to leave your group to help others. Try to create a climate of independence in which children are praised for having a go at solving problems without constant recourse to the teacher.

### Managing writing sessions: extended, paired

Although some older primary pupils are able to concentrate on writing for long periods, it is generally unreasonable to expect that all can do this. Skilful teachers recognise the signs when children become restless and intervene quickly. They try to break the lesson up occasionally and use the opportunity to focus children's attention on the task and to share good work and good ideas. (See also the sections on shared, guided and independent writing in Chapter 11.) The following suggestions may be helpful in planning for successful classroom management in writing sessions:

- Discuss the 'rules for writing' with children at the beginning of the lesson and ask for their suggestions. Note these on the board and use them as a reference point when infringements occur.
- Occasionally write something yourself, and make the point that you need peace and quiet to be able to do so.
- Allot a writing partner to each child and ensure that the pairs sit near to each other.
- Look for opportunities during extended writing for partners to read each other's work and offer constructive criticism.
- Rather than repeatedly telling children that they are too noisy, stop them to discuss common problems, make teaching points and read aloud good work. This has the effect of quietening them down, but achieves it in a more positive and task-related way than constant rebukes.
- Be explicit about the level of noise which is acceptable. This is much easier for children to relate to than being told they are 'too noisy'. For example, you could say that no one should be able to hear what they are saying except the person whom they are addressing, or no one from another table should be able to hear their conversation. You may also want to insist that any talk is task-related.
- Try to catch children being good. Look for opportunities to praise those who are doing the right thing and draw the rest of the class's attention to this.
- Go to the children who have problems rather than having them queuing at your desk. Tell them that they must not simply sit doing nothing with their hand in the air, but should carry on with the parts of the work which they can do and wait for you to help them with any insurmountable difficulties.
- Probably the greatest source of disruption to any writing lesson is the child's spelling dictionary. Do not allow children to pursue you with these. Insist that they try out spellings and that they check that they do not already have the word they need in their books.
- If you discover that several children are experiencing similar problems, stop the class and use these to make a teaching point, perhaps writing words which cause spelling problems on the board.
- Encourage children to use dictionaries and other reference materials as a first rather than a last resort.

### Managing class discussions

Class discussions often occur at the beginnings of lessons and can set the tone for the rest of the lesson. It is, therefore, vital that they are orderly yet productive and lively. The problems most frequently encountered include the following:

- Children calling out or not taking turns to speak.
- Children showing a lack of interest.
- Minor irritations caused by children sitting too close together or being uncomfortable.

- Dominance of discussions by a few people (sometimes including the teacher).
- Restlessness brought on by lengthy periods of sitting on the floor (this is especially so after a long assembly or hymn practice or a wet playtime).

The solutions to the problems are simple, but can be difficult to deploy where inexperienced teachers lack the confidence to assert themselves. Children are generally very forgiving and accept rebukes and reprimands as part of daily life. It is important that the teacher makes clear the type of conduct which is acceptable and sticks to it. Children, when asked to define rules for class discussions, usually make up the same ones that teachers wish them to adhere to, and most accept that transgressions deserve to be reprimanded. Skilful teachers are able to do this in a positive way without upsetting children or creating a negative atmosphere. Some of the strategies for successful discussions may appear obvious:

- Insist that children put up their hands and wait to be invited to speak.
- Try to involve everyone in discussions and avoid allowing a minority to dominate.
- Differentiate questions so that everyone is capable of answering something.
- Ensure that there is sufficient space for everyone to sit in comfort and provide a limited number of chairs for those who behave especially sensibly.
- Ensure that everyone can see and be seen by you.
- Avoid lengthy discussions if children are restless after a long assembly or wet playtime.
- Use visual aids to stimulate interest and try to involve children physically by asking them to hold things or write on the board.
- Maintain order in discussions by asking questions and varying your voice level and tone. Avoid using 'Shhh', which is ineffective and gives the impression that you are struggling. Dropping to a whisper can be especially effective!
- When children transgress the rules, try to criticise their behaviour rather than the children themselves.
- If everyone seems desperate to contribute but you simply do not have time to allow this, ask children to tell their neighbours their views and then invite a few children to say what the key points were.
- Devise a signal which children know and understand in order to gain their attention. In cooperative learning the teacher raises her hand and as children notice this they stop what they are doing and raise a hand too. The class quietens in a few seconds and the teacher does not need to raise her voice to gain their attention. This also has the advantage that children can finish the sentence they were saying rather than stopping abruptly.

## Successful strategies for class management

Most elements of successful classroom management are commonsensical and seem obvious when one observes a skilled teacher at work. However, if you are faced with thirty or more children when you are not confident about the subject matter and are having difficulty remembering the sequence of the lesson, and the children are restless after a long, indoor lunch break, sustaining order and creating a working atmosphere can seem very difficult. The key to success is to watch experienced teachers and learn what does and does not work for them and then adapt successful strategies to suit your own personality and situation. There is no definitive, correct way to manage a class well. Some people achieve success by being loud and assertive while others are very quiet and calm and convey their calmness to the children.

What is certain is that every teacher experiences some problems at some time and all can recall the lessons from hell as well as those which were heavenly!

---

**Activity: Dealing with classroom management problems**

How would you deal with each of the following? Discuss your ideas with a partner or small group.

- Your class includes four children whose behaviour is a problem when they are asked to move from one part of the classroom to another during lessons.
- During class discussions, some children tend to dominate and most children don't listen when others are making contributions.
- It is difficult to keep the rest of the class on task when you work with a group on guided work.
- Although you often manage to enthuse children about independent work during introductions to literacy hours, it often takes them a long time to settle down to work.
- You find it difficult to sustain children's enthusiasm during plenary sessions.

---

## Key points

- Many behaviour problems can be avoided if we consider class management when planning lessons and anticipate potential difficulties, and if we organise our classrooms well.
- It is worthwhile considering what our ideal scenario for a lesson might be before we teach, as this may inform our planning and anticipation of difficulties.
- There are many simple, practical ideas which can be used to improve class management.

## Further reading

Burnett, C. and Myers, J. (2004) *Teaching English 3–11*. London: Continuum.
Wragg, E.C. (1993) *Class Management*. London: Routledge.

# 3 Creative approaches to teaching literacy

## Purpose of this chapter

This chapter aims to:

- Examine how government strategies can promote literacy.
- Explore the impact of *Excellence and Enjoyment* in primary schools.
- Examine the concept of creativity.
- Discuss the impact of multimodal texts, including the moving image.
- Look at the role of popular culture in promoting literacy development.
- Present examples of creative approaches to teaching literacy and their impact across the primary age range.

## Government strategies to promote literacy

In an environment of heavily prescriptive government strategies, developing a creative approach to the teaching of literacy, at least in England, may seem an oxymoron. Yet, the government's *Excellence and Enjoyment* initiative (DfES 2003a) purports to do just that and encourage creativity. What this initiative entails and more recently, implications of the renewed Primary Framework for Literacy (DfES 2006b) are discussed in this chapter. We also discuss divergent approaches to literacy, including multimodal formats, popular culture and how the widest interpretation of 'texts' can motivate and challenge pupils. In essence creative teaching incorporates the three modes of English – speaking and listening, reading, and writing – using methods that are multisensory. It is as one teacher tells her class: 'Expect the unexpected in my lesson'. Some of the examples of pupils' responses in this chapter illustrate the power of such risk-taking.

### Primary National Strategy

The Primary National Strategy was launched in 2003 under the title *Excellence and Enjoyment: A strategy for primary schools* with the stated goal to 'combine excellence in teaching with enjoyment of learning' (DfES 2003a: 4). Key themes of the Strategy were set out as follows:

- To develop the distinctive character of schools by encouraging ownership of the curriculum and to be creative and innovative in teaching.
- To build on excellent primary teaching from the Literacy and Numeracy Strategies and extend this to Foundation subjects, and Modern Foreign Languages.
- Focus on learning – ensuring all children are catered for through tailored approaches underpinned by assessment for learning.
- Partnership beyond the classroom, extending work with parents and the provision of extended schools.
- Leadership in primary schools developed through the National College of School Leadership and local authorities and the power of collaboration through networks of schools.
- Managing school resources: workforce reform in primary schools and the use of classroom support staff.
- Realising the vision with support from local authorities, the DfES and stable funding arrangements for schools.

### Core principles: learning and teaching

The Primary National Strategy set out core principles that underpinned learning and teaching, and interestingly, 'learning' was emphasised over 'teaching'. These core principles were stated as follows:

- *Ensure every child succeeds:* provide an inclusive education within a culture of high expectations.
- *Build on what learners already know:* structure and pace teaching so that students know what is to be learnt and how.
- *Make learning vivid and real:* develop understanding through enquiry, e-learning and group problem solving.
- *Make learning an enjoyable and challenging experience:* stimulate learning through matching teaching techniques and strategies to a range of learning styles.
- *Enrich the learning experience:* infuse learning skills across the curriculum.
- *Promote assessment for learning:* make children partners in their learning.

Extensive professional development materials were provided to schools to support these core principles, which centred around three themes:

- Planning and assessment for learning.
- Creating a learning culture.
- Understanding how learning develops.

**Activity: Key themes of *Excellence and Enjoyment***

Working with a colleague, read the following quotation and highlight key words that exemplify the main aims of *Excellence and Enjoyment.*

> High standards and a broad and rich curriculum go hand in hand. Literacy and numeracy are vital building blocks, and it is right to focus attention on them. But it is important that children have a rich and exciting experience at primary school, learning a wide range of things in a wide range of different ways. Our new Primary Strategy will support teachers and schools across the whole curriculum, building on the lessons of the Literacy and Numeracy Strategies, but moving on to offer teachers more control and flexibility. It will focus on building up teachers' own professionalism and capacity to teach better and better, with bespoke support they can draw on to meet their particular needs. There will be extra support and challenge for the schools that need it most.
>
> (*Excellence and Enjoyment: A strategy for primary schools.* DfES 2003a: 27)

Now using the words you have identified (for suggestions, see page 43), map this onto the core principles above.

*Critical reactions to* Excellence and Enjoyment

While many of the themes of *Excellence and Enjoyment* encompassed in the Primary National Strategy are generally regarded as laudable, there has been a range of critical responses to the rationale of having a further major national strategy, this time to promote excellence and enjoyment. Jones and Wyse (2004: 6) state that at the time of the introduction of the Primary National Strategy there had been a 'growing consensus that educational policy in England was too prescriptive and that this was impacting negatively on things like creative teaching and creative learning'. Interestingly, as Jones and Wyse (2004) point out, it is not until page 18 of the document that the word 'creativity' appears. One issue that hinders teachers' creativity is the continued emphasis on high stakes assessment and the restrictive frameworks of the Literacy and Numeracy Strategies. Jones and Wyse conclude:

> Evidence that government has responded to the growing complaints about the prescription in the curriculum is shown in the changes of language evident in the primary strategy document but not in substantial action.
>
> (Jones and Wyse 2004: 8)

As this chapter will demonstrate with examples of practice, where teachers are really creative and deliver the curriculum in exciting and innovative ways, results are impressively enhanced.

## Creativity and literacy

The first question to clarify is: what is creativity? Research conducted at Manchester Metropolitan, Bath Spa and Goldsmiths Universities in 2004 (Davies et al. 2004) examining teacher trainees' views of creativity, showed a real lack of understanding of 'creativity' consisting of a narrow arts-based view. The research also showed that these views could however be challenged through exploring definitions and observations in school and then to begin to teach with, and for, creativity.

One of the problems with creativity is that the concept is ethereal. As Fisher (2004) states:

> Years of research has gone into trying to specify what creativity is, but despite all the checklists, models and tests, researchers admit that we do not know how fully to explain the creative power of the brain.
>
> (Fisher 2004: 7)

---

**Activity: Defining creativity**

Review the statements below and discuss with colleagues what the key ingredients of 'creativity' consist of:

- 'The ability to solve problems and fashion products and to raise new questions.' (Gardner 1997, cited in Fisher 2002)
- 'A state of mind in which all our intelligences are working together.' (Lucas 2001, cited in Fisher 2002)
- 'Imaginative processes with outcomes that are original and of value.' (Robinson 2001, cited in Fisher 2002)
- 'An act that produces effective surprise.' (Bruner 1962, cited in Fisher 2002)

---

### *Principles of creativity*

Fisher (2004) argues that the processes that underpin creativity also underpin the evolution of life, namely generation, variation and originality. In essence creativity is 'making, forming or bringing something into being' (Fisher 2004: 8) There are in effect three key interlinked principles concerned in the concept of creativity:

- generating ideas, outputs, etc.
- differentiating: varying of products
- being original: as an individual, group or community.

There have been many attempts to define the term 'creativity'. Csikszentmihalyi (1996) advanced the idea that it is not an individual attribute but a product of a person with the interaction of a specific situation or stimulus. Csikszentmihalyi (1992) also developed the concept of 'flow' where during creative activity in a state of total absorption and mental challenge; many people experience their greatest joy.

Creativity can therefore improve individual's emotional state of mind and quality of life. Fisher states:

> Creativity is developed through intellectual engagement, purpose, energy and interaction tension with others. These positive, creative attributes are essential to citizens living in any increasingly complex, changing and challenging social environment and essential for teachers in schools.
>
> (Fisher 2004: 11)

It is also important to value what Craft (2002) calls 'the creativity of everyday life' or little 'c' creativity, otherwise many of us may feel inadequate and lacking in achieving 'sublime' creativity (Cropley 2001). Einstein or Picasso we may not be, but in a myriad of ways we can be creative or support it in others.

Jones and Wyse (2004: 5) summarise creativity as something that is 'novel, created with understanding of the field and valued as creative by observers'. Perhaps the final word should be the definition by a 10 year old cited in Fisher: 'Creativity is not just art. It is thinking deeply and having original thoughts about something' (Georgie Eccles, aged 10, cited in Fisher 2004: 6).

### Developing creativity in children

There are several ways that teachers can develop creativity in pupils:

- fostering curiosity and exploration
- encouraging risk-taking
- having high expectations about pupils' diverse talents and abilities and enhancing their self-image
- providing choice and independence
- giving time and responsibility for creative activity
- encouraging collaboration with others.

The Qualifications and Curriculum Authority (QCA) has developed materials, *Creativity: Find it, promote it*, which provide information and case study examples in order to encourage teachers to promote pupils' creativity. These materials can be found on the QCA website (http://www.qca.org.uk). Over three years, a creativity project investigated how teachers can promote pupils' creativity across all National Curriculum subjects at Key Stages 1, 2 and 3. This project found that, by making small changes to their existing planning and practice, teachers can promote pupils' creativity, which can:

- improve pupils' self-esteem, motivation and achievement
- develop skills for adult life
- develop the talent of the individual.

Teachers found that when they actively planned for and responded to pupils' creative ideas and actions, pupils became more curious to discover things for themselves, were open to new ideas and keen to explore those ideas with the teacher and others. Promoting creativity is a powerful way of engaging pupils with their learning.

*Examples of creativity across the curriculum*

The professional development materials as part of *Excellence and Enjoyment: Learning to Learn: Progression in key aspects of learning* (DfES 2004c) cite creative thinking as a key aspect which can

> enable pupils to generate and extend ideas, to suggest hypotheses, to apply imagination, and to look for alternative innovative outcomes.
>
> (DfEE/QCA 1999: 22)

It also cites some indicators of creative thinking (DfES 2004c: 22). Children may demonstrate that they can:

- generate imaginative ideas in response to stimuli
- discover and make connections through play and experimentation
- explore and experiment with resources and materials
- ask 'why', 'how', 'what if' or unusual questions
- try alternatives or different approaches
- look at and think about things differently and from other points of view
- respond to ideas, tasks and problems in surprising ways
- apply imaginative thinking to achieve an objective
- make connections and see relationships
- reflect critically on ideas, actions and outcomes.

Examples of working creativity across the curriculum in literacy are cited in *Excellence and Enjoyment: Learning to learn* (DfEE 2004c), derived from the QCA's *Creativity: Find it, promote it* project. These can form the starting point for other cross-curricular work in school.

## The changing face of literacy

Literacy in the twenty-first century presents a very different picture from the text-based concept, traditionally associated with reading and writing. We need to start by understanding that children from a very young age are driven to make meaning from the many forms of stimulus around them. Gunther Kress (1997) describes how a young child comments of a father's deliberate attempt to shape a piece of toast by taking careful bites: 'You made it like a crocodile'. Children develop their own meanings and do this in a multiplicity of modes, means and materials: 'Children act multimodally' (Kress 1997, cited in Grainger 2004: 75). This supports children's paths into literacy, helped by a rich environment of print. Central to this is what Anne Haas Dyson (2001) describes as a 'patchwork quilt' of children's literacy development with a range of home and cultural influences. It is unfortunate that as Kress (1997) notes, young children's imaginative drive is often not supported and states:

> The brain's capacity for translation from one mode into another is not seen as a quality to be fostered. If it were, the imaginative capacity of humans in western culture would be entirely different.
>
> (Kress 1997, cited in Grainger 2004: 82)

## Multimodal texts

Eve Bearne's work on 'multimodal texts' describes how we need to redefine what 'literacy' involves, to include combinations of modes with not just words and images but also moving images and sound (Bearne et al. 2004). The Essex Writing Project (2003) found it important to challenge and redefine teachers' perceptions of 'texts' and that by so doing we can show significant improvement in children's literacy skills, particularly impacting on boys' writing.

Multimodal texts combine word, image and often sound and have been made possible through digital technology. This has increased the number of screen-based texts: three-dimensional animations, websites, DVDs, playstation games, hyper-textual narratives, chat sites, email, virtual reality representations and so on. Numerous books and magazine texts use image, word, layout and typography, echoing screen-based technology.

Reading changes due to the screen image. Hyperlinks enable readers to flit from one text to another through links – developing their own pathway. The key point is that reading is not linear and readers choose routes and their own sequence. One example of an on-screen interactive text that demonstrates this is entitled 'Jack's choice' (developed by the Primary National Strategy). It powerfully shows not only the different ways in which the text can be read, but also the engagement and inter-action that such text stimulates. Here the text presents characters and scenarios and as the title depicts, the readers are invited to choose from different routes presented on the screen or change the outcome by making choices for the main character at key points.

The reading of on-screen text

- engages the reader in a very active (dynamic) way
- requires the 'orchestration' of information from non-linear, multimodal sources
- facilitates focus on some key aspects of text (sequence and structure, author/ character perspective, etc.)
- extends reading into the 'new literacy' of the ICT medium.

In addition, the creation of on-screen text has key differences. Peter Hannon (2000) comments that the production of graphics has been difficult for ordinary writers, but due to software packages this is now changing. How it is transmitted is also very different due to electronic transmission and use of internet. Creating on-screen texts

- brings the content and structure of writing into a new and very dynamic relationship
- involves strong elements of design as well as language and style considerations
- requires particularly careful consideration of the potential readers, and how and why they will access the content
- extends writing into the 'new literacy' of the ICT medium, facilitating multimodal communication.

## Email and text messaging

How we create texts for email or as text messages contrasts with other forms of writing, which can be productive to explore in the classroom. The often criticised use of shortened language in text messaging, which can lead to children not knowing conventional spelling, can be analysed. A dictionary of correct spellings and text messaging formats can be developed, or text messages can be translated into conventional format. Other possible activities can be devising rules for the use of mobile phones on buses and trains, or stories about mysterious text messages appearing.

## Using visual texts: picture books

Picture books are a common part of the repertoire of young children, and their value is often underestimated. They provide a powerful introduction to reading through the many outstanding examples of the attraction of the visual image. Indeed, many adult readers experience the draw and select books because of the attractive cover or illustrations. Merchant and Thomas (1999: 2) describe picture books as an 'art-form through which authors and illustrators communicate what concerns them and how they reflect on the experience of childhood'. These books are 'characterised by the dynamic relationship between print and visual image (Merchant and Thomas 1999: 2). It is this relationship and the multilayers of meaning that can be created through this medium that make picture books valuable for young and old alike.

---

**Activity: Analysing how picture books contribute to children's understanding**

For this activity you will need access to a range of picture books. Some texts are given below, or see the list of suggested authors on page 44. Look at the following ways in which picture books support children's understanding of text and find examples that match. Notice as you do the meaning created from the interplay of pictures and text.

- They introduce us to narrative in pictures and written text.
- They introduce different types of text in interesting ways, such as the use of the letter in *Dear Greenpeace* (Simon James), links to children's comics in Colin McNaughton's work or visual symbolism in Anthony Browne's work.
- They help in understanding different cultures, as in *Handa's Surprise* (Eileen Browne) and *Amazing Grace* (Mary Hoffman).
- They develop closer and critical reading of images as in *Each Peach Pear Plum* (Janet and Allan Ahlberg).
- They support inter-textuality (of references to other texts) as in *The Jolly Postman* (Janet and Allan Ahlberg).

---

Some outstanding examples of this genre by authors such as Janet and Allan Ahlberg, Anthony Browne, Maurice Sendak, John Burningham and Pat Hutchins, to name but a few, provide not only a clear incentive for young children to develop a love of reading, but also can support a deeper layer of meaning for older children (for example *The Highwayman* by Alfred Noyes illustrated by Charles Keeping). *Rosie's Walk* by Pat Hutchins is a prime example of the power of this genre for young children, using only thirty-two words, but it is what the text does not say and the pictures do that is significant.

Anthony Browne (1996) made the following comment about creating picture books which illustrates the link with other multimodal texts:

> Making a picture book, for me, is not like writing a story then painting some pictures. . . . No, it is more like planning a film, where each page is a scene that includes both words and images inextricably linked. What excites me is working out the rhythm of the story and seeing how much it is told by the pictures, how much by the words, and how much by the gap between the two.
> (Browne 1996)

Arizpe and Styles (2002) investigated how children aged from 4 to 11 years actually read pictures, and showed how in addition to providing access to a story that would otherwise be denied younger or less competent readers, the visual image can be better than spoken or written language in evoking an affective response. The project found that children were very good at analysing the visual features of texts, aided by the input of teachers in discussing the texts and pictures thereby giving the children the opportunity to operate at a higher cognitive level. Reader-response theory (Rosenblatt 1978) also shows the importance of children making personal connections in reading to actively engage in texts and draw on their own experiences.

### Supporting children's understanding of picture books

To support children, begin from the understanding that a good picture book is multi-layered and may be used for a variety of readings at different levels. The use of shared reading is the Primary National Strategy's recommended method of support-ing (or scaffolding) children and a common introduction to text. How this is done is important, primarily to ensure that the joy of the text is not lost. At times this will include extended reading aloud without deconstructing the text. It should also enable children to respond in an open and unstructured way. With picture books it will involve the close examination of visual elements and their interplay with the written text, supporting children's ability to 'read' the images.

Guided reading allows the teacher to explore the text with a small group and focus on particular elements. This allows the opportunity for pupils to practise skills that they have learnt in shared reading and for the teacher to support individuals or groups. In addition, it is important that children are given the opportunity to read a range of picture books independently and with a partner. The use of 'storysacks' or 'storybags' can promote the use of picture books still further, incorporating props, characters, audio tapes and games. This can provide opportunities for pupils to really inhabit the text and further their understanding.

## Moving image: film, television and video

Picture books illustrate the power of the visual image to aid our enjoyment and understanding of texts. The moving image is a development of this. It also ensures that we are relating to children's home experiences. Most children appear to watch television for about eighteen hours a week (Livingstone and Bovill 1999), but only a small proportion of the population visits the theatre, opera or ballet. We thus need to recognise children's 'cultural capital' (Bourdieu 1977).

The British Film Institute (BFI) has provided a range of resources for use in primary schools to support the effective use of film. Its teaching guide entitled *Look Again!* (BFI 2003) is available online (see web resources on page 44) and contains some key arguments for building moving image education into the learning experiences of primary pupils. These are summarised as follows:

- The necessity for active learning – using the moving image can involve children because it is familiar. Starting with what they know and building on this can support a deeper level of understanding.
- Linking home and school – helps form a bridge through the use of familiar moving image texts. For pupils with English as an Additional Language, work with moving images can be central to developing understanding.
- Deepening the understanding of the nature of texts – film can help understanding of all texts and their role in creating our culture. It can also develop higher order skills such as inference.
- Creativity and the moving image – it supports the need to provide rich and varied contexts for learning and can help pupils to develop ICT skills by producing their own media texts.
- Understanding culture and society – moving image media have a unique capacity for the development of cultural understanding, for example by watching films set in different cultures.

Resources from the British Film Institute for Key Stages 1 (*Starting Stories*) and 2 (*Story Shorts*), consisting of short video clips of about five minutes and accompanying lesson ideas, have demonstrated the impact of using film to develop literacy skills. One teacher involved in the pilot work commented: 'I have been more surprised by the children's reactions to the films than anything else I have ever seen' (cited in Jones and Wyse 2004: 14). Here the film *Growing* stimulated 'the strongest poetry ever written by children.' It is also possible to download free resources from the BFI website. For other useful resources, see the list of websites on page 00.

The Film Education Working group (FEWG 1999) outlined a curriculum framework for work on the moving image consisting of

- Stage 1 – access to a range and discussion, using film language.
- Stage 2 – moves to deconstruct complex narratives.

This also stresses the importance of giving children the opportunities to produce media texts such as video diaries, watching and analysing reports (e.g. weather) and filming their own. These can provide rich opportunities for oral and literacy work as they plan and write scripts, etc.

*Teaching techniques when using moving images*

When using film, different techniques need to be taught to broaden children's understanding. The British Film Institute cites eight basic techniques to help understand the codes and conventions of the moving image. The first three concentrate on the language of the moving image and help pupils to see that everything in a moving image contributes to the overall meaning.

- *Freeze frame:* pausing the film and using focused questions.
- *Sound and image:* examining separately the sound and image.
- *Spot the shots:* after viewing a short sequence, they guess number of shots, view again and mark each change in shot, examine transitions and timings.

The next two deal with the way the moving images are produced.

- *Top and tail:* show title sequence and then using one of the three techniques above help pupils to identify the genre.
- *Attracting audiences:* examine merchandising or promotional material.

The next three techniques help explore ways of recognising the conventions of moving image texts.

- *Genre:* what happens next – short clip of recognised genre (western, sci-fi, soap opera), pupils then make predictions about how a scene will end.
- *Generic translations:* translate a moving image into a print genre.
- *Simulation/production:* pairs or groups of pupils placed in role as producers and produce plans for a particular film.

*Vocabulary for analysing films*

Analysing film requires knowledge of film language. Six elements (3Ss and 3Cs) are recommended by the British Film Institute to explore and interrogate a film text:

- story
- setting
- sound
- colour
- character
- camera.

Many of these are self-explanatory; however, the use of camera requires clarification. In film the camera acts as a 'narrator', leading the viewing through the story. Different types of camera shots fulfil different purposes:

- extreme close up – for moments of high drama
- close up – for detail
- medium or mid shot – to allow for more sense of what character looks like and of setting/action

- long shot – for an overview of location and/or action
- point of view – narrative perspective
- zoom – change in size of subject
- pan – moving horizontally left to right or vice versa
- tilt – moving up or down.

*Moving images and literacy*

The popular misconception is that watching films is bad for literacy. However, used effectively, utilising some of the techniques above, research has shown (Robinson 1997; Mackey 1999; Marsh and Hallett 1999) how film, TV and video can be incredibly empowering. As the BFI (2003) comments in *Look Again!*:

> Children who are able to draw on connections and parallels between film and print are more likely to become confident and critical readers across different media, including print.

Moving images can support literacy development in the following ways:

- illustrating genres or types of story
- motivating children to read related printed texts
- supporting the concept of narrative is key in linking print and moving image media
- developing sequencing skills
- offering great depth for literacy work based around character and setting
- enhancing oral skills through linked retelling, storytelling and drama
- extending children's vocabulary
- enabling children to compare and contrast narratives across media, thus developing their critical skills
- analysing the moving image helps children to understand more fully and gives them tools to shape their writing.

Using short, film clips can easily be incorporated within most literacy lessons. The power of the visual image to support creative approaches to literacy teaching can be easily demonstrated. Activities could include using soap operas, e.g. watching an extract with the sound removed and then for children to create their own dialogue. Marsh and Millard (2000) show how children often tap into their cultural capital of TV and mix genres. The following is one child's mix of fairy stories and soap operas in which couples indulge in pre-marital sex:

> One upon a time there was an old woman and a princess and one day the princess found a prince and they made love and one day they got married and lived happily ever after and the princess had a baby.
>
> (Marsh and Millard 2000: 158)

Incorporating children's TV experiences with literacy work can also impact on home–school links. Marsh and Millard (2000) cite the example of the popular TV programme *Who Wants to be a Millionaire?*, which has a more general appeal compared with other quiz shows such as *University Challenge*. In one school a teacher asked the children to write three questions each for a class version of the quiz. This produced an astonishing involvement by parents, who became engaged in researching and writing questions. These were then put into a class booklet and a class quiz was held at the end of term which had engaged the children and community in a literacy experience.

---

**Activity: Incorporating the moving image into a literacy lesson**

Download a film clip from the web resources recommended on page 44 and then take one aspect from the 3Ss and 3Cs (such as camera) to see how this impacts on the story.

- Work with a colleague to discuss how to incorporate within a literacy lesson.
- How could you build on this to support a unit of work?

---

## Popular culture

It is vital to tap into the rich experiences that children bring to the classroom. We can utilise this to act as a stimulus to engage with a range of literacy practices. Anne Haas Dyson describes the assortment of children's popular cultural texts as a 'tote bag' of 'symbolic material gleaned from the myriad of voices around them' (Dyson 2000: 362). We need to make use of this 'bag', not 'shut out the noise of society at work'.

### Computer games

The proliferation of computer games in many homes would seem an odd starting point for literacy, and yet it can be productively utilised. It has a strong appeal for boys, encouraging activity: 'Video games are better than books 'cos you can be player in games and you just have to read books' (Livingstone and Bovill 1999: 17). They can help develop a range of skills, such as:

- improving hand–eye coordination
- processing visual information from a number of sources
- developing problem-solving skills
- improving concentration
- developing understanding of narrative.

Computer games can be utilised in school through

- collecting data for class surveys
- providing discussion points
- designing own games

- developing characterisation
- making comic strips of computer games characters.

Critics of computer games cite the tendency for issues of race to be not well addressed, as well as the element of violence depicted. Such issues could form the focus for literacy work and discussion to encourage a critical response by children. Ignoring this popular pastime may be more damaging than including it.

### Comics: an inferior medium?

Comics have received scant attention from educationalists except to generally decry their use. Attitudes have changed however since the 1950s when our own experience meant that demands for a comic were answered by being allowed to read the *Children's Newspaper*. Marsh and Millard (2000: 101) sum up this attitude: 'There is something about the combination of cartoon images and racy colloquial language that distresses a significant proportion of adults'.

Many educationalists argue that children deserve better material than comics. Features such as the language which often seems to be coarse or show lack of respect (e.g. Bart Simpson, 'Eat my shorts') are cited. Also drawings which predominate with relatively few words indicate a correlation with deficient literacy. However, Helen Bromley (2000) has demonstrated that comics can help in critical knowledge of how texts work with use of jokes and understanding of multilayering and inter-textuality of texts. Millard and Marsh's (2000) project in creating a home–school comic library in two Sheffield schools showed an enthusiastic response and children found it motivating. Most popular was the interactive nature and inclusion of puzzles and games. One effect was the communal reading experiences with families. They were also integrated into school work with shared reading and writing. Activities such as cutting up versions of comic strips to sequence can support a range of literacy skills such as recognising the complication in a story, developing understanding of character, use of puns, alliteration and onomatopoeia.

### Toys and media characters

A key aspect of popular culture for young children are the proliferation of toys and associated artefacts that are linked to computer games, films or fast food chains. Despite the commercial interests that undoubtedly make substantial profits from such crazes, tapping into children's cultural capital should not be ignored. Where such items can be used to motivate, excite and engage children, teachers are very justified in employing them.

How can they be used? The following are a few ideas:

- Use of superheroes in role-play (e.g. Superman and Batman, Rugrats' home, Gladiators' gym, etc.).
- As starting points for different literacy activities, e.g. write to a Teletubby.
- Collections or current crazes can be used (historically Dinky toys, trolls, gonks, beanie babies, tamagotchis, pokemon, etc.) to write narrative histories of collectors' crazes. Collectors' websites can be consulted. Children can write descriptions, list features, or instructions of how to look after them.

- Use of toys for literacy – one example was providing Star Wars figures and children constructed a story, first arranging the figures, taking photographs and then using these to write stories.

Marsh and Millard (2000: 51) ask 'How many children living in high-rise flats in inner-city areas of poverty visit garden centres?' Too often teachers set up role-play areas in a Foundation Stage setting without such considerations. In contrast, one teacher explored what existed in the local area and then set up a fish and chip shop in the nursery.

## Popular music

> What Bart Simpson, Madonna, M.C. Hammer, or New Kids on the Block have to say about the world is far more important to youth than the social and moral lessons teachers extract from literacy and basil readers.
>
> (Luke and Roe 1993: 115)

Again this relates to children's common experiences and motivates them to engage with literacy. The world of popular music is as Marsh and Millard (2000: 165) state 'inescapable'. Very young children learn lyrics to pop songs and enjoy singing them. Cultural boundaries can be transcended by sharing enjoyment of such music and more recently musical forms have shown an element of cross-over with rap, hip-hop and bhangra. Concerns over sexual overtones in such music, or violent and sometimes misogynistic content of some lyrics are undoubtedly justified. However, with careful selection and thought, pop music can be utilised effectively, for example:

- using rap to support engagement in poetry
- using karaoke to support children's reading (one study used this effectively with children having reading difficulties)
- carrying out surveys of popular artists or songs
- compiling Golden Oldie charts that incorporate parents' and grandparents' views
- practising handwriting by copying a verse from a song
- analysing lyrics.

## Advantages of including popular culture

By including popular culture when teaching literacy, we are clearly relating to children's everyday experiences.

- It is meaningful: in literacy it is essential if school practices are to be seen as meaningful reflections of home experiences.
- It is motivational: there are a range of studies to show that inclusion of popular cultural texts into the literacy curriculum has increased motivation.
- It can introduce children to a more recognised canon of texts.
- It can be a useful means of developing critical literacy skills.

---

**Activity: Using popular culture**

Working in a group of four, each select an area of popular culture to investigate (comics, computer games, toys or pop music), plan an activity, or series of activities for use in the classroom with an age group you are familiar with. Now share your ideas with others and see if you can combine the different forms of popular culture in creative ways.

   After planning and, if possible, carrying out the activity with children, consider:

- How did this motivate the children?
- Did it promote good opportunities for talk?
- Did it support their growing vocabulary?

---

## Creative approaches to teaching literacy

This section provides a diverse range of creative approaches to teaching literacy. As you read each one, note what is innovative and motivational and how creative responses are fostered.

### *Linking drama and writing: a research example*

Research carried out by the Centre for Language in Primary Education (Barrs 2000) looked at the link between the quality of what children read and the quality of what they write. Working with Year 5 pupils and exploring the difference between oral and written storytelling, one of the project's main findings was the effect on children's writing of writing in role. The pupils began work on a text with a drama workshop. This delayed the introduction of the text itself until the fictional world and the themes of the story had been prefigured through drama. Barrs states:

> This had a big impact on the children, who seemed to relate much more closely and personally to this text because they had already 'lived through' some of the events and situations.
>
> (Barrs 2000: 56)

Barrs (2000) reported that the writing was almost universally well done with children filling in a range of detail and also developing a real sense of authorial 'voice'. One example is based on *Fire, Bed and Bone*, a historical text about the Peasants' Revolt, by Henrietta Branford (1997), where a child writes as Humble the Cat:

> I am a creature of very different worlds.
> I know where the dormice nest in the oat fields. I know valleys that have deep blue rivers with the silver fish.
> I know the house and the warmest place in front of the fire. I know where the rats play at the back of the house. I know the tops of the tall pine trees. I know where the plumpest birds nest. I know the comfiest branch.

### Raising Boys' Achievements in Writing project

This project found similar results to Barrs (2000). Here teaching units were designed to raise boys' engagement, motivation and achievement in writing, using either visual stimuli (integrated technologies – video, DVD and other computer texts), or drama and other speaking and listening activities (United Kingdom Literacy Association (UKLA) and PNS 2004). The project found very positive results with the following being significant:

- The importance of planning longer units of work, typically three week blocks.
- The impact of speaking and listening being employed to scaffold children's learning, particularly linked to the use of drama. One teacher stated: 'I've realised that the drama needs to match the writing in order to get the maximum from both.'
- Integrating visual approaches was another significant feature with the most success showing how the use of varied media was woven into planning. This integration of film, DVD, still images or pupils' own drawings into units of work and an ongoing use of three-dimensional stimulus, including music, and videos alongside books for both fiction and non-fiction writing, made one teacher comment:

> I have seen the difference that using film makes to motivating and involving boys and I will work to make sure it is part of my practice . . . the 'wow factor' works as the films are so much part of what my children know, they are starting from a stronger knowledge base.

### Linking performing arts to children's literacy development

Airs et al. (2004) described studying war through drama and using a range of media to promote responses. These included photographs, re-enacting everyday scenes, use of sound (air raid sirens), music, movement, freeze framing and thought tracking. From this the children created scores of music to depict the scene and, using photographs, they worked in groups to describe it. Having worked on issues around evacuation, children wrote letters home in role, which demonstrated the power of this method of teaching.

### Using drama imaginatively

This example used *Where the Wild Things Are* by Maurice Sendak (Colleen Johnson, cited in Fisher and Williams 2004: 62). A Year 2 class had been reading this story of Max sent to bed without any supper as a punishment for his misbehaviour. From his room he embarks on a journey to a different land where the 'wild things live'. Later Max befriends huge scary monsters and becomes their 'king', but finally goes home. When he returns to his bedroom he finds his supper; it is still hot and time appears to have stood still. Using drama strategies the teacher re-enacts scenes from the story such as the first time Max sees the monsters. She first divides the class into two and asks the second group to choose a monster from the pictures in the text. She instructs them to make themselves into a 'wild thing' and after moving in role, on the signal they freeze. The other group wander around the still images, the teacher joining them speaking her thoughts aloud and encouraging the children to do the same: 'I'm terrified!', 'They'll kill me with their spiky teeth!', 'Is this a nightmare?' etc. The teacher then froze this group, asking them to remember their facial expressions. The group as monsters were then unfrozen so they could look at the images of Max. Groups were swapped over and in each case children could describe the expressions they saw and speculated what Max might do next. Out of role the children were asked to think of a time they were frightened. Further work on different scenes in the story took place and having really inhabited the setting and characters, the children could attempt a range of activities, such as writing a script of the story, or a diary of Max's feelings.

### Responding to a work of art

Using a painting as a stimulus (Andrew Green, cited in Fisher and Williams 2004: 49) with a Year 6 class is described (although other stimuli could be a map, object, piece of music, photograph, etc.). The class collectively, in small groups and individually, considered the picture (*Evening Thoughts* by Robert Herdman, National Gallery of Scotland) and were asked to focus on the young girl's expression in the picture, her clothing, the background and her likely emotional state, developing, as they did, banks of vocabulary and devising a story map for their piece of writing. One exceptional example showed the authentic response to such stimulus:

> Her mouth was an arch leading to a place full of sorrow and her eyes were a vortex trailing away to a distant place. She was a complete picture of total misery along with her life I thought suddenly.

### Using props to create narrative

Russell Jones (in Jones and Wyse 2004) reproduces a conversation with a teacher that demonstrates how creativity is achieved in the classroom. The teacher describes how s/he was working with a Year 3 class looking at Native American Indians and read *The Indian in the Cupboard*. Using a papier mâché figure of an Indian, the teacher asked the class to write about the Indian in the classroom and what happened if he came alive. Mindful of the National Literacy Strategy objective regarding adjectives, the teacher asked the children to think about the adjectives they used. The weakest child in the class, who was working towards level 1 in literacy, produced an 'amazing' story. The teacher stated:

> it gave me goosebumps. Some of the class are quite clever children, they came up on level 3, but for this child not only was the spelling quite good, the structure was there and her use of adjectives was amazing. When I read it out as it should have been read, her face . . . her smile just got bigger and bigger and bigger!

> (cited in Jones and Wyse 2004: 15)

## Common elements in creative approaches

Creative responses by pupils require creative approaches. What are some of the common elements in the examples above?

- using a range of stimuli for writing
- ensuring that children inhabit the text and that it becomes a 'lived' experience making any subsequent literacy activities authentic and real
- using talk and drama as a first step and part of the total learning experience
- combining a range of genres
- linking multimodal texts.

In addition, other triggers for creativity in this chapter have included the use of screen-based text, visual literacy, moving image and popular culture. All of these excite, engage and draw children into literacy practices. The renewed Primary Framework for Literacy (DfES 2006b) advocates the use of multimodal digital texts, together with an emphasis on speaking and listening. Let us hope that this inspires real excellence and enjoyment.

## Key points

- The Primary National Strategy promotes a 'rich and exciting experience' for pupils, yet there are inherent difficulties in a heavily prescriptive approach.
- Creativity involves generation, variation and originality of ideas and approaches.
- Multimodal texts combine word and image and often sound to create rich and varied contexts for learning.
- Popular culture, including computer games, comics, toys and popular music can act as a springboard into motivational literacy experiences.

---

**Answers for the activity on key themes of *Excellence and Enjoyment* on page 27**

Key words include 'rich and exciting experience', 'across the curriculum', 'teachers', 'control and flexibility', 'meet their particular needs'.

---

## Further reading

Craft, A. (2000) *Creativity across the Primary Curriculum: Framing and developing practice.* London: RoutledgeFalmer.

DfES (2003a) *Excellence and Enjoyment: A strategy for primary schools.* Nottingham: DfES Publications.

Jones, R. and Wyse, D. (eds) (2004) *Creativity in the Primary Curriculum.* London: David Fulton.

Marsh, J. and Millard, E. (2000) *Literacy and Popular Culture: Using children's culture in the classroom.* London: Paul Chapman.

## Resources for teaching

BBC film website – http://www.bbc.co.uk/film/
British Film Institute (BFI) dowloadable resources – http://www.bfi.org.uk/education/teaching/primary.html
BFI *Starting Stories* – http://www.bfi.org.uk/education/teaching/startingstories/
BFI *Starting Stories 2* – http://www.bfi.org.uk/education/teaching/startingstories2/
BFI *Story Shorts* – http://www.bfi.org.uk/education/teaching/storyshorts/
BFI *Story Shorts 2* – http://www.bfi.org.uk/education/teaching/storyshorts2/
Digital video (a *Guardian* supplement) – http://www.education.guardian.co.uk/digitalvideo/
Film education study resources – http://www.filmeducation.org/
Film trailers – http://www.apple.com/trailers/
National Curriculum in Action – http://www.ncaction.org.uk/creativity/index.htm

## Suggested authors of picture books

Janet and Allan Ahlberg (particularly *The Jolly Postman, Each Peach Pear Plum*)
Jez Alborough (*Where's My Teddy*)
Quentin Blake (particularly *Mrs Armitage on Wheels, Mr Magnolia*)
Anthony Browne (particularly *Changes, The Tunnel, Through the Magic Mirror, Gorilla, Voices in the Park*)
Eileen Browne (*Handa's Surprise*)
John Burningham (*The Shopping Basket, Oi Get off our Train!, Granpa, Mr Gumpy's Outing*)
Mary Hoffman (*Amazing Grace*)
Pat Hutchins (*Rosie's Walk*)
Mick Inkpen (particularly *Blue Balloon*)
Simon James (*Dear Greenpeace, Sally and the Limpet*)
Colin McNaughton (*Suddenly, Boo!, Have You Seen Who's Just Moved in Next Door to Us?*)
Alfred Noyes (*The Highwayman*)
Michael Rosen (particularly *We're Going on a Bear Hunt*)
Jon Scieszka and Lane Smith (*The Stinky Cheese Man and Other Fairly Stupid Tales, The True Story of the Three Little Pigs*)
Maurice Sendak (*Where the Wild Things Are*)
Colin Thompson (*Falling Angels*)
Martin Waddell (*Owl Babies, Can't You Sleep, Little Bear?, Farmer Duck*)
Kit Wright (*Tigerella, Dolphinella*)

# 4 Communication, language and literacy in the early years

## Purpose of this chapter

This chapter aims to:

- Provide a broad overview of early language development and a range of theories that seek to explain this process.
- Present a range of ways of supporting early language development.
- Discuss links with language and literacy at home.
- Examine ways of developing literacy through play and creativity.
- Support early reading development, particularly through phonological awareness.
- Examine ways of supporting children's early attempts at writing and how to scaffold (support) the process.

## Early language development

The development of language is one of the most remarkable developmental achievements that human beings make. As Hetherington (1999) explains:

> Language is one of the most complex systems of rules a person ever learns, yet children in a wide range of different environments and cultures learn to understand and use their native languages in a relatively short period.
>
> (Hetherington 1999: 274)

The new Early Years Foundation Stage (EYFS) (DfES 2007b), due to come into force in September 2008, has been designed to support this process and it states: 'As children develop speaking and listening skills they build the foundations for literacy, for making sense of visual and verbal signs and ultimately for reading and writing' (*Practice Guidance for the Early Years Foundation Stage*, DfES 2007b: 39). Having a clear understanding of how early language is acquired and knowing how to support the development of speaking and listening is therefore crucial to working with young children.

## Theories of language development

A wealth of research into language development has produced a range of different theories to explain the emergence of communication, language and literacy skills.

Essentially these theories revolve around the role of genetics and environment although many now agree it is a combination. This section summarises the main theories that explain language development (for more information, see further reading at the end of this chapter).

---

**Activity: Theories of language development: implications for practitioners**

Read the brief summaries of theories that follow and, together with colleagues if possible, make notes on the role of the practitioner according to each view.

---

### *The behaviourist view*

Traditional learning theorists invoke the principle of reinforcement to explain language development. According to this view (e.g. Skinner 1957) the carers selectively reinforce a child's sounds that are most like adult speech and by showing approval encourage their child to repeat them. Other learning theories, e.g. Bandura (1977), propose that the child learns primarily through imitation or observational learning. According to this, the child picks up words, etc. by imitation from what he/she hears. Then through reinforcement or generalization the child learns to use the words when appropriate.

### *The nativist view*

This theory originated from the work of Noam Chomsky (1957) who proposed that children are born with an innate mental structure that guides their acquisition of language and in particular grammar. This he terms a *language acquisition device* (LAD). The justification for this is that certain universal features are common to all languages (e.g. sentences in all languages contain a verb, subject and object). Children then use a set of innate language hypotheses to derive rules from the language data that they hear. Children acquire complex language quickly, which indicates that they could not learn this from fragmented and incomplete environmental input; this skill must be partially innate.

### *The cognitive view*

According to this view, language development was seen as part of general cognitive development. It links to Piaget's (1954) description of mental structures or schemas, which are created by the child's explorations with the environment. This perspective sees the child as a meaning maker, actively seeking to make sense of the world. This suggests that cognitive development precedes language development and therefore, for example, children understand the concept of an object before they learn the word for it. From this perspective children's language development is dependent on their cognitive development.

*The social interactionist view*

This view sees the interplay between biological and environmental factors in the acquisition of language. Language is learned in the context of spoken language but also humans are biologically prepared for learning language. Factors that are important are the child's active role; they formulate, test and evaluate hypotheses concerning the rules of language, plus the role of carers in supporting the process. Jerome Bruner (1986) proposed a *language acquisition support system* (LASS) which contrasts to Chomsky's language acquisition device and emphasises the role of the carer/parents as facilitators of language acquisition. This consists of a series of techniques that adults use to facilitate language – playing non-verbal games, using simplified speech, and elaborating or rewording children's utterances.

## Development of language in children

Before considering further the impact of such theories on practice, it is important to be aware of the common developmental sequence that children encounter as they become proficient language users. It is vital to bear in mind that the sequence is only a guide; children are all individuals with varying home contexts. Table 4.1 provides a brief summary of the main features.

*Table 4.1* Stages of language development

| Developmental stage | Common features |
| --- | --- |
| Pre-verbal communication | From birth: parent/carer, sounds, movements, smiles and other facial expressions show a type of dialogue – early conversation. From 3 to 12 months: increased ability to use gesture to communicate and respond to adult. About 7 to 8 months: adults point to draw attention to objects. By 1 year: children are highly skilled at non-verbal communication, e.g. point to request something. As they learn language they combine words and gestures. At 3 years onwards: they reduce their use of gesture and rely more on verbal skills. |
| Early language comprehension – receptive language | Even pre-natally children may develop a preference for own language. Understanding begins very early. Babies show a preference for human speech rather than other sounds. Even 2-day-old infants can distinguish their mother's voice. From 1 month old: ability to discriminate speech sounds develops. From about 6 months: children more able to engage in turn taking games involving sounds and body movements. From 18 to 24 months: children learn new words at a rapid rate, mapping the concept to the word. |

*continued on next page*

*Table 4.1* continued

| Developmental stage | Common features |
| --- | --- |
| | From 24 to 36 months: developing conversation skills. From 5 years: understanding develops of non-literal speech. |
| Babbling and other early sounds – productive language | End of first month: vowel-like sounds start. Middle of the first year: babbling (strings of consonant-vowel combinations), common across all languages. End of first year: patterned speech begins – strings of words made up of phonemes from own language which sound like speech but are not. Middle of second year: cultural differences in pre-speech sounds begin to emerge. |
| Semantic development acquiring words | Vocabulary acquisition proceeds in bursts. From 10 to 15 months: children usually utter first words. About 18 months: rapid increase in vocabulary (typically about 50 words). Average child 2 years: ranges from 600 to 900 words. About 6 years: about 8000 words. To learn a word – requires appropriate concept and sound and to link the two, called 'fast mapping'. This is helped by interacting and reading to children. Errors illuminate the learning process, for example: over-extension – a single word to cover many different things, e.g 'doggie' for cows, horses, etc. Under-extension children use a single word in a highly restricted way – e.g. a child may use 'car' only for her family car. |
| Acquisition of grammar – learning the rules | First words not just naming, but expressing ideas. Between $1\frac{1}{2}$ and 2 years: two-word sentences – telegraphic speech. Stages in learning rules, e.g. use of plurals and past tense. In third year: children show signs of understanding the rules and use sentences so complex that it is difficult to analyse all the rules they have learned. |

### Key learning principles in communication

Guidance for practitioners from the DfES (2005a), entitled *Communicating Matters*, refers to these stages as strands and presents *key learning principles* (KLP) within each strand.

#### Knowing and using sounds and signs

This involves having the ability to recognise, comprehend and produce the distinct sounds critical for oral language behaviour, or to recognise, comprehend and produce the individual signs and symbols of alternative modes of communication.

- KLP: Sounds are heard in the interactive context of language in regular use in social life.
- KLP: Infants continuously seek and construct patterns of language and communication.
- KLP: Having common ground for communication, and learning to share attention with other people, gives a context for children's developing language.

*Knowing and using words*

This involves having the ability to recognise, comprehend and produce the particular units of language, in particular words or phrases, which carry independent meanings sufficiently distinct for them to be demarcated from other words or phrases.

- KLP: Words start to be produced in line with a child's increasing ability to share attention and identify common communicative ground with others in a variety of situations.
- KLP: There is a broad timespan for the production of first words within the normal frame of development; some children might do this at 9 months, others not until they are nearly 2 years old.
- KLP: Word combination starts when children know between 50 and 100 words; it is the number of words they know that is significant rather than their age; adults know an average of between 50,000 and 100,000 words.

*Structuring language*

This involves having the ability to recognise, comprehend and produce longer units of language that are organised in systematic ways and which generate more complex units of communication appropriate for many different purposes.

- KLP: The wider communicative environment in which children find themselves provides the resources with which they learn to construct language; this happens through their increasing experience of social and interactive situations.

*Making language work*

This involves having the ability to recognise, comprehend and produce language appropriate for a range of different social interactions, recognising social conventions and their variations, and combining different modes of communication for full effect.

- KLP: Features of adult–child interaction are culturally determined, and conventions for interaction vary, both within and across speech communities. This does not affect the final outcome, in the sense that all these children learn to speak and communicate.

### Becoming an effective communicator

Not only is it important to be aware of the common sequence that children go through in learning language, but also it is important to realise that to be an effective speaker requires a complicated set of skills. These require the child to

- engage the attention of listeners
- be sensitive to listeners' feedback
- adjust speech to listeners, e.g. age, cultural and social factors (a school child learns to speak differently to a teacher and a classmate)
- understand it is a two-way process and there is a need to be a good speaker and listener
- recognise their own communication skills and be able to evaluate their own messages.

Considering the complexity of the above, it is remarkable that by 2 years old children are generally very adept. They have learned to adjust speech when talking to other children of different ages, for example they use more repetitions when talking to baby brothers or sisters than older children or parents. The crucial factor to bear in mind is the interaction they have with others: children learn from direct instruction and by observing others.

*Table 4.2* Supporting children's language development

| Key factors | Examples |
| --- | --- |
| **People** <br> Play, talk and interaction with other people are the key. | Listen carefully to the child and respond accordingly. |
| **Places** <br> School settings – small rooms or the creation of safe areas. | Provide a changing range of play-based areas that encourage talk. |
| **Activities** <br> Varied opportunities for talking, singing, listening and watching and helping. | Expand and model conversations supported with visual material. |
| **Subjects** <br> Ample opportunities for talk about topics that are relevant and meaningful to children. | Read, tell and talk about stories. |

---

**Activity: Supporting language activities**

Review the key factors to ensure rich linguistic beginnings in Table 4.2. Under each of the key factors

- people
- places
- activities
- subjects

provide further examples of ways to encourage and support children's rich linguistic beginnings in the Foundation Stage.

---

### Knowledge and practitioners

Practitioners working with young children should therefore:

- Understand, as Marian Whitehead (2004) summarises:
  - all children are linguists
  - all languages are complex grammatical systems
  - all natural languages, are or have been spoken
  - language and thinking are inextricably linked
- Support children with symbolic representation of ideas through playing, gesturing, drawing, building, labelling, naming, storytelling and writing.
- Support children with significant aspects of the language curriculum:
  - playing with language
  - telling stories and sharing books
  - writing
  - using 'words about language' (e.g. word, letter, etc.).

One of the key issues is the importance of the relationships that are built up with young children. Marian Whitehead highlights the importance of providing 'genuinely mutual conversations between children and adults, and between children and children' (Whitehead: 2004: 106).

The Early Years Foundation Stage (DfES 2007b) Practice Guidance stresses the importance of this and states:

> To become skilful communicators, babies and children need to be with people who have meaning for them and with whom they have warm and loving relationships, such as their family or carers and, in a group situation, a key person whom they know and trust.
>
> (DfES 2007b: 39)

### Speaking and listening

Language is a tool for thinking as well as being vital for communication and this process is facilitated by interaction with others and through appropriate stimulus. Practitioners therefore need to support children's speaking and listening skills as this is crucial to their ability to learn effectively. Speaking and listening also underpins children's ability to deal with written language; to read it and to write it.

The Curriculum Guidance for the Foundation Stage does not specifically use the term 'Speaking and Listening'; instead it calls this 'Communication, Language and Literacy', perhaps a more apt term. This term is also used by the Early Years Foundation Stage (DfES 2007b). The renewed Primary Framework for Literacy (DfES 2006b) has now placed speaking and listening firmly at the centre of 'literacy' and shown a clear progression from Foundation Stage to Key Stage 3. Further discussion of this will be examined in Chapter 6. In the Foundation Stage, it is important that this builds on an understanding of children's early language development and that teachers consider how they may support children in the following ways:

- Acknowledge and build on the invaluable contribution that home makes to the development of language. Gordon Wells' study found that at schools children had fewer interactions with adults than at home and stated: 'for no child was the language experience of the classroom richer than that of the home' (Wells 1986: 87).
- Understand the value of talk and the potential it provides for children's learning. The danger is to value a piece of written work as more tangible evidence of learning and to feel that a noisy classroom is evidence that not much work is taking place, and yet the contrary is the case.
- Model the use of talk in a variety of ways and particularly model the art of being a good 'active' listener. This is clearly signalled by really listening to children and what they have to say and building on their understanding sensitively by asking relevant and challenging questions.
- Engage in meaningful dialogue. This notion of encouraging dialogue has become known as 'sustained shared thinking' as a result of the lengthy research undertaken by Sylva et al. (2004) known as the EPPE (Effective Pre-school and Primary Education) study, which found that 'excellent' settings encouraged relatively more 'sustained shared thinking' which consists of an episode in which two or more individuals 'work together' in an intellectual way to solve a problem, clarify a concept, evaluate activities, extend a narrative etc. Both parties must contribute to the thinking and it must develop and extend.

---

**Activity: What is sustained shared thinking?**

Read the two extracts from the EPPE study which illustrates interaction between an adult and children.

- Which example provides evidence of sustained shared thinking?
- Which example illustrates the adult really 'tuning in' to the children's discussion?

**Extract 1**

Eight children aged 4–5 years and nursery teacher:

*Teacher:* What area of science did we cover last week?

*Joe:* The skeleton.

*Teacher:* What is the name of it?

*Lucy:* Biology.

*Teacher:* This week we are going to be looking at zoology. A zoologist is a person who studies animals. What does a zoologist study?

*Joe:* Animals.

*Teacher:* A biologist studies?

*Ganesh:* Animals.

(Teacher reads from a book about zoology)

*Teacher:* What's the backbone called Ganesh?

*Ganesh:* Th- The spine.

*Teacher:* Animals with a backbone are called vertebrates.
  – I need you to know that animals with backbones are vertebrates, animals without backbones are called invertebrates.

*Teacher:* Harry, an animal with out a backbone is called a . . .?

*Harry:* Reptile.

*Teacher:* No, a vertebrate. I've got some things for you to have a look at and then we're going to put them into categories.

*Teacher:* Do you think crocodiles have got a backbone?

*Ganesh:* A backbone.

*Teacher:* What kind of animals are they?

*Ganesh:* Vertebrates.

(All the children are invited to look at a poster of vertebrate/invertebrate.)

*Teacher:* We are going to look at the different groups these animals fall into. We're going to talk about mammals.

*Harry:* It's like a reindeer.

*Teacher:* Yes it is, but what's the difference between a reindeer and a starfish?

*Harry:* It's like a star.

*Ganesh:* The reindeer is a vertebrate.

*Teacher:* The female mammal feeds the baby with their own milk. This makes the mammal special. What else feeds with its own milk?

*Charlotte:* Cows.

*Ganesh:* Tigers.

*Teacher:* What are we called? Are we mammals?

*Joe:* No.

*Teacher:* Why Ganesh?

*Ganesh:* No we are. We have a backbone.

*Teacher:* Did Mummy feed you? What with?

*Joe:* Cows.

*Teacher:* No, breast milk.

*Ganesh:* And very good it was too.

**(Later . . .)**

*Teacher:* Something else I forgot to tell you, mammals are warm-blooded. If you cut yourself the blood that comes out is . . .?

| | |
|---|---|
| Harry: | Cold. |
| Teacher: | Tomorrow we are going to look at where mammals and arthropods live. What are we going to do tomorrow? |
| Ganesh: | Look at where they live. |

## Extract 2

The following interaction shows what may be achieved by children of the same age when they are supported and encouraged:

| | |
|---|---|
| Tom: | (boy 4:8) How did God make himself? |
| Teacher: | Well in most of the books about God, it says God just is. |
| Tom: | Well how did God make us? |
| Teacher: | I don't know. What do you think? |
| Tom: | I don't know. |
| Teacher: | Well how would *you* make yourself? |
| Grace: | (girl 4:9) I would make myself happy. |
| Tom: | I think when God made us, we made God. |
| Grace: | He putted [sic] our bones in first and then he putted our blood on the bones and then he putted our skin on. |
| Tom: | No – he opened up our bones and put the blood in us. |
| Grace: | No – if he put it in our bones, the blood wouldn't come out. |
| Tom: | (changing subject) You don't know what's there (pointing to throat). These are microphones to talk. My dad told me. |
| Grace: | You're wrong. |
| Tom: | No! I'm right! |
| Grace: | No *and* your dad's wrong. |
| Tom: | No he's not! He's right . . . I want to draw. |

(He goes to get paper and pencils.)

(Tom returns and begins to draw 'a bone'.)

| | |
|---|---|
| Grace: | That's a funny bone. |
| Tom: | Yes – but it *is* a bone. |
| Grace: | (drawing) He's got long arms to let him make his dinner. Cos my mum's got long arms like me. (pauses and thinks) . . . If the blood was inside your bones . . . |
| Tom: | (interrupting) I know your blood is out of your bones . . . |
| Grace: | (ignoring Tom's comment and pointing to a blood vessel in her finger) Look! So why are you telling me blood's in the bones? . . . I know God's got blood. |
| Tom: | No he hasn't. |
| Grace: | Yes he has. Why do you think we have blood and everybody has blood and he doesn't? . . . |
| | (Showing her picture to Sophie – girl 3:11) Look I done [sic] God. |
| Sophie: | That's not God. . . . It's too little. |
| Tom: | So how did God make eyes and eyelashes? |
| Teacher: | I don't know. |
| Grace: | I know – he does the bone in the eye (pointing to the iris) and then he paints the white. |
| Teacher: | So God paints you does he? |

| | |
|---|---|
| *Grace:* | He painted your eyes. |
| *Tom:* | No it's not. |
| *Grace:* | It is. |
| *Tom:* | How does the paint stay on anyhow? |
| *Grace:* | (chanting) Easy peasy lemon squeezy. |
| *Tom:* | I hate 'easy peasy lemon squeezy'. |
| *Teacher:* | So you don't think Grace's right then? |
| *Grace:* | I am right and Tom's wrong. |
| *Tom:* | We're both wrong – well you're wrong and I didn't say anything. |

(The following week the teacher brings in a dog's skull and the following week a skeleton – the discussion about bones and blood continues in detail and in an equally dramatic fashion!)

### Supporting children's talk

To support children's learning through talk, a teacher should not merely take over the conversation, but instead guide the children. The teacher should:

- focus on the child and listen to what he or she is saying
- summarise what the child has said to check the message has been understood
- help the child to focus on significant aspects
- show respect for the child's views and support him/her in the next steps
- help with sequencing a particular issue, where appropriate
- ask genuine questions that respond to what a child has said
- treat the child as an equal
- make tentative suggestions, e.g. 'Perhaps if . . .'
- let the child do most of the talking.

### Providing an environment for talk

To develop a climate of meaningful and valued talk, certain prerequisites are necessary. Children need to feel secure and free to make mistakes without being judged. They need to feel their culture or home background is acknowledged and their views are taken seriously. The next step is to ensure that the environment lends itself to talk.

Review the bullet points below with colleagues and decide which are particularly important.

### Classroom areas

- There should be a rich environment of print, for example with signs and labels including the home languages of pupils, which encourages children to interact.
- Role-play opportunities are provided that encourage talk, in which adults take part.
- A listening area should be included.
- Furniture should be arranged to support interaction.
- Writing areas should permit sharing.

- Class noticeboard is provided where children are encouraged to interact with their attempts at mark-making (i.e. when children make representations through drawing or attempts at writing).
- Reading corners support interaction with a range of books and print displayed and related to play activities (e.g. a letter from Goldilocks saying she is sorry to the Three Bears).
- Other areas of learning help to develop collaboration.

*Opportunities for partner or small group work*

- Children have a talk partner and this has been modelled and discussed with them.
- They share ideas with their partner before the rest of the class.
- Specific tasks for children in pairs are set up.
- Children are encouraged to discover specific aspects about a class topic and then share with partners/groups and the rest of the class.

*Resources*

- Tape recorders and tapes.
- Telephones.
- Dressing-up clothes.
- Puppets.
- Storysacks or storyboards.
- Visitors to the classroom.
- Opportunities to explore first hand a range of materials and practical equipment.
- Use of various games that support interaction.

*Activities*

- Topics are chosen with opportunities for talk highlighted.
- The teacher takes part in role-play.
- Storytelling or activities result from stories read.
- Drama techniques such as hot-seating are used. (*Hot-seating* is a drama device where one person acts in role and others ask questions related to the role.)
- Circle time is provided that encourages everyone to talk.
- Classroom routines encourage talk.

**Lesson planning**

Opportunities for talk need to be carefully planned for: bear in mind the following:

- Key questions are decided in advance and noted in planning.
- Focused group or whole-class work should provide opportunities for discussion with partners/peers.
- Clear structure is given to oral tasks.
- Careful support and monitoring are provided by the teacher.

Useful resources and ideas for planning lessons are provided in *Talk Box: Speaking and Listening Activities for Learning at Key Stage 1* by Lyn Dawes and Claire Sams (2004). In particular the use of an actual box with a range of props to provide a visual focus is recommended, including resources that relate to a particular lesson, for example items from a story to be read, or pictures that depict scenes that promote discussion.

## Links with language and literacy at home

For opportunities for talk and the development of literacy to be really effective in the classroom, it is important to build on children's experiences at home. A number of detailed long-term ethnographic studies have revealed the richness and intellectual power of young children's language development in secure and familiar domestic settings (Heath 1983; Tizard and Hughes 1984; Campbell 1999; Whitehead 2002).

The way the child interacts with his or her own family in relation to literacy is important. It is therefore necessary to tune into the child's family literacy and use this as a springboard to help his or her development. This was clearly acknowledged in the Curriculum Guidance for the Foundation Stage, and now in the Practice Guidance for the Early Years Foundation Stage (DfES 2007b), which includes an underlying principle:

> Parents are children's first and most enduring educators. When parents and practitioners work together in early years settings, the results have a positive impact on children's development and learning.
>
> (DfES 2007a: 2.2)

It is interesting to note that this has not always been the case and it was not until the late 1960s and early 1970s, following the Plowden Report (Central Advisory Council for Education 1967) that the case for parental involvement was argued and innovative programmes began to be disseminated and have effect. Following this a series of legislation (Education Acts of 1980, 1981, 1986 and 1988) all strengthened the rights of parents to be involved in their children's schooling.

### Advantages of involving parents

Legislation requires schools to involve parents, but the advantages of doing so can support children's development in the following ways:

- supporting practitioners in developing a fuller picture of the child
- helping transition from home to school
- supporting two-way communication from school to home and vice versa
- sharing with parents what a child is learning
- helping parents to support children at home
- extending the curriculum to include contributions from the parents and community.

Many schools have developed home/school diaries that support this process and have an open-door policy to encourage parents to come into school to help and work with their child. Particular projects that involve parents can support this, so that children may be asked to find out about the history of their name or provide pictures of themselves as a baby, etc. With the increasing development of Children's Centres as a 'one-stop shop' for families and a range of services available at one site, enabling partnerships with parents should be facilitated.

The DfES materials entitled *Involving Parents, Raising Achievement* (2003b) presents a clear rationale and summary of research into the benefits of involving parents. This provides materials for schools to audit their work in this area with ideas to improve activities. A range of research has been cited by the DfES (2003d) in *The Impact of Parental Involvement on Children's Education* to show the value of parental involvement for the development of literacy skills including:

> The frequency with which the child plays with letters/numbers at home was linked with attainment in all measures.
> Parents' drawing children's attention to sounds and letters was linked to literacy skills, early number skills and non-verbal attainment.
>
> (DfES 2003d: 1)

### Environmental print

Environmental print is the print found in the local environment, such as road signs and street names. It can be an effective bridge between children's experience of literacy at home and their learning in school. Literacy development begins very early as babies are surrounded by print, and children begin to understand the symbolic awareness of print. Thus 'C Beebies', 'Toys 'R' Us' or 'McDonald's' are recognised at an early age. At home children are surrounded by writers (of shopping lists, birthday cards, tax forms, cheques, letters, etc.): from this children begin to develop rules about writing. The task of the teacher is to help those implicit understandings to become explicit. Role-play provides frequent opportunities for literacy, for example children writing prescriptions in the context of a role-play area as a health centre. Classrooms should be print-rich and culturally diverse to build on the fertile world of print outside school. This needs to include digital literacy, a growing literacy source in most homes, and ensure that socio-dramatic play includes different forms of ICT, such as a computer-based inventory, or internet link for information searches.

Children can take part in 'print walks' around the classroom, school or the local area, looking for examples of print. Making use of digital photography by the children as well as the teacher can support a range of literacy work in the classroom, encompassing labelling, describing, citing areas of interest or areas for improvement, and actively interrogating the print around them. Many early years classrooms demonstrate a print-rich environment with examples of labels and signs clearly displayed: in guided print walks around the classroom, teachers can point out examples of print and what they say. This needs to be ongoing to show what is constantly added to the classroom. By such means children can be alert to the classroom as a rich resource for literacy activities.

Using the awareness of print around them can be a powerful incentive to beginning reading and one very useful activity is to create environmental scrapbooks consisting of a range of captions and advertisements that children readily recognise.

A scrapbook could include wrappers from items such as cornflakes, crisps, chocolate bars or popular toys. Children loved to 'read' the book and parents were encouraged to make their own. This supports the use of print around children and helps develop their confidence as print users.

The most significant piece of writing in a child's life is his or her name. How often do you hear young children say, 'Look, Mummy, that is in my name!' as they point to a particular letter on a sign or poster. As many Foundation Stage teachers know, 'games with names' are a good way into early writing. Most classrooms have children's possessions labelled with their name and often an accompanying picture. They can then sort their name cards according to those that begin (or end) with the same letter and use them to record who is here, playing in a certain area, etc. When this is accompanied by the child's picture, either current or as a baby, this can generate real interest. It is often illuminating to ask parents to tell the story of the child's name: how it was chosen and where it came from. Names can be a powerful motivator for children, especially when slipped into stories or songs.

### *Play, drawing and narrative*

Children gradually assimilate their everyday experiences into their play. Loris Malaguzzi's (1998) inspirational work with early years children in the Reggio Emilia area of Italy describes this as the 'hundred languages of children'. These 'languages' may consist of storytelling, singing, dancing, patterning, model-making, drawing or talking. For children, it is through play that meaning is negotiated and symbolism is used.

The importance of early mark-making and drawing to the development of literacy stems from children's attempts to fix their play in time. These attempts to symbolically represent aspects of their play are driven through natural need and by mirroring the examples of literacy they experience at home and in the environment. Thus a child learns that a shopping list consists of a series of words, each written on a separate line, while a note to someone consists of continuous print (see Figure 4.1).

## Developing literacy through play and creativity

There is a strong tradition in early years education regarding play as the key way in which young children learn. Research has shown that play is important socially, emotionally, physically, intellectually and linguistically. This is supported by the Practice Guidance for the Early Years Foundation Stage (DfES 2007b) which states:

> Providing well-planned experiences based on children's spontaneous play, both indoors and outdoors, is an important way in which practitioners support young children to learn with enjoyment and challenge.
>
> (DfES 2007b: 8)

This is not always well understood by parents who feel that school should be 'work' and not 'play'. This is encapsulated by Timothy Mo in *Sour Sweet* (1982). Here a Chinese mother is aghast at her young son's description of school:

Punjabi

a list of clothes for a
service wash, with cost
and time.

jumper
socks
scarf
tights
leggings
dress
shirt
apron
2p
10 minutes

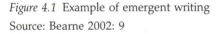

Out of order + signature
of manager.

*Figure 4.1* Example of emergent writing
Source: Bearne 2002: 9

> She couldn't believe that Son dropped in an aside that they played with plasti-
> cine and flour and water in the classroom. He had been doing that at home
> for years.
> 'Bad to tell lies, Son,' she admonished him gently.
>
> (cited in Hall and Robinson 2003: 5)

Later in the story, the mother discovers that her son has no difficulty working with
money when helping in the family shop. He tells her that he has played shops at
school with plastic meat and pretend money. But she can't believe he could be learning in this way and retorts: 'Clever Boy.' Kiss. 'But bad to tell lies, Son.'

Play is diverse and consists of different forms. Corinne Hutt et al. (1989) have
shown that play consists of epistemic play and ludic play. Epistemic play concerns
children exploring and learning by doing. Ludic play includes socio-dramatic play
and offers more opportunities for language play, creativity, and literacy development. Hall and Robinson (2003) suggest that planning opportunities should take
the following into account:

- A theme that naturally has a range of literacy activities.
- A setting that is relevant to the children's lives but also can extend their
  knowledge.
- Where possible visit a real-life example of the intended setting.
- A setting that can have more than one possible area, e.g. a zoo park with an
  animal care centre and a customer care centre.
- A setting that has a range of literate character roles.

- A setting in which there are different kinds of print for different purposes.
- Allow the children to design and build the setting.
- Join the children and play in the setting from time to time.

An example cited by Hall and Robinson (2003) involves visiting a garage:

- A visit to a local garage to examine what happened there and with a focus on types of environmental print.
- Whole-class discussion of the visit including the kinds of jobs they had seen and the roles that would be needed in the classroom, plus the necessary props.
- A thank you letter to the garage owner following the visit.
- Applying to the council for planning permission to build a garage. Here the children wrote to the Town Planning Department and in response were asked to fill in a form. The teacher read the form and wrote the children's responses.
- Drawing up plans for building the garage with labels.
- Lists of things needed to set up a garage.
- Response to a letter of complaint about plans to build a garage.
- Planning the opening with a notice, advertisement, programme of events, and name badges.
- Job advertisements and applications.
- Playing in the garage encourage the following: notices, clipboards, lists, instructions (e.g. how to change a wheel), estimates for repairs, etc.

Summing up the impact of the project, Hall and Robinson stated that:

> During the entire course of the case study the children demonstrated massive engagement in, and enjoyment of, the experience . . . the children engaged in the writing with considerable intensity and purpose.
>
> (Hall and Robinson 2003: 124)

The project promoted considerable engagement with parents, who contributed in many ways such as making child-sized overalls, coming to the opening and listening to the children's recounts, all of which involved many literacy experiences.

## Developing a love of reading in the early years

In order for children to develop as readers, they need to have experienced the delight that books can bring. This should begin early and initiatives such as 'Books for Babies' have helped to promote it. These first experiences may be multisensory when books contain tactile surfaces and other sensory delights. Books such as *The Very Hungry Caterpillar* by Eric Carle or *Dear Zoo* by Rod Campbell contain visual features which extend the playful possibilities. These first experiences are shared with an adult, and for children represent a time of warmth, security and pleasure.

Children develop favourite books which must be read again and again and in turn the child retells, turning the pages as if actually reading the words. Here the young child is switching on to book language, rehearsing for later reading and importantly being introduced to the unique voices of many authors. As experience of literary texts grows, it supports a range of skills and principally the desire to create meaning by questioning and commenting on events. The role of the adult or practitioner is crucial here in mediating their understanding, and many authors support the process by encouraging the children to interact by creating spyholes as in *Peepo* by Janet and Allen Ahlberg, or other picture clues as in *Rosie's Walk* by Pat Hutchins. One of the key skills that young children develop is the ability to predict what will happen next. Prediction is a key skill for readers in order to constantly search for meaning in the text. It is from the early enjoyable experiences of the wealth of children's literature that reading skills are formed. It is also by playing with words and language, another commonly enjoyable occupation with young children, that the basic building blocks of mapping the sounds and symbols of our language are developed.

### Developing phonological awareness

Research (e.g. Bryant and Bradley 1985; Adams 1990) has shown that through playing with sounds, children develop the ability to understand that the stream of sounds that represents speech is made up of individual words, which are made up of individual sounds or phonemes. Phonological awareness is the ability to distinguish individual sounds and in turn is the foundation for mapping the sounds (phonemes) to their letters (graphemes). This is a powerful predictor for later literacy success and, importantly, it can be taught through a range of suitable activities for young children. A lack of phonological awareness can considerably hamper children's progress and it is therefore important to ensure that children are adept at discriminating and manipulating sounds.

Phonological awareness also consists of different steps. These can be thought of as ranging from larger to smaller units:

- word awareness: understanding that sentences consist of individual words
- rhyme awareness: being able to identify words that have identical final sound segments
- syllable awareness: being able to hear parts or segments of phonemes that comprise the rhythm of the word
- phonemic awareness: being able to attend to, identify, and manipulate the sounds that are representative of graphemes in the English language.

Children find it easier to begin with the larger units (words and rhymes) and then begin to break these into smaller units (syllables and phonemes). Table 4.3 describes a programme of activities to support children's phonological awareness.

Early experiences with a range of books and playing with sounds and words all support the development of reading. This is explored fully in Chapter 7, which discusses the teaching and learning of reading.

### Emergent writing

Reading and writing are closely interlinked, supported by speaking and listening. It is by supporting these links that children best learn to become literate. The term 'emergent' literacy refers to the phase when a child is in the process of becoming literate, between approximately six months and school entry. Marie Clay (1979)

*Table 4.3* Developing phonological awareness

| Step | | Objectives | Suggested activities |
|---|---|---|---|
| Listening | 1 | To listen attentively | Stories and role-play<br>'Simon Says' game<br>Follow my leader<br>Songs and tunes |
| | 2 | To identify environmental sounds | Taped sounds<br>Water play<br>Songs, e.g. 'Old MacDonald had a Farm' |
| | 3 | To identify speech sounds | Songs, e.g. 'Tommy Thumb'<br>Play activities with telephones<br>Read *Polar Bear, Polar Bear What do You Hear?* by Eric Carle<br>'Chinese Whispers' |
| Rhyme | 4 | To hear examples of rhymes | Nursery rhymes – familiarity with hearing a range of rhymes<br>Songs, e.g. ' Fox in a Box'<br>Rhyming books, e.g. Dr Seuss |
| | 5 | To identify rhymes | Same or different – rhyming pictures<br>Deliberate mistakes – children have to spot the deliberate mistake in the nursery rhyme |
| | 6 | To generate rhymes | Alternative nursery rhymes – substituting different rhyming words<br>Rhyming couplets<br>Songs, e.g. 'Row, row your boat' |
| Words | 7 | To identify individual words | Count the words using counters<br>Track the words – use a pointer<br>Poems and songs that emphasise individual words, e.g. 'POP goes the weasel!' |
| Syllables | 8 | To identify syllables | Clapping games<br>Tap your name |
| | 9 | To maintain a syllable pattern | Musical instruments – copying a pattern demonstrated and continuing the pattern |
| Phonemes | 10 | To learn the alphabet | Alphabet songs and rhymes |
| | 11 | To identify lower- and upper-case letters | Alphabet matching – cards: one set for upper-case letters and one for lower-case to hang on washing line or to play a series of matching/pairs games |
| | 12 | To identify initial letter sounds | Songs and rhymes, e.g. 'To market, to market to buy a fat pig'<br>'I Spy'<br>Alliteration – alliterative sentences, e.g. Wayne wears Wellies, alliterative names, Big Brian, Tall Thomas |

Source: adapted from Jolliffe 2006a

introduced this term when she described the knowledge and awareness that young children have about print before starting school. Clay emphasises the interrelationship between speaking, listening, reading and writing.

Children begin the process of mark-making early, representing their thoughts about experiences and cultural images. This starts with the way in which young children attach special importance to a toy or blanket. From then on marks using a range of media are common, from smearing food on a high tray to daubing with paint or crayons. Drawings and writing are produced together and many researchers (Ferreiro and Teberosky 1982; Kress 1997; Hall and Robinson 2003) emphasise the significance of these early drawings that precede and accompany writing.

Understanding early writing is supported by three principles (Goodman 1984):

- *functional principle:* writing has a purpose for the writer (e.g. putting up a notice)
- *linguistic principle:* writing is a system which is organised into letters and words
- *relational principle:* there is a connection between the spoken and written word.

Emergent writing develops children's creativity and encourages them to experiment. It is this experimentation that helps children not only to 'find the frontier that differentiates drawing from writing' (Ferreiro and Teberosky 1982), but also to crack the writing code and begin to understand the correspondence between letters and sounds. It is a backwards step if when children start school at 5 years old, they feel that only by tracing and copying will they come to learn how to write. It is not, however, a matter of leaving children alone to learn to write. They need support from teachers who can respond, monitor and help development as children learn about the writing system. The process also encourages children to try spellings and work out how to represent sounds rather than rely on the teacher.

## Supporting early writing

A key factor in success is to place writing in a meaningful context and to provide a real purpose in order to make those crucial links with literacy at home. Providing a supportive environment that encourages early writing involves the following:

- Modelling writing for children in a range of forms, for example writing letters, notes or filling forms, in addition to scribing for children in shared writing.
- Providing a range of writing materials for children to investigate. For example, a variety of paper, from different colours to little notes, lists and large pieces of paper which can be stuck to the floor or table with large pens. Other items that can be motivating are diaries, postcards, envelopes, stamps, computers and a range of forms of print displayed including junk mail with opportunities to complete forms etc.
- Creating a workshop area, for example for making small books with a range of supporting materials, such as glue, staples, lists of words, name cards etc.
- Displaying examples of writing in a range of languages and scripts.
- Producing published examples of the children's work using computers, printers and digital cameras.
- Supplying a real purpose and audience for writing.
- Giving positive feedback that supports children's learning in manageable ways.

- Having opportunities to practise writing in various ways.
- Providing natural ways into writing alongside play (such as prescription pads in the health centre, telephone message pads in the home corners, shopping lists, etc.).
- Accepting children's tentative attempts at writing.
- Supporting children's fine motor skills in the development of handwriting through a range of exercises.

Above all, it is important that children see themselves as writers and are not dissuaded from attempting it due to the complexity of correct written English.

### Talking before writing

One of the keys to encouraging children to write is to provide the time and opportunity to talk about the subject first, either with a partner or adult. The advantages of this have been shown to be:

- It has been shown by research to improve standards.
- Storytelling gives experience of story forms and helps narrative writing.
- Talk partners help shape writing.
- Even very young writers can express their ideas after talk, role-play and guided storytelling.
- It guides how the text should sound – its style and voice.
- It helps children to sequence and structure their writing.
- It helps to check if it makes sense.

### Narrative writing

Children's exposure to storytelling from infancy establishes a body of knowledge which can be used to develop a writer's voice. It is important for children to become aware that fiction has a recognisable pattern with a chronological structure focusing round a complication or a problem.

This does not follow a simple structure or formula, e.g. a beginning, middle and end. Stories can cover a wide range of structures, for example, linear stories (e.g. Jill Murphy, *On the Way Home*, or Colin McNaughton, *Suddenly*), circular stories (e.g. Pat Hutchins, *Rosie's Walk*, or Eric Carle, *The Bad Tempered Ladybird*), journey stories (e.g. John Burningham, *The Shopping Basket*, or Michael Rosen, *We're Going on a Bear Hunt*).

It can be useful in making progress in narrative to borrow the models of known stories as starting points. Through this, writers learn to use a prop for a while which then can lead to creating their own writing. Using prompts and aids such as storyboards and story maps can help oral retelling and also assist planning a story.

### Early writing development

The following factors are crucial in developing proficient writers:

- a rich oral experience of telling and retelling texts in preparation for writing

- frequent rehearsal of sentences orally
- varied stimulating writing contexts and experiences, often within play settings
- adults (not just teachers) modelling writing for a range of purposes
- systematic teaching of phonics
- direct teaching of handwriting with daily practice
- regular shared writing to teach the skills of text composition directly
- displays of variety of writing, including word lists and work in progress
- valuing emergent writing.

The process of writing for young children is a complex one, but as a child develops increased skill with transcriptional skills, i.e. spelling and handwriting, then he or she can pay more attention to the content. However, these skills should be taught in real writing contexts in order to enable the child to transfer the acquired knowledge. The process of shared writing with the teacher is an effective teaching strategy.

### Scaffolding (supporting) the process

Supporting young children as writers can be done powerfully by modelling the process. Geekie et al. (1999) describe 'blackboard stories' and chronicle the development of two girls aged 5 in a Kindergarten/Reception classroom, who within the first year of school become competent readers and writers. Aided by the teacher modelling 'blackboard stories' which consisted of a considerable amount of oral rehearsal of each child's 'story' prior to individual writing, each child has a clear 'story' to tell and knows how to go about the process of writing it, using at first a combination of drawing and writing, but gradually developing orthographic spelling. This is similar to the process used in the Success for All literacy scheme where children see examples of sentences modelled by the teacher, then share ideas with a partner and, having orally rehearsed their sentence, they say it to their cupped hands. Figuratively holding this sentence in their hands, children go to tables and then individually write their sentences. This symbolic action provides a real aid to the authoring process. Geekie et al. (1999) describe the process thus:

1   Make a clear statement about what is going to be written.
2   Identify each word in succession.
3   Either recall words from memory, find them in the print environment of the classroom, or segment into phonemes and make sound-symbol matches.
4   Reread the developing text in order to remember what has already been written and what remains to be written.

(Geekie et al. 1999: 40)

At the heart of the ability to support children's emerging literacy is the need to respond contingently to children. This is described by David Wood (1988), based on a series of research studies, as follows:

> Contingent teaching . . . involves pacing the amount of help children are given on the basis of their moment-to-moment understanding. If they do not understand an instruction given at one level, then more help is forthcoming. When they do understand, the teacher steps back and gives the child more room for

initiative. In this way the child is never left alone when he is in difficulty nor is he 'held back' by teaching that is too directive and intrusive.

(Wood 1988: 81)

## Enhancing communication, language and literacy

As the Practice Guidance for the Early Years Foundation Stage states:

> As children develop speaking and listening skills they build the foundations for literacy, for making sense of visual and verbal signs and ultimately for reading and writing.

(DfES 2007b: 39)

Communication, language and literacy are enhanced by the following key factors:

- practitioners who understand the development process
- opportunities for meaningful talk and interaction
- clear links to home and the community
- provision of a secure environment with sensitive adults who really listen and respond appropriately to children
- a print-rich environment
- learning through play
- first-hand experiences
- frequent engagement with the wealth of children's literature
- playing with sounds, words and rhymes
- modelling by adults of different forms of literacy
- celebration of home cultures and languages.

## Key points

- Early language acquisition is a remarkable achievement and there are a range of theories to explain the developmental process.
- The support and interaction of adults and peers are crucial to this development and particularly to encourage sustained shared thinking.
- Providing an environment to promote talk needs careful consideration.
- It is important to acknowledge children's rich language experiences at home and create meaningful links with language and literacy.
- Play is seen as the key way in which young children learn and providing opportunities for play in the classroom is important.
- Children need opportunities to explore the wealth of children's literature and thus develop early reading skills.
- The development of phonological awareness is a key skill in the reading process through playing with words and sounds.
- Early mark-making and writing should be encouraged through a range of resources, opportunities and modelling by adults.

## Further reading

Browne, A. (2001) *Developing Language and Literacy 3–8* (2nd edn). London: Paul Chapman.

Buckley, B. (2003) *Children's Communication Skills: From birth to five years*. London: Routledge.

Geekie, P., Cambourne, B. and Fitzsimmons, P. (1999) *Understanding Literacy Development*. Stoke-on-Trent, UK: Trentham Books.

Pugh, G. (1999) 'Young children and their families', in L. Abbott and H. Moylett (eds) *Early Education Transformed*. London: Falmer.

Whitehead, M. (2004) *Language and Literacy in the Early Years* (3rd edn). London: Sage.

# 5 Knowledge about language
## Grammar and punctuation

### Purpose of this chapter

This chapter aims to:

- Discuss reasons for learning about language.
- Examine problems associated with teaching and learning about language.
- Present classroom activities to develop children's knowledge about language.
- Describe the role of punctuation and how to teach it.
- Provide classroom activities to develop children's ability to punctuate accurately.

In this chapter we will look at issues related both to our own development of subject knowledge about language and to ways in which children's knowledge about language can be improved through enjoyable and meaningful activities.

### Reasons for learning about language

'We never learned no grammar when we was at school.' What might you think if you heard this said by someone about to embark upon an English course? You might agree with the gist of it and think, 'No, neither did I', or you might hear only the grammatical errors. You might form an opinion about the speaker. George Bernard Shaw (1916, Preface to *Pygmalian*) wrote: 'It is impossible for an Englishman to open his mouth without making some other Englishman hate or despise him', and examples of deviations from Standard English such as the above might lead us to draw conclusions about social status and even intelligence.

Some 'mistakes' occur when people use regional dialects rather than Standard English. A common error for trainee teachers in many regions is: 'Who is sat nicely?' Then there is the confusion over when to say 'John and I' or 'John and me'. However, we do all have quite a sophisticated understanding of English grammar, even if we happily deviate from Standard English several times a day.

Even young children have an understanding of grammar before they begin to read or write. Listen to them talking and note the mistakes they make. For example, 'we wented' or 'we goed' instead of 'we went', 'we runned' instead of 'we ran'. In using such constructions, children demonstrate that they are aware of the past tense endings of regular verbs, but make the mistake of applying these to irregular verbs. They do similar things with plurals, assuming that all plurals end with s, as most do.

Therefore, we hear of 'mouses' and 'mans', instead of mice and men, because children know about houses and cans and blouses and fans.

Learning about language and acquiring the terminology necessary to discuss it is rather like taking a course on car mechanics. We may be good drivers but have no knowledge of what makes a car work, but when the car breaks down, a rudimentary knowledge of what happens under the bonnet can be useful, and we may save ourselves from being charged for unnecessary work by an unscrupulous garage. If we tell people who regularly ask if children are 'sat nicely' that they should ask if they are 'sitting nicely', it is helpful if we can explain why and perhaps provide other examples to reinforce the point (would they ask 'who is ran nicely?').

---

**Activity: Analysing grammatical errors**

- Which grammatical errors annoy you and why?
- Make a list and write corrected versions.
- Can you explain the reasons for the errors?

---

One of the problems that teachers face when teaching children about language is that many teachers (including us) were not given any explicit instruction during their own schooldays and may lack confidence in their own abilities. There is also a feeling among some teachers and trainee teachers that they managed to achieve good results at school and university without having had any training in grammar, so why could it be important for others? David Crystal (1990) suggests six reasons why we should learn about language:

- 'Because it's there.' We are curious about the world and wish to understand it and grammar is 'no different from any other domain of knowledge in this respect'.
- Because language 'is involved with almost everything we do as human beings' and 'grammar is the fundamental organising principle of language'.
- Because we already have an extraordinary grammatical ability and it may be helpful to describe the rules which govern grammar.
- Because we need to be aware of what went wrong when we have made grammatical errors in speech or writing.
- Because 'Learning about grammar provides a basis for learning other languages'.
- Because after studying grammar we should be 'more alert to the strength, flexibility and variety of our language, and thus be in a better position to use it and to evaluate others' use of it'. Crystal sounds a cautionary note here: 'Even after a course on car mechanics, we can still drive carelessly'.

## Problems associated with teaching and learning about language

Modern Foreign Languages (MFL) are increasingly a feature of the primary curriculum in England and all pupils will be entitled to receive tuition in MFL by 2009. Many secondary school teachers of modern languages assert that before they can begin to teach children a new language, they have to spend time teaching them about their own language. The National Curriculum for English and the Primary National Strategy should help children to become more aware of their own language and how it works, but this will depend upon teachers having the subject knowledge to teach about it effectively. Wilson (2005) unequivocally states:

> I feel absolutely certain that only by building on their own language knowledge can teachers hope to foster the skills and the enthusiasm for language, and confidence in engaging with it, that children need.
>
> (Wilson 2005: 6)

### Why does English present problems?

English is a rich language that has developed over hundreds of years and is an amalgamation of languages from other parts of the world, particularly Europe. This has led to a variety of spellings and some sound symbol correspondences which can be baffling for English speakers let alone for foreigners. For example, the 'k' sound in 'kit' is made in different ways in different words such as cat, sock, queen and school. Add to this the number of homophones (words which sound the same but have different spellings and meanings) in English and it is no wonder that many people struggle with spelling (see Chapter 5). However, homophones provide us with great scope for humour: puns and misunderstandings are central to many jokes. For example:

- Two peanuts walk into a bar, and one was a salted.
- I walked into a seafood disco last week . . . and pulled a mussel.
- Two fish swim into a concrete wall. One turns to the other and says, 'Dam!'

While some of these subtle (or not so subtle) differences in meaning of words can make us laugh, it can also lead to exasperation when we try to learn more about our language. The language is littered not only with homophones, but also with homonyms, which are words which have the same sound and perhaps the same spellings as others, but different meanings. For example, let us look at the word *fast*:

- fast is a noun when one takes part in *a fast*
- fast is a verb when one decides *to fast*
- fast is an adjective as in *a fast driver*
- fast is an adverb in *to drive fast.*

This inevitably leads to problems when we try to teach children about parts of speech. The presence in English of *word class mobility* means the words may be different parts of speech according to the context in which they are used. And it is not only children who find this a difficult concept to grasp: teachers and trainee teachers sometimes have to address their own misconceptions before they can attempt to teach children about parts of speech. Those who may have been taught about nouns and adjectives by being given lists of each were done a disservice by teachers who failed to discuss parts of speech in the context of texts. Thus, we can look at a list of words which can be adjectives and consider how each may be a different part of speech according to how it is used in a sentence. Try this with the list below:

- green
- fat
- light
- club

As adjectives these words could be part of phrases such as:

- A green dress
- A fat cow
- A light meal
- A club sandwich

However, they could also be nouns as in:

- They played on the village green.
- He wanted to lose some body fat.
- She switched on the light.
- They met at the tennis club.

And three could be verbs as in:

- The leaves began to green in the spring.
- She decided to light a fire.
- They had to club together to pay the bill.

---

**Activity: Using words as different parts of speech**

Look at the following words and experiment with using them as different parts of speech:

- mirror
- drink
- table
- farm
- mate

- run
- foot
- boot
- chair
- face

---

You may feel that understanding parts of speech is rather more challenging than you first thought! However, if you have a basic understanding of parts of speech and are aware of word class mobility, you will be well equipped to use the terms with children in the context of whole texts. What will confuse both children and teachers is teaching parts of speech in isolation by using lists on the board and asking children to decide which words are nouns, which are verbs etc. Apart from being misleading for learners, it just takes one child to give an answer which the teacher does not expect, but which is correct, for confusion to reign for everyone.

# Classroom activities to develop children's knowledge about language

## Nonsense sentences

Children should learn grammatical terms in the context of texts and of the language they use in speech and writing. For example, try asking children to read nonsense sentences and then work in pairs or small groups to produce their own. This activity not only forces children to consider and discuss the roles played by different words in sentences, but also enables them to be creative and to engage in an enjoyable task. Sentences can be simple and short for younger children, but can become increasingly complex for older and/or more able pupils.

Begin by writing a simple nonsense sentence and showing it to the whole class or group. For example:

The blue carrot ate the red dustbin.

Ask the children to look at the sentence carefully and discuss it and then to suggest another sentence which is equally nonsensical and which follows exactly the same pattern. Children who do not know the names of parts of speech will probably talk about the words in terms of their function and so may say things like: 'It needs *the* at the beginning then a word that describes something and then a thing . . .'. For the time being, this is fine and children *should* be encouraged to think carefully about the functions of words in sentences. However, if, when you discuss sentences which you compose with the children's help, you explain that words which describe things are called adjectives, this will gradually enable them to develop a vocabulary for their discussions.

Having introduced simple nonsense sentences, you might go on to introduce adverbs and then subordinate clauses so that children could be asked to replicate structures such as:

The pink elephant, who was riding a bike, carefully drank the purple pond.

Having mastered a few different sentence structures, children could go on to make their nonsense sentences more interesting by making them alliterative (The boring banana bashfully bought a beautiful brick) or putting them together into a rhyme. They could be introduced to nonsense verse by writers such as Spike Milligan (for example, *The Ning Nang Nong*) and Lewis Carroll (for example, *The Jabberwocky*) and might go on to write their own versions of the poems. Again, in exploring the poems children will need to understand the functions of different words if they are to replicate the style.

---

**Activity: Using nonsense sentences**

Why use nonsense sentences rather than 'sensible' sentences?
(See page 85 for an explanation.)

### Replacing adjectives and other words

Another activity which focuses attention on the functions of parts of speech involves replacing adjectives in a text. Many teachers tell children to vary the adjectives they use and to avoid more mundane ones such as *nice*. Try presenting children with a text similar to the following as a shared reading activity:

> The weather was nice when we went to Hornsea. We had a really nice time on the beach and we ate some very nice sandwiches. Mum helped us to build a really nice sandcastle and we put some nice flags in it which we bought at a nice little shop next to the beach. Dad played with us while Mum and Gran went for a nice cup of tea and we had a really nice time with him.

Invite children's comments about the text: it is almost certain that they will mention the frequent use of *nice*. Ask them to consider what the purpose of the word *nice* is in the text, and encourage them to discuss alternatives. Edit the text with the children's help, and then produce a *Nice Chart* with the word nice in the middle and a range of alternatives around it. This can lead to a discussion on context, with children being asked to think about the different situations in which an adjective like nice might be used. For example, in the text above it is used to describe weather, food, various objects, and a passage of time. The *Nice Chart* might, therefore, include a collection of adjectives to describe food, weather, clothing, places etc.

Another activity to promote consideration of varied vocabulary focuses on alternatives to *said* in dialogue. A shared reading passage could be a starting point:

> 'Leave me alone,' said Chloe.
> 'No!' said Tom. 'I won't leave you alone until you tell me where you've hidden my book.'
> 'And I won't tell you where it is until you give me my pen back,' said Chloe.
> 'Oh please can I have my book back?' said Tom.
> 'You know what you have to do first,' said Chloe.
> 'Oh all right,' said Tom. 'Here it is.'
> 'Thank you,' said Chloe. 'Your book is under the table.'

Children should be asked to consider how the text might be improved. On this occasion, the punctuation can be studied and can act as a guide to the kind of verbs which might be used instead of *said*. There is, of course, no reason why *said* cannot be perfectly acceptable in many situations, but its repeated use can make dialogue dull and does not always enable the reader to gauge how characters' words were spoken. As an extension activity, children could introduce some adverbs to give a further indication as to how words were spoken. For example, *shouted angrily, whispered secretly, muttered crossly*. They could also be asked to look at examples of dialogue from story books in the classroom and could make a collection of alternatives to *said* as well as a collection of adverbs used with such verbs.

Activities can begin with reading whole texts and moving on to study aspects of the text, which teachers can choose in line with the learning objectives they wish the children to meet. A natural progression is then to move on to shared, guided and independent writing which allows children to reinforce their understanding by using what they have learnt and making it a focus of their writing. For the *nice* adjective work, children could write descriptions of days out or walks around the school grounds, using a range of adjectives to embellish their writing. For work on dialogue, children could be given imaginary scenarios in which a conversation takes place, for example, a parent speaking to a child who has arrived home late. They could hold the conversations in role and could go on to work in pairs to write dialogue for the conversations. Having done this, they could read the dialogue to others before inviting their audience to guess which verbs they used to show how the words should be spoken. After showing the words they actually used, they could consider editing their work to make use of any suggestions which they feel might enhance it. By paying close attention to the meanings of the verbs in this way, children will be much more likely to remember them.

### A problem-solving/discovery approach to developing knowledge about language

We need to teach children grammatical rules, but we should also encourage them to discover rules for themselves by looking at different texts and discussing them. The children's conclusions can then be tested by presenting them to the teacher and to classmates. For example, here is a mini saga, a story condensed into exactly fifty words.

> Three bears, Mummy, Daddy and Baby, awoke. Breakfast was too hot, so they took a walk. Goldilocks, little girl, sneaked into their house, ate their porridge, sat on their chairs and broke Baby Bear's. She slept on the small bear's bed, but ran away in terror when the family returned.
>
> (Waugh with McGuinn 1996: 118)

By presenting children with the story in this format we can encourage discussions not only about the key elements of the story, but also about ways in which we can express them concisely through careful use of language. When asked to write their own mini sagas, children should be encouraged to consider different sentence structures, and the use of punctuation both to separate and to draw text together.

Children can also look at ways in which words which are unnecessary to the meaning of a sentence might be eliminated. For example:

'I have not got any money,' said Tim.

could be rewritten as:

'I have no money,' said Tim.

Children could go on to look at other examples of sentences which include the word *got* to see how often it is really necessary. Other convoluted phrases could be explored, such as:

I myself personally think that it is not unlikely that rain will fall tomorrow.
I think it is likely to rain tomorrow.

At this present moment in time we have an ongoing period of sunshine.
It is sunny.

Sasha has got a new bicycle and Daniel has got one too.
Sasha and Daniel have new bicycles.

In spite of the fact that it was raining, Ruth had not got her hat on.
Despite the rain, Ruth had no hat.

Skilled users of language can add to sentences to embellish them, or remove words to make them more concise and easier to understand.

### Use of texts: planned opportunities

While one of the great strengths of the literacy strategy is its emphasis on the use of texts as starting points for teaching and learning, this has also led to many children thinking that poems and extracts from stories and non-fiction texts are merely vehicles for learning about grammatical features. Some sample texts are contrived in order to reinforce grammatical concepts, but on the whole it is better to focus upon less contrived texts which provide some examples of word and sentence level concepts, but which are enjoyable and engaging in their own right, as well as on tests which are written to focus on particular grammatical features.

Excerpts should be seen by children as being part of whole texts and they should be introduced as such. Thus, if a Year 3 class is learning about pronouns you can find examples in almost any piece of continuous prose without relying upon contrived examples. However, you may wish to reinforce children's understanding by also looking at specially written passages in which a particular noun is frequently repeated so that they can discuss possible pronoun alternatives.

### Shared writing

Shared writing offers an ideal opportunity to focus children's attention on grammar, and demonstrates how writers can explore ideas and consider alternatives. Because the teacher is doing the writing, the children are free to discuss and suggest how it might be structured and the quality of the writing should be high, given the scope for drafting, editing and revising. Children should, therefore, look closely at what is written and question whether it is accurate. Teachers can encourage this by making occasional deliberate mistakes which children will enjoy spotting, and then justifying their alternative suggestions. Children will also experience and analyse structures which they might not use in their own writing.

A typical activity to develop children's appreciation of complex sentence structures could involve reading a text and then focusing on one sentence, for example:

There was a horrible moment when every breath was held as the ball sped towards the staffroom window, then there was a shattering, crashing sound as the glass exploded into a thousand pieces.

Unlike the work on nonsense sentences, the objective here is not to replicate the sentence structure exactly, but to replicate the sentence type. Children might read and reread the sentence to identify that there are two parts: the first describes a moment of tension, and the second a dramatic event. As a shared writing activity they could write similar sentences with tension followed by action. This could form part of a sequence of lessons on story opening and might lead to independent work in which complete stories could be written.

An understanding of language is, then, more than simply having a knowledge of parts of speech, important though that is. It involves looking at language usage, appreciating various possible ways of using language, and leads to an ability to experiment with language and to write in more interesting ways.

### What can teachers do to make children more aware of language?

We will now look at some of the key things which we can do to foster children's awareness of language.

- Look at a wide range of examples of written and spoken language.
- Make collections of words and texts.
- Discuss different registers (see Waugh 2000a: 125).
- Use terminology when exploring language (for example, 'tense': see Waugh 2000a: 118).
- Provide opportunities for children to write in different styles.
- Discuss language and vocabulary in other lessons besides English. For example: physical education, movement, geography, mathematics.
- Encourage children to look at examples of incorrect or misleading English and to analyse what is wrong with it (see Waugh 2000b: 119–20).
- Encourage children to rewrite texts in different ways (see Waugh 2000b: 128).
- Discuss the value of understanding the way language works.

---

**Activity: Rewriting incorrect sentences**

Consider your own knowledge about language. All the sentences below are incorrect. Can you work out why and then rewrite them correctly?
(See page 85 for answers and explanations.)

- Living in Hull has it's advantages.
- Give a child lots of books and they will learn to read.
- 'Whose the comedian who's catch phrase is "Turned out nice again"?' asked George.
- A packet of cigarettes are now very expensive.
- John knew he could of done better in the test.

---

## The role of punctuation and how to teach it

In this section we will look at the teaching and learning of punctuation. For some children, punctuating their writing is an obstacle when they are just beginning to write down groups of words. Those who experience difficulty with the concept of punctuation might take some comfort from its history.

Until around 1700, only limited amounts of punctuation were used and what was used was designed to help people to read passages aloud. The marks showed suitable places to pause, breathe, or change the tone of voice. Gradually, punctuation marks began to be used 'to mark grammatical structure – such as clauses and sentences – and to guide the reader's interpretation of a text' (Graddol et al. 1996: 63). It was not until the eighteenth century that punctuation began to look as it does today. However, legal documents have continued to be unpunctuated, probably because they were not intended to be read aloud, so early compositors did not bother to punctuate them (see Crystal 1987: 387).

When discussing the use of punctuation with children, talk about the reasons why it is necessary. We require punctuation when we write so that we can compensate for the lack of intonation that is possible in speech. However, punctuation can be a matter of style, and some people make greater use of commas, hyphens and exclamation marks than others in order to achieve a certain effect upon the reader.

Punctuation marks enable us to define the status of the sentences we write. Through its use we can indicate whether a sentence is a question, a statement, or direct speech, and whether a speaker is exclaiming. Punctuation also enables us to separate units of language such as phrases, clauses and sentences.

### What is punctuation?

The word 'punctuation' derives from Latin *punctuare* to prick (think of puncture). Bunting (1997: 44) maintains that there are two main aspects of punctuation: 'rules which must be used and conventions which are more open to interpretation'. She provides the following examples of rules in English:

- capital letters at the beginning of sentences
- full stops to end sentences
- question marks at the end of sentences which are questions
- apostrophes to mark elision (don't) and possession (John's) (its is the possessive exception).

(Bunting 1997: 44)

Punctuation is also used in a stylistic way to emphasise certain words, phrases and clauses and to make subtle, or sometimes not so subtle, changes to meaning. Thus, the same words may be given different meanings through varying the punctuation marks. An inability to understand that the effect that the placement of punctuation marks is significant can lead to confusion for a writer's audience and may result in ambiguity. For example, inserting a comma in 'Shoot Waugh!' alters the meaning of the phrase to 'Shoot, Waugh!' For more examples, see page 83. Linking the teaching of punctuation to meaning will enable children to regard it as important, whereas an approach which dealt with the subject separately from children's own writing might not convey the necessity for careful punctuation.

*Punctuation, the National Curriculum and the Primary National Strategy*

At Key Stage 1 children are taught to punctuate writing with consistent use of capital letters, full stops and question marks and to begin to use commas. At Key Stage 2 they should be using exclamation marks, inverted commas and apostrophes to mark possession and omission.

In order to achieve level 4 in the writing element of National Curriculum English, a piece of work must fulfil the following requirements:

> Full stops, capital letters and question marks are used correctly, and pupils are beginning to use punctuation within the sentence.
> (Department for Education and Employment (DfEE) 1999: 7,
> in Attainment Targets section)

The National Literacy Strategy is rather more demanding, requiring Year 1 children to understand full stops, question marks and speech marks and to understand commas and exclamation marks by Year 2. In Year 4 they meet colons, semi-colons and possessive apostrophes.

Some teachers will feel uncomfortable about their own knowledge of punctuation, while others will have strong views on the ways in which children should acquire skills in this aspect of language. The next section shows some of the ways in which punctuation might be taught and learned.

## Classroom activities to develop children's ability to punctuate accurately

Punctuation may be taught in stages, with teachers taking the opportunities presented in children's reading to explain commas, colons, and so on. Some class or group lessons may be used to discuss, for example, the use of capital letters and, whilst it is important to relate what is learnt to children's writing, it may be helpful to provide some illustrative exercises in order to reinforce concepts.

### Proof-reading

Encouraging children to proof-read their work can help with punctuation, especially when they work with response partners. Communicating with someone else through writing can provide the stimulus many children require to develop punctuation skills. Tape-recording work may help some children to realise where it is necessary to indicate pauses, in much the same way as early printers devised schemes for doing the same. Children may devise their own marks initially, before having conventional methods explained to them. Such proof-reading may be easier for children to manage if they are given a checklist for checking their work, for example:

- Have you put a capital letter at the beginning of each sentence?
- Does each sentence end with a full stop?
- Have you used speech marks to show when someone was speaking?
- Have you used commas to separate items in lists?

(For another example of a checklist, see Chapter 11 on 'Developing writing'.)

By providing a checklist, we can enable children to focus on specific aspects of their writing rather than expecting them to spot mistakes in a more general way. Often, children who are simply asked to check their work go away and return a few minutes later having either done very little, or having added punctuation in a random way.

### The sentence

The most basic concept in punctuation is the sentence. Kress (1982) suggests that a key element of learning to write is learning to write in sentences, but he cautions that the sentence is not the basic unit in which young children speak. Appropriate use of the comma, colon, semi-colon and paragraph can be taught only when children have an understanding of the nature of a sentence. In the early stages of writing, children place full stops in many places. Sometimes full stops appear at the end of each line of writing, because children have encountered books in which sentences are short and contained within single lines.

One activity that develops the concept of the sentence is to provide children with incomplete sentences and to ask them to use their imaginations to finish them. This could lead to a discussion of the nature of a sentence. They may be asked to join beginnings and endings of sentences, choosing from a list. This could lead to some interesting combinations and some discussion of what was possible and impossible, as well as what made sense and what did not. For example:

| The big, brown dog | flies over the hill. |
| The little sparrow | played football. |
| The children | begged for a bone. |

It can be seen that there are possible combinations here which might be nonsensical such as 'The big, brown dog flies over the hill', but which are grammatically accurate. However, one combination is not possible because the subject and verb would not agree ('The children flies over the hill'). Discussion about grammatical accuracy can, therefore, be linked to discussion about punctuation in such exercises.

### Commas

Much of children's early writing is made up of lists. The list may be a feature of preparation for writing for experienced writers too. Commas may be introduced when children begin to turn their lists into prose. They might be asked to write descriptions of members of the class using a series of adjectives separated by commas.

At a later stage, the children could examine the use of commas in their reading books and could try to work out why they were used in particular places. Teachers could help them to classify the different uses. For example, commas can be used:

- to separate words in a list
- to separate the name of a person being addressed in direct speech from the rest of the sentence
- to separate an adverbial from the rest of a sentence
- to separate clauses in a sentence.

A story about a comma which saved a human life (see Waugh with McGuinn 1996: 133) may be used to show how the insertion of a comma into text can change meaning dramatically.

### Question marks

Asking children to look at a list of sentences and identify which require full stops and which need question marks may help to reinforce the use of punctuation. Providing them with answers and asking them to write their own questions is a more creative way of developing their conception of the question and its punctuation. For example, children could be asked to think of questions which might produce answers such as:

> Half past nine.
> Yes, but only on Saturdays.
> Florida.

### Exclamation marks

Exclamation marks may be introduced through an oral activity in which children pass a word around and try to say it in different ways, such as loudly, angrily, softly or humorously. They then discuss which are exclamations and are shown that these can be denoted in writing by using an exclamation mark to help readers to understand how they were spoken. The children might go on to write short drama scripts in which there are frequent exclamations. Tabloid newspaper headlines are a rich source of exclamation marks and children could make collections of these for a classroom display.

### Speech marks

Many children are confused about the placement of inverted commas when writing dialogue, and may gain a greater understanding if they are introduced to them through speech bubbles in comics. They could be given copies of comic strip stories with the speech bubbles blanked out and then be asked to add dialogue. Subsequently, they could write the story using speech marks and adding text to show the identity of speakers.

### Walking and reading

Children might be presented with a short passage which is unpunctuated and be asked to read it through. They could go on to walk as they read, pausing briefly where the text seems to include a pause and the need for a comma, and for longer when a full stop might be required. They could begin working individually and go on to discuss with partners where punctuation may be needed.

### Apostrophes for abbreviation

Where apostrophes are used to abbreviate words, it is important that children understand that the apostrophes show where letters have been missed out. They might be shown examples and be asked to say what the longer versions would be. At this stage, words such as *won't* and *shan't* (*will not* and *shall not*) should be avoided, with the focus being on more regular abbreviations such as *didn't, shouldn't* and *isn't*.

Children could go on to look at examples of words abbreviated using apostrophes in newspapers and in shops. Football league tables often show teams' names in shortened form and may promote discussion and investigation into the complete spellings. For example, they may find:

N'castle, So'ton, B'ham City, Middlesboro' and Tott'm.

Collections can be displayed together with reference sources, so that children could try to find extended versions. They could also look at road signs with place names abbreviated and could be invited to create their own abbreviations for different places. A development activity could explore some of those abbreviations which tend not to have apostrophes such as 'Utd' and 'Tn'.

### Apostrophes for possession

Children often see examples of apostrophes being misused, so a good introduction to using possessive apostrophes can involve children being given examples of sentences which include apostrophes, or they could look for apostrophes in their reading books. They could discuss the reasons for the presence of the apostrophes, both together and with the teacher, before being given some examples of sentences which require apostrophes to be added. They might go on to attempt short pieces of writing which include possessive apostrophes.

Bunting (1997: 54) maintains that 'It may help children to understand that the apostrophe *s* to mark possession represents the *es* form of Old English'. For examples, see Chaucer's *Canterbury Tales* which were written in the fourteenth century and include *The Nonnes Preestes Tale* (*The Nun's Priest's Tale*) and *The Cokes Tale* (*The Cook's Tale*).

---

**Activity: Using apostrophes**

Look for examples of apostrophes in the environment.

- Make a list of those which are used correctly and those which are not.
- Can you explain why particular errors are made?

---

### Making use of children's reading

The influence of reading in the environment is evident in the misuse of apostrophes, which seem to appear in children's writing before they are taught about them. It is useful to discuss punctuation marks by showing examples in reading books in order to demonstrate correct usage. Group reading sessions can reinforce concepts in punctuation. For example, give children a copy of the same book and ask them to read in turn, changing reader after each sentence or paragraph. They may be assigned different characters in a story and be asked to read dialogue without using words such as 'said John' or 'asked Jill'. This develops an understanding of the purpose of speech marks and their placement.

### Using incorrectly punctuated text

One method of teaching punctuation which is frequently employed is to use unpunctuated or incorrectly punctuated passages which pupils are asked to punctuate. This draws attention to ambiguities which can arise when punctuation is absent or inappropriate and, if used sparingly and as a follow-up to marking of writing, can be effective. Children may be presented with pieces of writing and asked to punctuate them in different ways in order to alter their meaning. For example:

the boy sat down on the television there was a herd of elephants in his bedroom his father was tidying up

This could be punctuated in different ways:

The boy sat down on the television. There was a herd of elephants in his bedroom. His father was tidying up.

The boy sat down. On the television there was a herd of elephants. In his bedroom, his father was tidying up.

Similarly, a simple sign could have its meaning changed through variations in punctuation:

PRIVATE.                    PRIVATE?
NO SWIMMING                  NO!
ALLOWED.              SWIMMING ALLOWED.

(Waugh 1998: 17)

Another example invites the reader to show how the same words, punctuated differently, may be used to portray a person as generous or as mean:

At Christmas, Hayley was going to buy lots of things for herself. She was going to buy nothing for everyone else. It was going to be a wonderful time.

At Christmas, Hayley was going to buy lots of things. For herself, she was going to buy nothing. For everyone else, it was going to be a wonderful time.

(Waugh with McGuinn 1996: 69)

### Identifying necessary punctuation

Another activity could involve the use of a passage presented on the whiteboard, a flipchart, or an overhead transparency with the punctuation covered. Children would listen to the passage or read it aloud, and then reread it and try to decide what the hidden punctuation marks were (see Barnes 1997: 18).

## Approaches to teaching punctuation

Punctuation may be developed through a variety of approaches which include:

- discussion of punctuation in children's reading
- discussion of punctuation in children's writing
- the use of response partners in the drafting process
- the use of group reading sessions
- the use of class or group teaching reinforced by exercises.

The first four approaches have formed the bulk of many children's experience of learning about punctuation since the mid-1970s. The use of exercises seemed to fall out of favour with many teachers during the 1960s and 1970s, but there appears to have been a revival of interest recently, perhaps because of the demands of the National Curriculum and the Primary National Strategy. Exercises need not be dull. Indeed, they may involve children in producing imaginative writing. They enable us to reinforce what has been learned and provide an opportunity for us to check if children have grasped concepts. However, they cannot, in themselves, teach children very much. They should be regarded as an adjunct to teaching rather than as a method of teaching, and should not be used in isolation.

Punctuation has been neglected in many works on children's writing and may have been inadequately taught and learned by some teachers. A combination of approaches, with an emphasis on the vital role which punctuation plays in helping us to derive meaning from text, should enable us to raise its status and improve its usage.

---

**Activity: Responding to children's problems with punctuation**

Study each of the following and decide upon your response:

- A Year 1 child puts a full stop at the end of every line, regardless of whether one is needed or not.
- The majority of your class of Year 2 pupils seem to have little idea about the use of commas.
- A Year 3 child puts apostrophes before every terminal s in her work.
- A Year 4 child uses no punctuation whatsoever, but writes at length.
- Many of your Year 5 pupils do not understand the concept of the paragraph.
- A Year 6 child uses speech marks, but he places them around whole sentences including within them 'he said' and 'she said', etc.

This chapter has looked at the importance of developing knowledge about language, both for pupils and teachers. While it has been shown that the English language's complexities can prove challenging for both pupils and teachers, it should also be clear that there are many interesting and engaging ways in which language can be studied and explored as we develop our understanding. We do not need to be graduate linguists to be able to teach children about their language, but a good working knowledge will help us to explain their errors and challenge them to develop their skills.

## Key points

- If we learn about language, we are better able to understand our errors and avoid them.
- An understanding of language can help us to develop and improve our writing.
- There are many interesting classroom activities to develop children's knowledge about language and their punctuation skills.
- Punctuation needs to be understood if we are to use it effectively to convey meaning when we write.

---

**Explanation for the activity on using nonsense sentences on page 73**

The use of nonsense sentences makes the activity creative and enjoyable and motivates children to want to produce sentences which will entertain their classmates. It also provides a good link to a genre of writing which can be explored by the class.

---

**Answers and explanations for the activity on rewriting incorrect sentences on page 77**
- Living in Hull has it's advantages.
- Living in Hull has its advantages.

('*its*' has an apostrophe only when short for *it is*. Only pronouns ending in *one* (*someone, anyone* etc) have apostrophes when possessive.)

- Give a child lots of books and they will learn to read.
- Give a child lots of books and he or she will learn to read.

OR

*continued on next page*

- Give children lots of books and they will learn to read.

(*A child* is singular and so the pronoun should not be they. However, because we do not have a suitable gender neutral pronoun in English, it has become quite common for people to speak of one person as *they*.)

- 'Whose the comedian who's catch phrase is "Turned out nice again"?' asked George.
- 'Who's the comedian whose catch phrase is "Turned out nice again"?' asked George.

('*who's*' is short for '*who is*' – try replacing *whose* and *who's* in the sentence with *who is* and you will see why the sentence is incorrect.)

- A packet of cigarettes are now very expensive.
- A packet of cigarettes is now very expensive.

OR

- Cigarettes are now very expensive.

(Even though *cigarettes* is a plural, it is the packet which is the subject of the sentence and this is singular, so the verb must be singular too.)

- John knew he could of done better in the test.
- John knew he could have done better in the test.

('could of' is a common mistake made because people hear *could've* (short for *could have*) and assume of should be used. *Have* is a verb and *of* is a preposition, and a verb is clearly needed.)

## Further reading

Bryson, B. (1990) *Mother Tongue: The English Language*. Harmondsworth: Penguin.
Medwell, J. and Wray, D., with Moore, G. and Griffiths, V. (2001) *Primary English: Knowledge and understanding*. Exeter: Learning Matters.

## Resources for teaching

Waugh, D. (1996) *Curriculum Bank Writing at Key Stage 1*. Leamington Spa, UK: Scholastic.
Waugh, D. (2000a) *Further Curriculum Bank Writing at Key Stage 1*. Leamington Spa, UK: Scholastic.
Waugh, D. (2000b) *Further Curriculum Bank Writing at Key Stage 2*. Leamington Spa, UK: Scholastic.
Waugh, D. with McGuinn, N. (1996) *Curriculum Bank Writing at Key Stage 2*. Leamington Spa, UK: Scholastic.

# 6  Talking to learn

## Purpose of this chapter

This chapter aims to:

- Clarify the link between talk and learning.
- Summarise the key aspects of cooperative learning and present this as a vehicle for promoting talk and effective learning.
- Analyse the use of teachers' questioning to promote talk.
- Discuss the use of talk to support children's development of reading and writing skills.
- Examine the different forms of speaking and listening and how these can be planned and managed effectively in the classroom.
- Involve children in self-assessment of their speaking and listening skills.

## The importance of talk for learning

A wealth of research has shown that talk is a key ingredient in the learning process (Barnes and Todd 1977; Slavin 1983; Corson 1988; Johnson et al. 1988; Wells et al. 1990). One powerful example of the social and collaborative nature of learning is a transcript of a mother and child completing a jigsaw puzzle (Geekie et al. 1999). The way in which the mother scaffolds the unfamiliar process by modelling, thinking aloud and talking to the child, followed by the child attempting to complete the puzzle alone and demonstrating what he has learned is a vivid illustration of supporting the learning process. Geekie et al. (1999: 116) describe learning as *collaborative puzzle solving* and *provide* seven principles that are involved in learning:

- Learning is often a mutual accomplishment.
- Children learn through guided participation.
- Children profit from the support of more competent people.
- Effective instruction is contingent instruction – the involvement of adults does not imply simply direct instruction or control of learning.
- It is the quality of the interaction that is important, ensuring that the child is involved in planning activities and decision-making.
- Language is the means through which self-regulation of learning behaviour develops.
- Learning depends on the negotiation of meaning.

Adults can therefore support children's understanding by performing a number of functions. These include focussing the child's attention on what is relevant, simplifying and interpreting information, holding information in working memory for the child, reminding the child of what is known and what the goal is, alerting the child to success or failure and shifting the child to an alternative procedure.

---

**Activity: Using talk to support learning**

Examine the transcript below of paired counting with an older child (Kay, 14 years) and Antonia (3 years), cited in Mercer (1995: 11). Discuss the following questions with a colleague:

- How does talk support the learning?
- How does the older child support the younger child's learning?
- What would be the next step for the older child in order to support the learning process?

| | |
|---|---|
| *Antonia:* | I do one first. No you do one first. |
| *Kay:* | OK. One. |
| *Antonia:* | Two. |
| *Kay:* | Three |
| | (and so on up to . . .) |
| *Kay:* | Fifteen. |
| *Antonia:* | Seventeen. |
| *Kay:* | Sixteen! Yours is sixteen. |
| *Antonia:* | Sixteen. |
| *Kay:* | Seventeen. |
| *Antonia:* | Eighteen. |
| *Kay:* | Nineteen. |
| *Antonia:* | Tenteen. |
| *Kay:* | No! (*laughs*) Twenty. |
| *Antonia:* | Twenty. |
| *Kay:* | Twenty-one. Keep going. |

---

The activity illustrates the use of language as a tool, or a social mode for thinking. As Mercer (1995: 19) says, 'Knowledge is neither accumulated nor discovered by learners: it is shaped by people's communicative actions.'

The role of talk in learning was explored by the Russian psychologist Lev Vygotsky (1962), who looked at the link between language and thinking. He saw our use of language as serving two purposes, first as a 'cultural tool' for sharing and developing our knowledge to support our social life and second as a 'psychological tool' to help organise our individual thoughts. He also felt that these two aspects are integrated to help us become active members of communities. Vygotsky also developed the concept of the *zone of proximal development* (ZPD) which is:

the distance between the actual development level as determined by independent problem solving and the level of potential development as determined through problem solving under adult guidance or in collaboration with more capable peers.

(Vygotsky 1978: 86)

In addition Vygotsky (1986: 188) stated that 'What the child can do in cooperation today, he can do alone tomorrow'. The concept of zone of proximal development has been widely used (and differently interpreted) and one teacher commented that if ZPD had not been invented by Vygotsky, teachers would have needed to invent it! In other words, teachers (and fellow pupils) support the learning by guiding the child's next step in their understanding.

Bruner (1985) has built on this concept and suggests that the learner passes through mental developmental phases which are supported by structured learning experiences. In addition, Bruner asserts that speech is a primary mechanism for thought and therefore it is vitally important for children to have the opportunity to talk through their ideas. Bruner's term for the support that adults provide in the learning process is 'scaffolding', whereby an adult varies the level of support, gradually withdrawing it as the child gains in competency.

Central to the work of Vygotsky and Bruner are the following strategies, as described by Corden (2000: 10):

- *Modelling:* showing children examples of work by experts.
- *Demonstrating:* illustrating the procedures experts go through in producing work.
- *Supporting* children as they learn and practise procedures.

Neil Mercer (2000) in discussing the zone of proximal development says he is more interested in understanding the quality of teaching and learning as an 'intermental' or 'interthinking' process:

> For a teacher to teach and a learner to learn, they must use talk and joint activity to create a shared communicative space, an 'intermental development zone' (IDZ) on the contextual foundations of their common knowledge and aims'. This is facilitated by dialogue: 'If the dialogue fails to keep minds mutually attuned, the IDZ collapses and the scaffolded learning grinds to a halt.'
>
> (Mercer 2000: 141)

Like the original zone of proximal development, it still focuses on the guidance of a more experienced peer or adult for a learner but relates more to the contributions that both make in a reciprocal process. It is a process of 'interthinking'. Mercer (1995: 104) also presents three ways of talking and thinking:

- *Disputational talk:* this is characterised by disagreement, short exchanges that consist of assertions or challenges and decisions being reached by individuals, not collaboratively.
- *Cumulative talk:* here pupils work together, often in pairs, to construct 'common knowledge' by accumulation.

- *Exploratory talk:* here pupils work collaboratively and engage critically but constructively with each other's ideas. Challenges are justified and alternatives offered and progress is made towards a joint agreement. In exploratory talk 'knowledge is made more publicly accountable and reasoning is more visible in the talk' (Mercer 1995: 104).

Lyn Dawes (2001), describing a project that built on the work of Mercer and the idea of 'interthinking', says it is:

> the situation that exists when two or more people achieve real communication with each other, when mental resources are pooled through the medium of talk.
>
> (Dawes 2001: 128)

The project (Raising Achievement through Thinking with Language Skills, cited in Dawes 2001: 129) took place in the late 1990s and involved classes of Year 5 pupils. It consisted of the following:

- developing ground rules for talk
- devising a series of ten one-hour talking lessons
- using exploratory talk (from Mercer)
- employing ICT with specially written software to support exploratory talk
- using talk across the curriculum.

Results of the project showed that children who had received talk training did better in non-verbal reasoning tests and the conclusion was that 'Talk-focused children had learnt how to engage more effectively with one another's ideas' (Dawes 2001: 131).

---

**Activity: Understanding the zone of proximal development**

Spend some time ensuring you understand the link between talk and learning based on the concept of ZPD.

- Explain this to a colleague to support your understanding.
- Discuss also the impact that this has on teaching.

---

The status of talk has been considerably raised by a range of research (for example, Mercer 1995, 2000; Alexander 2000, 2004) which has shown that:

> Reading, writing and number may be the acknowledged curriculum 'basics', but talk is arguably the true foundation of learning.
>
> (Alexander 2004: 5)

Following Alexander's (2000) comparative research of primary education across five countries, he has developed the concept of *dialogic teaching* to support the use of talk.

This teaching approach aims to harness the power of talk to stimulate and extend pupils' thinking and understanding. Dialogic teaching is being trialled in schools in London and Yorkshire, and is becoming influential in other parts of Britain and with the national agencies, notably the Qualifications and Curriculum Authority (QCA) and the government's Primary National Strategy. Dialogic teaching consists of the following five elements:

- It is *collective*: children work together on tasks, as a group or class.
- It is *reciprocal*: teachers and children listen to each other and comment/share ideas.
- It is *supportive*: children are supported to discuss their views freely.
- It is *cumulative*: teachers and children build on each other's ideas to create coherent lines of thinking.
- It is *purposeful*: teachers plan and steer classroom talk with specific purposes.

## Cooperative learning

One ideal vehicle for the development of talk and 'interthinking' in the classroom is through cooperative learning. This requires pupils to work together in small groups to support each other to improve their learning.  Group work is certainly not new; indeed putting children together to work in groups is a common occurrence in the United Kingdom. But putting children together and then assuming they will interact and support each other's learning is another matter altogether. However, when implemented properly, cooperative learning presents an ideal method of supporting not only children's learning, but also the effective use of talk. First, ensure that pupils are supported with the necessary interpersonal and small group skills to cooperate; second, structure the tasks to maximise this. Extensive research (Sharan 1990; Slavin 1995; Johnson et al. 2001) has shown three main categories of advantages: improved achievement, greater interpersonal skills, and improved self-esteem.

There need to be certain key ingredients for the learning to be cooperative. Johnson and Johnson's (1999) extensive work in this field states that five basic elements are needed to be in place for it to be effective:

- *Positive interdependence:* students must feel that they need each other in order to complete the group's task; they 'sink or swim' together.
- *Face-to-face interaction:* the interaction patterns and verbal exchanges that take place among students in carefully structured cooperative learning groups benefit their learning.
- *Individual accountability:* cooperative learning groups are successful only when every member has learned the material or has helped with and understood the assignment.
- *Interpersonal and small group skills:* students do not necessarily come to school with the social skills they need to collaborate effectively with others; teachers need to teach the appropriate communication, decision-making and conflict management skills to students and provide the motivation to use these skills, in order for groups to function effectively.

- *Group processing:* this involves giving students time and procedures to analyse how well their groups are functioning, and how well they are using the necessary skills. The processing helps all group members achieve while maintaining effective working relationships among members.

---

**Activity: Create a graphic representation**

Work with colleagues to devise words and symbols to represent each of these five key elements of cooperative learning, to act as an aide-memoire.

- Positive interdependence
- Face-to-face interaction
- Individual accountability
- Interpersonal and small group skills
- Group processing.

---

## Teaching cooperative learning skills

Teachers can establish the correct ethos of a 'cooperative learning classroom' by:

- creating a safe environment where risks can be taken without fear of ridicule
- celebrating diversity and valuing everyone
- establishing conflict resolution strategies.

To create this ethos, give students opportunities to build relationships, encourage them to support each other in learning, give students self-responsibility for aspects of the classroom and, above all, ensure that learning experiences are enjoyable.

By creating a safe and supportive learning environment, the teacher will have built the *will* to work together. However, this is not sufficient, unless the skills of group work are also taught. Teamwork skills can be divided into task skills and working relationship skills and need to be explicitly taught in stages, as follows:

- establish the need for the skill
- define the skill
- guide the practice
- generalise the application of the skill.

Specific teamwork skills that are necessary include:

- active listening
- being aware of volume of voices
- helping and encouraging each other
- everyone participating
- completing tasks
- resolving conflicts.

A range of structures, principally derived from Spencer Kagan (1994), to facilitate paired and/or group work can be applied to different activities across the curriculum. Some of these include: think, pair share, round robin, doughnut, rally table, line up, three-step interview, two stay and two stray, roam the room, and jigsaw groups, many of which are explained in the DfES (2003c) *Speaking, Listening, Learning* materials. For further guidance on these structures and others, see Kagan (1994) and Jolliffe (2007).

### The National Curriculum and Primary National Strategy

The importance of talk was not recognised until the 1960s when the Schools Council Project (Halliday et al. 1964) and the work of Wilkinson (1965) and Barnes et al. (1969) promoted an interest in spoken language and literacy in primary schools. The Bullock Report (DES 1975) was devoted entirely to language and welcomed the growth in importance in oral language. It argued that schools should prioritise the speech needs of their pupils. The Oracy Project in the late 1980s further built on this and involved over half of England's local education authorities, using case studies of classroom practice, usually written by teachers themselves. This showed the relevance of understanding the role of talk for learning in *all* curriculum subjects. This project particularly revealed how teachers and children alike undervalued the role of talk for learning at the time. As Mercer (1995) states:

> one of its main achievements was to raise teachers' awareness of the potential value of talk, and so improve the status of classroom talk amongst both teachers and pupils.
>
> (Mercer 1995: 92)

This research was instrumental in speaking and listening becoming a separate component in the English 5–11 National Curriculum:

> Our inclusion of speaking and listening as a separate profile component in our recommendation is a reflection of our conviction that these skills are of central importance to children's development.
>
> (Her Majesty's Inspectorate (HMI) 1989)

### Requirements of the National Curriculum

Speaking and listening in the National Curriculum is divided into the following areas:

Knowledge, skills and understanding

- Speaking
- Listening
- Group discussion and interaction
- Drama
- Standard English
- Language variation

Breadth of study: this shows the range of activities, context and purposes through which pupils should be taught the above knowledge skills and understanding.

## The National Literacy Strategy

The importance of talk for learning took a backwards step in 1998 with the introduction of the National Literacy Strategy, where speaking and listening were largely omitted from the wealth of teaching objectives. The result of this, as Smith et al.'s (2004) research showed was that:

> In the whole class section of literacy and numeracy lessons, teachers spent the majority of their time either explaining or using highly structured question and answer sequences. Far from encouraging and extending pupil contributions to promote high levels of interaction and cognitive engagement, most of the questions asked were of a low cognitive level designed to funnel pupils' response towards a required answer.
>
> (Smith et al. 2004: 408)

In 2003, the Qualifications and Curriculum Authority (QCA) produced a document *Planning for Speaking and Listening in Key Stages 1 and 2* (QCA/DfES 2003) to support speaking and listening and, in response to widespread criticism of the National Literacy Strategy, a revision of this QCA document was made in order to integrate Speaking and Listening and the National Literacy Strategy Framework for teaching, entitled *Speaking, Listening, Learning: Working with children in Key Stages 1 and 2* (DfES 2003c). The guidance sets out four teaching objectives for speaking and listening each term from Year 1 to Year 6, covering speaking, listening, group discussion and interaction and drama. These objectives can be linked to other curriculum areas as appropriate. Examples of activities are provided for different year groups. The guidance also emphasises the importance of

- modelling appropriate speaking and listening
- encouraging sensitive interaction
- setting goals with clear success criteria
- providing opportunities for pupils to practice and reflect on language used.

Speaking and listening has been given more emphasis with the *Excellence and Enjoyment* professional development materials and in the revised Primary Framework for Literacy from the Primary National Strategy (DfES 2006b). The Rose Review (DfES 2006a) of the teaching of early reading has also emphasised the key importance of speaking and listening:

> The indications are that far more attention needs to be given, right from the start, to promoting speaking and listening skills to make sure that children build a good stock of words, learn to listen attentively and speak clearly and confidently. Speaking and listening, together with reading and writing, are prime communication skills that are central to children's intellectual, social and emotional development.
>
> (DfES 2006a: 3)

## Teachers' questioning to promote talk

Research (Galton et al. 1999) shows that teachers usually ask closed questions, such as the 'guess what I am thinking' type, where the teacher has a clear idea of the answer, and the children have to guess it, rather than open questions that genuinely seek to explore children's understanding and views. David Wood (1986) argues that teachers often constrain classroom discussion through inappropriate questions. One of us listened to some teachers describing an action research project on 'thinking skills', a key aspect of which is developing good questioning by teachers and pupils. A teacher described how in one school, the children had been involved in interviewing for a new teacher. At the end of the interview, a child had asked if the applicant had any questions to ask. The reply was 'No'. Later, when discussing the different applicants, the children had commented: 'We don't want the teacher who didn't think of any questions. We know in this school that good questions are really important.'

The Primary National Strategy *Excellence and Enjoyment: Learning and teaching in the primary years. Professional development materials* (DfES 2004b) has a section on developing a learning culture; questioning is one aspect of this. It says: 'We should try, therefore, to ask fewer but better and more demanding questions – and to use alternatives to questions to stimulate their thinking' (Conditions for Learning: DfES 2004b: 64). There is a place for the 'quick, closed, fact-finding questions of the quiz type', but it is important to consider whether the questions used provide a cognitive challenge for the children. There should be a balance between closed 'quick fix' questions and open questions that demand more complex and higher-order thinking. Examples are provided of open questions that 'genuinely invite children to think'.

There are a range of ways of promoting thinking skills recommended in the guidance some of which incorporate partner or cooperative group work, as well as activities to encourage children's questioning. Using a taxonomy or scheme of classification of thinking to support higher-order thinking can be helpful when deciding how to challenge children. Bloom's (1956) taxonomy shows a progression in thinking (see Figure 6.1). Using this hierarchy of thinking skills can help teachers to plan more effective questions with appropriate cognitive challenge.

## The centrality of talk to reading

Speaking and listening are important not only for learning and developing effective communication skills, but also for developing reading and writing skills. Palinscar and Brown (1984) have shown the value of dialogue in supporting children's comprehension skills when reading. The method they suggest involves the reciprocal teaching of comprehension strategies, which was designed to provide a simple introduction to group discussion. The basic procedure is that a teacher and a group of pupils take turns leading a discussion on the content of a section of text they are jointly attempting to understand. Four strategies are practised: questioning, clarifying, summarising and predicting. Throughout the teacher provides guidance and feedback to the group. This process can be modified so that the essential features can be used in whole-class discussion; success has also been achieved with training peer tutors. A further development could be the use of *cue cards* within groups to replace the role of the teacher.

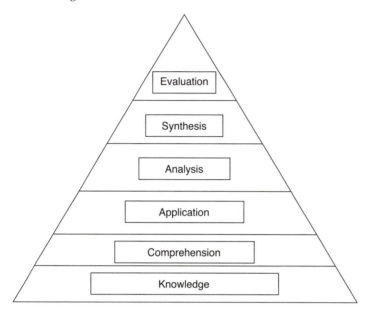

*Figure 6.1* Bloom's taxonomy of thinking skills
Source: adapted from Bloom 1956

Dialogue has been shown to be powerful by Rosenblatt (1989), who demonstrated that teacher–pupil and peer–peer dialogue and interaction is an important part of the reading and writing process:

> Group interchange about the texts of established authors can also be a powerful means of stimulating growth in reading ability and critical acumen. When students share their responses and learn how their evocations from transactions with the same text differ, they can return to the text to discover their own habits of selection and synthesis and can become more critical of their own processes as readers. Interchange about the problems of interpretation and a collaborative movement toward self-critical interpretation of the text can lead to the development of critical concepts and criteria of validity of interpretation. Such meta-linguistic awareness is valuable to students as both readers and writers.
>
> (Rosenblatt 1989: 173, cited in Corden 2004: 139)

One example of this is demonstrated in the National Literacy Strategy video (DfES 2004b) of guided reading discussion in Year 5 using *The Firework-maker's Daughter* by Philip Pullman (1995). Here we see the power of discussion both in pairs and as a group really exploring and empathising with a character in a book.

### Talk and writing

The advantages of talking before writing were discussed in relation to the early years in Chapter 4. These advantages persist throughout Key Stages 1 and 2. Giving children the chance to talk about the subject with a partner, in groups or with the teacher can substantially improve the motivation and the quality of what children write.

The effective use of shared writing can support this process, particularly using *teacher scribing*, where the teacher takes contributions from the children and helps mould it into effective writing or *supported composition*, where the children work, usually in pairs, to write short sections, building on what the teacher has modelled. Guided writing also provides valuable opportunities to use talk to support the writing process, with a clear focus on a particular aspect of the writing and the chance to engage in meaningful dialogue with small groups of pupils.

The concept of writing workshops is derived from the work of the National Writing Project (1989b), which showed the value of children getting responses from their peers. From that the use of response partners became widespread. Where children already have an established 'talk partner' then this is easily put in place. Children often need prompts to aid their responses to partners. Using a range of prompts can be very beneficial in supporting children's comments and questions on one another's work. This process needs clearly establishing, ensuring that children are positive about one another's work and can make some helpful suggestions. Modelling the process for children would be beneficial. Here are some examples of prompts:

- The best bit was ........................................................................................... ?
- I liked how you ............................................................................................. ?
- I would like to know more about ................................................................. ?
- What do you mean by .................................................................................... ?
- Do you think you could add .......................................................................... ?
- Could this part be cut/moved ....................................................................... ?

Using models from literature can be a powerful springboard into writing, but this needs to be supported by real interactive learning through talk. Roy Corden (2000) provides some vivid examples. In a Key Stage 2 class children were working on responding imaginatively to characters in stories. The teacher had read extracts from *Matilda* (1989) to show how Roald Dahl uses direct action and dialogue description to develop characters. After examining the words that Dahl uses, the children developed lists of words to describe characters. For example:

Character:  Miss Trunchbull
Book:       *Matilda*, Author: Roald Dahl
awesome     loathsome
barbaric    mammoth
bossy       mean
blobby      mountainous
cruel       muscular
ferocious   macho
fierce      spiteful
formidable  strict

gigantic     terrible
grumpy       terrifying
grotesque    ugly
hideous      vicious

(Corden 2000: 59)

This practice eventually led to the children developing a character portfolio with a range of lists of words to describe characters to support their own writing. Such a wealth of material had evolved from the effective use of talk. The research of Bereiter and Scardamalia (1987) demonstrated that successful writers 'think aloud', needing to elaborate and revise as they write. Primary age children need to see this modelled by teachers. The process of 'metacognition', that is understanding and examining the thinking process, can be demonstrated by teachers verbalising such thoughts. For example, during shared writing, the teacher might think aloud: 'Let me see, how shall I start this paragraph? Yes, perhaps some dialogue. . . . One word would be good to emphasise the suspense . . .' and so on.

### Boys' underachievement

Many boys underachieve in writing. In Chapter 3, the *Raising Boys' Achievements in Writing* project (UKLA/PNS 2004) gave examples of how the use of visual stimulus, drama or speaking and listening can engage boys in writing. One might sum this up by saying 'Let Jack climb the beanstalk, before he writes about it'. Action and talk are critical to motivate boys to write.

## Distinctive features of speaking and listening

Understanding the distinctive features of speaking and listening can support planning for it effectively in the classroom. The Primary National Strategy (DfES 2003c) cites the following differences with other modes of language:

- It is collaborative: meaning is mainly constructed collaboratively and it is fluid and open-ended.
- Spoken language is more varied in terms of purpose, context and levels of formality.
- Social relationships are mostly enacted through talk.

The key factors to consider for effective talk are topic (the subject matter), audience (who is being spoken to affects the level of formality) and purpose (the underlying reason for the talk). All these will inform the format of the talk.

### Progression in speaking and listening

Progression in speaking and listening relates to the following features:

- the ability to contribute
- the ability to sustain speaking and listening with appropriate language
- the use of standard English when appropriate

- adaptability to different contexts with confidence
- understanding and verbalising of own progress.

The Primary National Strategy's guidance (DfES 2003c: 24–7) provides clear guidance on the features of progression for Years 1–6 for all four areas (speaking, listening, group interaction and drama), which can be used for assessment purposes.

One of the key aims of the renewed Primary Framework for Literacy (DfES 2006b) is to integrate speaking and listening with the reading and writing strands. It sets out twelve strands for teaching literacy, four of which relate to speaking and listening as follows:

1  Speak and listen for a wide range of purposes in different contexts
   Children learn to:

   - speak competently and creatively for different purposes and audiences, reflecting on impact and response
   - explore, develop and sustain ideas through talk.

2  Listening and responding
   Children learn to:

   - understand, recall and respond to speakers' implicit and explicit meanings
   - explain and comment on speakers' use of language, including vocabulary, grammar and non-verbal features.

3  Group discussion and interaction
   Children learn to:

   - take different roles in groups to develop thinking and complete tasks
   - participate in conversations, making appropriate contributions building on others' suggestions and responses.

4  Drama
   Children learn to:

   - use dramatic techniques including work in role to explore ideas and texts
   - create, share and evaluate ideas and understanding through drama.

The Primary Framework for Literacy also provides a clear progression from Foundation Stage to Year 6 with continuity into Year 7.

Another resource that provides valuable guidance is First Steps Oral Language continuum (Education Department of Western Australia 1994), which identifies phases of development. This supports teachers to decide on a 'best fit' for a child's phase of development. It also provides very useful advice on the major teaching emphasis for each phase.

## Planning for speaking and listening

Opportunities for speaking and listening need to be carefully planned. The revised Primary Framework for Literacy (DfES 2006b) provides clear objectives from Foundation Stage to Key Stage 2 and links into Year 7. This builds on the earlier work from the Qualifications and Curriculum Authority (QCA 1999) and DfES (2003c) to ensure a range of activities to supporting children's progression in speaking, listening, group discussion and drama. Links are made in the exemplar units of work to show the integration of speaking and listening with reading and writing. Also bear in mind links across the curriculum, with speaking and listening as a springboard for a range of activities. The use of paired and group work can support this process.

### Managing children's talk

The importance of talk for learning has been discussed, but for many teachers the problem is more a matter of how to stop children talking. Table 6.1 lists a range of common issues which you could review and, if possible, discuss with colleagues, adding and amending where appropriate.

### The role of the teacher

There are many ways that the teacher can promote the necessary classroom ethos for developing talk:

*Table 6.1* Potential difficulties managing talk in the classroom

| Difficulty | Possible solution |
| --- | --- |
| High noise level when pupils are working in pairs or groups | Work through the issue with pupils and help them to understand the need for talking in appropriate voices (20 cm voices for working with a partner, i.e. voices that cannot be heard more than 20 cm away). |
| | Have a noise meter (a dial in the classroom which shows zones – green: acceptable, orange: getting unacceptable, red: unacceptable). |
| | Appoint a 'noise monitor' or monitors. |
| Some pupils dominating in small groups | Have a specific target of everyone participating in lessons. |
| | Reward pairs or groups where this is happening. |
| | Provide tokens for talk, so that every member of a group must use their token before members can speak again. |
| Encouraging shy pupils to participate | Ensure careful pairings. |
| | Give roles to pupils in groups to ensure all participate. |
| Gaining the attention of the class | Have a zero noise signal, such as a raised hand. |
| Pupils talking off task | Monitor when pupils are working in pairs or groups with reminders about task, time limits, etc. |

- Considering carefully the type of questions asked that promote pupils' engagement and thinking.
- Genuinely listening to pupils' ideas.
- Providing 'think' time and then opportunities to share with peers (often extended to a 'no hands up' rule).
- Displaying warmth and interest in pupils and particularly considering body language (e.g. smiling, eye contact, reassuring gestures).
- Showing empathy for pupils' feelings and a caring attitude.
- Being alert to pupils who are regarded as outcasts and making efforts to help.
- Having a sense of humour: this can be crucial in developing the right atmosphere; but sarcasm should be avoided at all times.

One way to support this is the use of circle time (Mosley 1996); however, it is important to ensure that this is carried out in the way Jenny Mosley sets out. Schools often pay lip service to establishing genuine circle time. Guidance on this is also provided by the DfES in *Excellence and Enjoyment: Social and Emotional Aspects of Learning* (SEAL) (DfES 2005b).

## Opportunities for talk: activities and resources

Separating spoken language into different areas is helpful as it focuses on specific ways of using talk and helps ensure that these important areas are provided for in a balanced way. This can be linked with the genres of texts in the Primary National Strategy known as narrative, recounts, explanations, instructions, reports, and persuasion. The following are a range of suggested activities for different categories of spoken language. You may like to discuss with a colleague which activities are suitable for different age groups.

### Narrative

- *Story box:* using a story box or bag of objects, children make up a story to fit.
- *Story basket:* the teacher models the use of a story basket containing the associated objects or props to bring the story alive. Pupils work in pairs or groups to use them.
- *Picture stories:* provide with a series of pictures for children to make into a story and then tell to others.
- *Story ingredients:* provide a selection of pictures on card for different characters, settings and objects. In pairs children choose one or two from each category and make up a story together.
- *Group stories:* teacher reads the beginning of a story and in groups, pupils decide how it will end.

### Recounts (personal experiences)

- *Memories:* recall things such as their earliest memory; some things that made them happy or sad; something exciting, something worrying.
- *Lost:* pupils talk about a time they were lost. (Use 5Ws – where, why, when, what, who – to promote children providing details).

- *Wishes:* talk about three wishes they would love to have granted. Could be followed by discussion of the most sensible, exciting, etc.
- *Making excuses* give examples of situations and excuses people give, e.g. when late home from school or forgetting to do something. Provide some funny examples. Children recount an experience and add an excuse for something that happened.

## Explanations

- *Explain an object to a Martian:* pupils choose an everyday object from a selection and put in a box or bag so other pupils cannot see it. They then describe it as if the person(s) listening were Martians and had no experience of it or its function. The other pupils have to guess what the object is.
- *The food game:* using a set of 15–20 different pictures of food, sort into different groups, e.g. foods that should be eaten hot, food that is in liquid form, food that you eat as a desert, etc. In groups pupils explain reasons for their choices.
- *Explain how it works:* pupils are provided with a diagram, such as the water cycle, and they then take turns to explain it to a partner.

## Instructions

- *Giving instructions:* in pairs, one pupil has a simple outline picture and then draws in features for which their partner has to give instructions.
- *Trust me!* Pupils work in pairs, one of the children is blindfolded and the other has to help their partner get to a designated place by using only verbal instructions.
- *Devise a game:* make up rules for a simple game and then teach them to a partner.

## Reports

- *The local park:* pupils prepare to give a verbal report on local facilities. They could also plan possible improvements.
- *The museum:* pupils record their own guided museum tour on audio tape, based on a visit made to a museum.
- *Talking tins:* pupils are provided with some interesting tins containing various artefacts. They work with a partner to prepare a short talk on the significance of the objects.

## Persuasion

- *Persuading parents:*
  - to have a pet (provide a situation, e.g. a child who lives in a small house with no garden and whose parents work all day). Groups discuss the pros and cons and come to a conclusion.
  - to watch a TV programme (provide a situation, e.g. it is late, a horror film, etc.).
  - to stay at a friend's house.
  - to buy a pair of expensive trainers.

- *Survival:* imagine a situation (e.g. a plane crash and only a limited number of objects can be carried): which five things would you need to survive? Working in groups, pupils have to persuade each other which they need.
- *Advertising:* collect a variety of adverts and discuss products and the wording of the advertisement. Consider what methods are being used to promote the product. Follow up with developing own advertisement, reflecting on, target audience, style of advert, wording, visuals, use of colour and layout. This could be in the form of a TV advert.

## Active listening

Closely linked to being a good communicator is the skill of listening and this also needs to be clearly taught. The following are important aspects:

- Use the term 'active': listening is not passive but something you need to be actively involved with.
- Discuss body language, expectations of what should be seen and heard in the classroom if children are listening.
- Explain that listening is a process that has three basic steps: hearing, understanding and judging (forming opinions on what has been said).

Teaching active listening requires clear steps. The following four steps will help the learning process:

- *Establish the need for active listening:* this can be done through role-play in pairs to demonstrate effects of not listening (e.g. showing lack of eye contact, bored body language (yawning, etc.), fiddling with other objects). This should be followed by discussion of key aspects of active listening.
- *Define the skill:* using a T chart (draw a large T on the board or large paper with either side of the T marked 'sounds like' and 'looks like'), work with the class to draw up a list of what the skill sounds like and looks like. This can then form a poster in the classroom for constant reference while the skill is practised and refined.
- *Provide guided practice:* make opportunities for pupils to practise with corrective feedback. The teacher monitors, observes, intervenes, coaches, reinforces and encourages. Groups reflect on how well they practised the skill and how they could become more effective.
- *Ensure generalised application of the skill:* once the skill has been established, the teacher provides opportunities for using the skill in a range of contexts.

## Drama and storytelling

Through hearing stories and telling tales, children develop awareness of story, character and plot and a range of narrative techniques, as well as expanding their imaginative capacity. The power of storytelling can be harnessed in the classroom only if teachers are prepared to develop their own storytelling skills and thereby model them for children. Demonstrating a range of techniques to recall the story shape can be empowering for children, such as skeletal summaries, 'seeds of the story', 'story hands' or 'story mountains'. In addition, by listening to a storyteller, children are more clearly able to recall and understand a narrative through experiencing the use of inflection, expression and eye contact. Encouraging children to tell stories gives them the opportunity to be listened to and develops skills such as oral competence, memory, vocabulary and use of different registers. In addition, once the story has been told, then the act of writing it is much more manageable and often far richer. As Teresa Grainger states:

> The oral tradition of storytelling underpins and complements the growth of language and literacy. Its spellbinding power can liberate children's imaginations, release their creativity and enable them to weave dreams together, as they journey along the road of never-ending stories.
>
> (Grainger 1997: 10)

### Developing storytelling skills

For many teachers, and particularly trainees, the thought of telling a story (rather than reading it out) is a daunting process. The following are some ways to gain confidence and competence in the art of telling stories:

- *Begin with a personal tale:* this could be a memorable moment perhaps triggered or supported by an object or photograph. One of us once told the true story of a parent's retreat at Dunkirk in the Second World War to an assembly of children, complete with a memento (a plate that he had been given by a French farmer's wife, stored in his knapsack, which still shows the marks from the ricochet of bullets). The children were absolutely enthralled. The experience came alive for them.
- *Try traditional tales:* we are all familiar with stories such as *Little Red Riding Hood.* Telling the story can free the teller to use body language and eye contact to really engage the audience.
- *Remember stories:* it is important to realise that no two retellings will ever be alike; that is part of the charm in embellishing and adapting the stories. Remember the story by distilling it into the key elements, perhaps through a series of keywords jotted on a piece of card. Interestingly once you are engaged in the story, it usually sweeps you away and you seldom refer to any notes. It is in the process of noting the keywords that you inhabit the story, ready to make it your own as you tell it.
- *Develop your use of voice:* change the expression, range, volume, etc. and use gesture. Provide pace by pausing from dramatic effect or speed to highlight action.

Once the skills are modelled, it is then that you can begin to develop these in children. Similar guidance to the above is needed. Start in a small way with something very familiar and build up to longer tales. Children will find it helpful to work with a partner to support each other. Telling the tale to a smaller audience is less daunting.

*Table 6.2* Talk diary for Key Stage 2

| Name: | Start date: | | End date: | | |
|---|---|---|---|---|---|
| | **Week 1** | **Week 2** | **Week 3** | **Week 4** | **Week 5, etc** |
| Talk activities this week: | | | | | |
| Given a talk or presentation to a large audience | | | | | |
| Explained ideas or processes | | | | | |
| Told a story | | | | | |
| Presented an argument with evidence | | | | | |
| Listened and contributed in a small group | | | | | |
| Worked with a partner and used good questioning and summarising | | | | | |
| Other | | | | | |
| How I have done this week: | | | | | |
| I listened well to my partner | | | | | |
| I spoke clearly | | | | | |
| I used some new and interesting words | | | | | |
| I can add detail to what I am saying | | | | | |
| I can speak to a large audience confidently | | | | | |
| I can speak to a group confidently | | | | | |
| I can ask useful questions | | | | | |
| I can summarise what someone has said | | | | | |
| I can talk appropriately for different occasions | | | | | |
| My targets for next week are: | | | | | |

Source: adapted from Grugeon et al. 2005: 206

## Assessing speaking and listening

Full guidance on methods of assessment for speaking and listening are contained in Chapter 16. Bear in mind the importance of involving pupils in this process. Table 6.2 illustrates a talk diary, which can be a useful means of doing this. Talk diaries are used weekly to record the types and range of speaking and listening activities the children have been involved in. See Grugeon et al. (2005) for further examples. Table 6.2 is an example for use in Key Stage 2; a simplified version could be used in Key Stage 1.

Providing rich and varied opportunities for talk in the classroom is the key to effective learning. Carefully planned with systematic teaching of skills, it will enhance not only the ability to communicate effectively, but also the ability to read and write effectively.

## Key points

- Talk supports learning through interaction, discussion and collaboration.
- Cooperative learning, correctly implemented, provides an effective vehicle for purposeful talk.
- The place of talk in the English Curriculum has been reinforced with the *Excellence and Enjoyment* professional development materials and the revised Primary Framework for Literacy.
- Teachers' questioning needs careful consideration to promote effective talk.
- Reading skills are supported through discussion and interaction.
- Talk prior to writing promotes greater engagement by pupils and higher quality of work.
- Planning for speaking and listening should reflect the distinctive nature of talk and provide for a range of opportunities.
- Storytelling can provide a powerful impetus for talk.
- Teachers need to establish clear strategies for managing talk.

## Further reading

Corden, R. (2000) *Literacy and Learning through Talk: Strategies for the primary classroom.* Buckingham: Open University Press.

DfES (2003c) *Speaking, Listening, Learning: Working with children in Key Stages 1 and 2.* Ref: 0626-2003 G. Nottingham: DfES Publications.

Goodwin, P. (ed.) (2002) *The Articulate Classroom: Talking and learning in the primary classroom.* London: David Fulton.

Grugeon, E., Dawes, L., Smith, C. and Hubbard, L. (2005) *Teaching Speaking and Listening in the Primary School* (3rd edn). London: David Fulton.

# 7 Teaching and learning reading

## Purpose of this chapter

This chapter aims to:

- Discuss literacy standards.
- Review historical perspectives on the teaching of reading.
- Summarise key research findings and theoretical perspectives.
- Describe models of the reading process and research into phonics.
- Examine the implications of the Rose Report (2006).
- Present an overview of research and effective practice in teaching phonics.
- Discuss how to teach comprehension skills.
- Provide guidance on teaching a comprehensive reading programme.
- Discuss effective shared and guided reading.
- Suggest methods of supporting children with reading problems and dyslexia.

## Literacy standards

Perhaps no aspect of educational policy has been as widely disputed as the teaching of reading. One reason is the status of reading as 'the key to educational achievement' (House of Commons 2005: 3). The Bullock Report thirty years previously stated that reading helps to 'shape the personality, refine the sensibility, and sharpen the critical intelligence; that it is a powerful instrument for empathy and a medium through which children can acquire their values' (DES 1975: 124).

Research shows that standards in literacy among English primary school children remained largely stable between 1948 and 1996. National Curriculum tests in 1995 and 1996 highlighted the concern and indicated that only 48 per cent and 57 per cent respectively of 11 year olds were reading at the level expected for their age group (i.e. National Curriculum level 4) (Brooks 1998). As Beard (2000) shows, evidence from inspection, surveys and research all suggests that, in the years prior to the National Literacy Strategy, early reading in English primary schools was largely taught by individualised methods, which consisted principally of the teacher listening to the child read (e.g. Cato et al. 1992). Indeed, Beard (2000: 246) notes that 'direct teaching of literacy skills was surprisingly rare'.

A research study in 1996 involved assessing the reading attainment of a nationally representative sample of 1817 9-year-olds (Year 4) in England and Wales (Brooks et al. 1996). This research has indicated that Britain is generally out-performed by countries like Finland, France and New Zealand. Britain is located within a 'middle' group of countries which includes Belgium and Spain. However, a distinctive feature of British performance is the existence of a long 'tail' of underachievement which is relatively greater than that of other countries (Brooks et al. 1996: 10). The much publicised Progress in International Reading Literacy Study (PIRLS: Ogle et al. 2003), of over 140,000 10-year-old pupils in thirty-five countries ranked England in 2001 as third in terms of reading achievement. The study also indicated that children in England are less likely to enjoy reading than those from other countries and that England still has one of the largest variations between its most and least able pupils.

Whilst there has been a significant improvement in the standards achieved by 11 year olds in schools in England since the introduction of the National Literacy Strategy in 1998, in 2005 about 20 per cent of children had still not achieved the expected standard for their age. This triggered a review of the approaches advocated by the DfES. The House of Commons (2005) report concluded that the government should undertake an immediate review of the National Literacy Strategy and the teaching of reading.

## Historical perspectives on the teaching of reading

The debate over the effective teaching of literacy has raged long and vehemently. One of us, as a newly appointed Literacy Coordinator in a primary school in the early 1990s, recalls being given the 'poisoned chalice' of conducting in-service training with the staff on the effective teaching of reading. In an attempt to highlight the need to teach a range of reading strategies, a fierce argument broke out over the virtues of teaching reading through the 'whole language approach', using 'real' books, versus the value of teaching the subskills such as phonics. The two positions seemed totally polarised and have been described as the 'reading wars' (Goodman 1998).

Harrison (2004: 28) noted that 'Since around the year 2000, peace has broken out in the UK in relation to the "reading wars" and the place of phonics in early reading instruction'. Harrison attributed this to the fact that the teaching of phonics is now in effect mandatory in the United Kingdom, although the situation he notes is different in the United States. Since then, however, as a result of the House of Commons (2005) report on the teaching of reading and the review by Jim Rose (DfES 2006a), war has broken out once more. Yet again, the place of phonics in the teaching of reading has been fiercely debated by academics and by those with only a limited knowledge, hyped by media interest.

## Summary of research findings

During the 1990s a wealth of research was produced on the effective teaching of literacy, most notably Adams' (1990) seminal work indicating the clear need for explicit teaching of phonics within a meaningful context of texts. Other key findings from Bryant (1993) and Goswami (1995) highlighted the need for developing phonological awareness. The work carried out by Clay (1979) through Reading Recovery emphasised the need to make explicit how print works, how to effectively link reading and writing, and to ensure swift intervention when children begin to exhibit a lack of effective progress. Holdaway's (1979) work, on using shared texts to enable teachers to re-create the experience of a bedtime story with a child and parent, began to be replicated to effect. Further work by Australian genre theorists (Littlefair 1991) made clear the need not only to introduce a range of genres to children, but also to make the features of each explicit, to enable a clearer understanding. All this research formed the background to the National Literacy Strategy in 1998.

## Theoretical perspectives on reading

The wide range of research on reading has led to very different theoretical positions or perspectives. Kathy Hall's book *Listening to Stephen Read* (2003) presents the example of 8-year-old Stephen, who is underachieving in reading and then views ways of helping him from different perspectives. The benefits of multiple perspectives, in providing a range of support, are thus displayed, rather than searching for a single right method of teaching reading. The four major perspectives are summarised below.

---

**Activity: Different theoretical perspectives on reading**

Read each of the four different perspectives on reading and then answer the following questions, working with colleagues where possible:

- According to the psycho-linguistic perspective, what would the teacher provide frequent opportunities for?
- According to the cognitive-psychological perspective, what specific skills would a teacher ensure are taught?
- According to the socio-cultural perspective, why are links to home and the community so important?
- According to the socio-political perspective, why is it important to carefully select texts for children?

---

### *The psycho-linguistic perspective*

Following the views of Noam Chomsky (1965) and his study of language development which suggested that humans are innately disposed to acquire language of their environment, psychologists began to question whether this applied to written language also. The work of Goodman (1973) and Smith (1971) used children's miscues to derive information about the reading process. Goodman's (1967) analysis led him to describe reading as a 'psycho-linguistic guessing game' and suggested that readers use three cues simultaneously to make sense of text: graphophonic, syntactic and semantic.

Frank Smith (1971) also argued that reading was not something that could be taught but rather you learn to read by reading. Teachers do not 'teach' reading but support children during the process. He placed more importance on the non-visual sources (context and prior knowledge) than the actual words. He claimed that readers do not use the alphabetic principle of decoding. The role of the teacher was to create the climate in which children would be motivated to learn and to provide an environment that is rich in natural language. This view can be described as a 'top-down' model whereby the use of text supports the learning rather than the subskills such as decoding. Dividing texts into smaller parts for this perspective can jeopardize the meaning. This led to the 'whole-language approach' to teaching reading using Breakthrough to Literacy materials (Mackay et al. 1970) which supported children creating their own texts to read based on their own experiences. In summary, according to the psycho-linguistic perspective, reading is not:

> a linear process of letter-by-letter deciphering, sounding out, word recognition and finally text comprehension. It is not a linear process, they insisted, but a meaning-building (constructivist), problem-solving one.
>
> (Hall 2003: 42–43)

### The cognitive-psychological perspective

This perspective sees reading as a staged developmental process. It views the alphabetical nature of written language as key and also a major hurdle for beginning readers. Different stage models have been presented (Chall 1983; Frith 1985; Ehri 1987) but they all share one important aspect, which is the importance of decoding words. This work suggests that sight word reading is not a flashcard method, but rather a processing of reading words by accessing them in the memory. It does not rely on the visual features of the word but relies on connections which link the words to their sounds and meanings which are stored in the reader's lexicon.

This theory has three main phases. First, the *pre-alphabet (or logographic) phase* is where children use the shape or look of the word and the reader stores in the memory visual cues to remember the word, such as the shape of two round eyes in the work 'look'. Second, the *partial alphabetic phase* is where learners have gained some alphabetic knowledge and begin to know the relevant letter–sound (grapheme–phoneme) correspondences. Phonemic awareness is necessary before this can progress and at first children focus on the most important letters. Third, the *full alphabetic (or orthographic) phase* is reached when readers understand fully the grapheme–phoneme correspondences. At this stage children are also beginning to store in their memories knowledge of common spelling patterns. In summary, the cognitive-psychological perspective sees reading as occurring in stages and highly dependent on alphabetic knowledge.

### The socio-cultural perspective

The emphasis here shifts from the individual to the social and cultural contexts in which literacy occurs. This perspective stresses the symbolic nature of language and thought. Meaning occurs through social interaction (Vygotsky 1978; Bruner 1996). For this perspective, learning to read is concerned with how reading is done in a particular context. The classroom, or school or home or community is in this view, a community of practice. Literacy becomes a multidisciplinary field which can be studied through ethnographic of literacies in their context. It follows that understanding the context and literacy practices in the home is crucial to supporting children's reading according to this perspective. For children it involves learning how to be like a reader in the context of the school. The research of Shirley Brice Heath (1983) who studied the differing literacy practices of different racial groups showed the real impact on the ways in which the children learned language. This can have a detrimental effect on low-achieving readers who come from lower socio-economic groups who may be offered a diet of reading that bears little resemblance to their own culture. One way to avoid this is to place more emphasis on meaning that is derived from print, than the decoding process. In summary, the socio-cultural perspective asks teachers to take note of the understanding of literacy gained in the home and community to inform the activities in the classrooms.

### The socio-political perspective

This view starts from the premise that no knowledge is neutral but is based on a group's perspective. The work of Comber (1999) and Marsh and Millard (2000) presents examples of this stance and shows the danger of demotivating pupils through not reflecting children's 'cultural capital' (Bourdieu 1977) in the classroom. This view (also called critical literacy) holds that learning to read includes being able to determine underlying assumptions and biases in texts. It requires the reader to take a critical stance of images that are portrayed, for example about gender, race, ability, etc. This stance is about making explicit the relationship between the language and the world. It is about learning how attitudes and beliefs about the world are presented by language. This view does not merely help the reader to spot stereotypes but also to understand how texts work to achieve certain effects. Hall (2003: 178) points out that 'Learning to read in this perspective is as much about learning identifies and values as it is about learning skills and codes.'

In summary, the socio-political perspective is about understanding the role of literacy skills in empowering pupils to fully participate in society. It sees literacy as bound up with ethnicity, gender, social class, disability, etc. and its purpose is social justice.

## Reading processes

The two main approaches to teaching reading are termed 'bottom-up' and 'top-down'. *Bottom-up approaches* view the reading process as building up from letters, spelling patterns and words to sentences and paragraphs. *Top-down approaches* stress the prime importance of the meaning of language for comprehension and for word recognition. Recent research-based models of early reading and fluent reading suggest that reading is neither top-down nor bottom-up in nature. Instead, sources of contextual, comprehension, visual and phonological information are simultaneously interactive, issuing and accommodating to and from each other (Adams and Bruck 1993). Related research is reported by Rumelhart and McClelland (1986) and Seidenberg and McClelland (1989). More recently, a US government report (Snow et al. 1998) analysed a large number of research articles and cited five areas of development associated with becoming a proficient reader: decoding, fluency, background knowledge, comprehension monitoring and motivation. Thus reading is viewed as a combination of bottom-up and top-down.

## Models of the reading process

One model of the reading process is the *Searchlights model* contained in the National Literacy Strategy *Framework for Teaching* (DfEE 1998a). The reading strategies or 'searchlights' help to shed light on the text. Successful readers use as many of these strategies as possible (see Figure 7.1).

When introduced in 1998, the Searchlights model represented the best practice in the teaching of reading. However, since then the model has been criticised. Ofsted (2002) noted:

> The 'searchlights' model proposed in the framework has not been effective enough in terms of illustrating where the intensity of the 'searchlights' should fall at the different stages of learning to read.
>
> (Ofsted 2002: para 58)

An alternative model known as the *Simple View of Reading* (Gough and Tunmer (1986) identifies two components: decoding and comprehension. *Decoding* means the ability to recognise words out of context and to apply phonic rules to this recognition. *Comprehension* means not reading comprehension but *linguistic comprehension*, which is defined as 'the process by which words, sentences and discourse are interpreted' (Gough and Tunmer 1986). They also state that the two interrelated processes are both necessary for reading. This view has been developed since first proposed in 1986 and is represented in the Rose Review (DfES 2006a: 77) as shown in Figure 7.2.

The advantages of this model are that:

- it shows children may not display equal performance in each area
- it enables clear identification of any strengths or weaknesses and supports appropriate teaching
- it demonstrates the importance of both word recognition and comprehension
- it shows the importance of teachers understanding the cognitive processes involved.

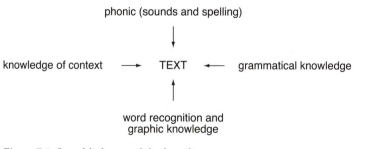

*Figure 7.1* Searchlights model of reading
Source: DfEE 1998a

**Activity: Relating the Searchlights model to the Simple View of Reading model**

Examine the two diagrams in Figures 7.1 and 7.2 and then, with colleagues if possible, answer the following questions:

- Where would word recognition fit in the simple view of reading?
- Where would contextual knowledge fit in the simple view?
- Where would phonic knowledge fit in the simple view?
- Where would grammatical knowledge fit in the simple view?

Now discuss the diagrammatic representation in Figure 7.3.

- What are the implications for teachers for this view?

In order to become readers as well as listeners, children need to develop processes that lead into their store of word meanings and their store of word sounds from language they *see*. The stores and processes that children need to set up to accomplish this are shown in the unshaded parts of Figure 7.3. The dotted lines leading to 'pronounce word aloud' indicate that reading aloud is optional, since probably most reading is silent.

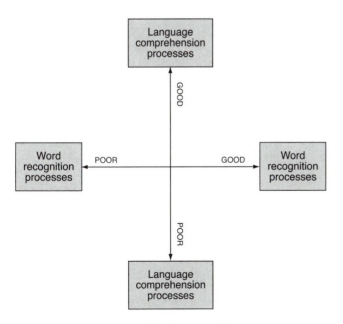

*Figure 7.2* Simple View of Reading model
Source: DfES 2006a: 77

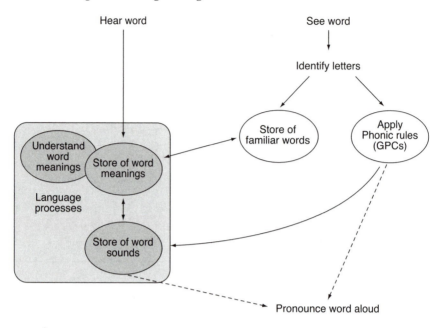

*Figure 7.3* Diagrammatic representation of the word recognition system
Source: DfES 2006a: 86

The Primary National Strategy (DfES 2006b) reinforces the concept of oral language underpinning the development of reading, and states:

> The idea that reading comprehension depends on oral language skill is captured in the 'simple view of reading'. According to this conceptual framework, comprehension means understanding of language whether it is spoken or written.
> (DfES 2006b: 5)

The implications of this are that:

> From an educational perspective what this means is that teachers must foster the development of oral language skills in order to safeguard children's reading comprehension.
> (DfES 2006b: 5)

### Research into teaching phonics

The teaching of phonics has also been subject to considerable debate. Harrison (2004) cites the example of Usha Goswami, now at the University of Cambridge, whose work (Goswami and Bryant 1990) was considered to be a milestone in reading research. However, during the period of her maternity leave from 1998 to 2000, Goswami was 'vilified' (Harrison 2004: 27) and the importance of rhyme and analogy was dismissed as *analytic phonics* (a term which she had not used to describe her position), which was attacked as a less systematic approach and instead the direct instruction of *synthetic phonics* was regarded as the Holy Grail of the teaching of early reading (Burkard 1999).

In a research study carried out in Clackmannanshire, Scotland, Rhona Johnston and Joyce Watson (2005) looked at 300 children in the first year of the Scottish primary school system. They compared three different teaching methods: synthetic phonics, analytic phonics, and an analytic phonics method that included systematic phonemic awareness teaching. At the end of the programme, those children who had been taught by synthetic phonics were found to be seven months ahead of the other two groups in reading.

- *Synthetic phonics* refers to an approach to the teaching of reading in which the phonemes (sounds) associated with particular graphemes (letters) are pronounced in isolation and blended together (synthesised). Synthetic phonics for writing reverses the sequence: children are taught to say the word they wish to write, segment it into its phonemes and say them in turn and write a grapheme for each phoneme in turn to produce the written word.
- *Analytic phonics* refers to an approach to the teaching of reading in which the phonemes associated with particular graphemes are not pronounced in isolation. Children identify (analyse) the common phoneme in a set of words in which each word contains the phoneme under study. Analytic phonics for writing similarly relies on inferential learning.

Ehri's (2003) systematic review of the teaching of phonics established that people used to think that readers learned to read sight words by memorising their visual shapes. However, research has led us to reject this idea. Now we know that sight word learning depends upon the application of grapheme–phoneme correspondences. These provide the glue that holds the words in memory for quick reading (Ehri 2003: 2). The findings of the meta-analysis support the conclusion that systematic phonics instruction helps children learn to read more effectively than non-systematic or no phonics instruction (Ehri 2003). The impact of phonics instruction on reading was also significantly greater in the early grades (kindergarten and first grades, i.e. from 5 to 7 years) when phonics was the method used to start children out than in the later grades (second through sixth grades, i.e. from 7 to 11 years) after children had made some progress in reading presumably with another method.

Researchers have associated phonological development with early success in learning to read for some years. One of the most influential publications is by Bradley and Bryant (1983), who reported a longitudinal study of 368 children and the finding that children's sensitivity to rhyme was a particularly important predictor of subsequent success in reading. Hatcher et al.'s (2004) research shows that phonological awareness training in conjunction with a phonics teaching programme was critical for those children at risk of literacy failure.

There are also strong links between children's 'orthographic' development on entry to school and their subsequent progress. Children's ability to write their name without a model has been found to be correlated with a number of aspects of writing at 7 years (Blatchford 1991). In addition, there is a strong link between children's early letter name knowledge and their subsequent reading development (Blatchford et al. 1987; Blatchford and Plewis 1990).

## Rose's Independent Review of the Teaching of Early Reading

The final report for the Secretary of State for Education and Skills produced in March 2006 by Jim Rose (DfES 2006a) drew on research findings, consultation with practitioners, teachers, trainers, resource and policy makers and visits to schools and training events. The remit for the review focused on five aspects and made recommendations as follows:

1  Best practice in the teaching of early reading and phonics.

   - The Early Years Foundation Stage (DfES 2007b) and the renewed Primary National Strategy Framework (DfES 2006b) for teaching literacy should provide, as a priority, clear guidance on developing children's speaking and listening skills.
   - High quality, systematic phonic work as defined by the review should be taught. The knowledge, skills and understanding that constitute high quality work should be taught as the prime approach in learning to decode (to read) and encode (to write/spell) print.
   - Phonic work should be set within a broad and rich language curriculum that takes full account of developing the four interdependent strands of language: speaking, listening, reading and writing and enlarging children's stock of words.
   - The Primary National Strategy should continue to exemplify 'quality first teaching'.

2  Relation to the Early Years Foundation Stage and the renewed Primary Framework for Literacy.

   - For most children, high quality, systematic phonic work should start by the age of 5, taking full account of professional judgements of children's developing abilities and the need to embed this work within a broad and rich curriculum. This should be preceded by pre-reading activities that pave the way for such work to start.
   - Phonic work for young children should be multisensory in order to capture their interest, sustain motivation, and reinforce learning in imaginative and exciting ways.
   - The Searchlights model should be reconstructed to take full account of word recognition and language comprehension as distinct processes related one to the other.
   - The Early Years Foundation Stage and the renewed Primary Framework for Literacy must be compatible with each other and make sure that expectations about continuity and progression in phonic work are expressed explicitly in the new guidance.

3  What range of provision best supports children with significant literacy difficulties and enables them to catch up with their peers, and the relationship of such targeted intervention programmes with synthetic phonics teaching?

   - It is not the purpose of intervention work to shore up weak teaching at Wave 1. Settings and schools should establish 'quality first teaching' to minimise the risk of children falling behind and thereby secure the most cost effective use of resources. High quality phonic work should therefore be a priority within Wave 1 teaching.

- Given that intervention work will be necessary, settings and schools should make sure that additional support is compatible with mainstream practice. Irrespective of whether intervention work is taught in regular lessons or elsewhere, the gains made by children through such work must be sustained and built upon when they return to their mainstream class.
- Leading edge interventions should continue to be exemplified in guidance showing how the best provision and practice are matched to the different types of special educational needs.

4   How leadership and management in schools can support the teaching of reading, as well as practitioners' subject knowledge and skills.

- Headteachers and managers of settings should make sure that phonic work is given appropriate priority in the teaching of beginner readers and this is reflected in decisions about training and professional development for their staff.
- Settings and schools should make sure that at least one member of staff is fully able to lead on literacy, especially phonic work.
- Those in leadership and management should make sure that the normal monitoring arrangements assure the quality and consistency of phonic work and that staff receive constructive feedback about their practice.
- Headteachers and governors should ensure that high quality teaching of reading in Key Stage 1 informs realistic and ambitious target-setting for English at Key Stage 2.

5   The value for money or cost-effectiveness of the range of approaches covered by the review.

- In order to ensure that initial training and professional development provide good value for money in the teaching of reading, including phonic work, the Training and Development Agency for Schools should consider all the steps set out under Aspect 5 of the remit.

It is as a result of this review that the Primary National Strategy has revised guidance on the teaching of phonics, which was incorporated within the renewed Primary Framework for Literacy in 2006. The strands of this framework integrate speaking and listening, reading and writing and with respect to reading they consist of:

- Word reading skills and strategies
- Understanding and interpreting texts
- Engaging with and responding to texts.

## Teaching phonics

As a result of the Rose Report (DfES 2006a) the provision of phonics in the Primary National Strategy has been revised. The report sets out the definition of high quality phonic work in which the key features are to teach beginner readers the following:

- grapheme–phoneme correspondences in a clearly defined, incremental sequence
- to apply the highly important skill of blending (synthesising) phonemes in the order in which they occur, all through a word to read it
- to apply the skills of segmenting words into their constituent phonemes to spell
- that blending and segmenting are reversible processes.

It recommends:

- High quality, systematic phonic teaching for most children should start by the age of 5.
- Children should have had the opportunity to engage in a range of activities and experiences to develop their speaking and listening skills and phonological awareness.
- A systematic programme of high quality phonic work which is time limited.
- Teaching should be both discrete and reinforced throughout the curriculum.
- Children's progress in developing and applying their phonic knowledge needs to be carefully assessed and monitored and, where necessary, additional support provided to ensure this learning is secure.

### Phonological and phonemic awareness

*Phonological awareness* is the ability to segment language aurally. *Phonemic awareness* is the ability to discriminate the individual phonemes within words – the sounds which make up that word. Instruction in phonological and phonemic awareness involves teaching children to focus on and manipulate phonemes in spoken syllables and words. The importance of children acquiring the ability to hear and discriminate sounds correctly is a necessary prerequisite for learning phonics. Harrison (2004) notes:

> how is it that some of the poorest readers in our schools are the ones who have had years of the teaching of 'phonics'? . . . The answer is simple and comes in two parts. One answer is that the reader may have been taught phonics is a poor and ineffectual way, but the second answer is that no child can profit from the teaching of phonics unless they have phonemic awareness.
>
> (Harrison 2004: 41)

The National Reading Panel (2000) looked specifically at phonological awareness particularly because studies have identified phonological awareness and letter knowledge as the two best school-entry predictors of how well children will learn to read during the first two years of instruction. In addition many experimental studies have been carried out to evaluate the effectiveness of phonological awareness training in facilitating reading acquisition. Overall, the findings showed that teaching children to manipulate phonemes in words was highly effective. Phonological awareness training was the cause of improvement not only in students' phonemic awareness but also in their reading and spelling.

Phonological awareness consists of different types. These can be thought of as ranging from larger to smaller units:

- *word awareness:* understanding that sentences consist of individual words
- *rhyme awareness:* being able to identify words that have identical final sound segments
- *syllable awareness:* being able to hear parts or segments of phonemes that comprise the rhythm of the word
- *phonemic awareness:* being able to attend to, identify, and manipulate the sounds that are representative of graphemes in the English language.

Teaching phonological awareness should bear in mind the following steps:

- *Listening:* ensure that children have developed the skills of listening attentively before teaching them to discriminate fine differences in sounds.
- *Rhyming:* this should be taught in steps, from rhyme exposure (lots of opportunities to hear rhymes), rhyme detection (same or different) and finally rhyme generation (children coming up with their own rhymes).
- *Identifying words:* ensure that children can identify individual words from the continuous stream of speech that they hear.
- *Syllables:* ensure that children can begin the process of breaking down words, first into syllables.
- *Phonemes:* once the above is secure, ensure children can identify individual phonemes, then the teaching of individual phonemes can begin.

---

**Activity: Teaching phonological awareness**

Examine each of the five steps in teaching phonological awareness and, with a colleague if possible, devise activities to fit each step:

- Listening
- Rhyming
- Identifying words
- Syllables
- Phonemes.

---

## Progression in teaching phonics

The pace of the teaching of phonics in the Primary National Strategy (DfES 2006b) has been revised as a result of the Rose Report (DfES 2006a) and the renewed Primary Framework for Literacy. The following six phases are recommended:

- *Phase 1:* developing phonological awareness
  Duration: Early Years Foundation Stage: Communication, Language and Literacy

  - Supports children's developing language structures and vocabulary
  - Helps children to distinguish between sounds through the use of rhyme, rhythm and alliteration

- *Phase 2:* beginning of systematic phonic teaching
  Duration: up to six weeks

  - Introduce small number of common consonants and vowels
  - Blend them together in reading simple CVC words and segment them to support spelling

- *Phase 3:* teaches one grapheme for each of the forty-four phonemes in order to read and spell simple regular words
  Duration: up to twelve weeks

  - Link sounds to letters (letter names and sounds)
  - Recognise letter shapes and say a sound for each
  - Hear and say sounds in the order in which they occur in the word
  - Read simple words by blending the phonemes
  - Recognise common digraphs
  - Read some high frequency words

- *Phase 4:* read and spell words containing adjacent consonants
  Duration: four to six weeks

  - Blend and segment adjacent consonants in words
  - Apply this skill when reading unfamiliar texts and in spelling words

- *Phase 5:* learn alternative ways of pronouncing the graphemes and spelling the phonemes already taught
  Duration: through Year 1

  - Learn alternative ways of pronouncing the graphemes and spelling the phonemes corresponding to long vowel phonemes
  - Identify the parts of two- and three-syllable words and be able to read and spell phonically decodable two- and three-syllable words.
  - Recognise an increasing number of high frequency words automatically

- *Phase 6:* develop their skill and automaticity in reading and spelling
  Duration: begin in and continue through Year 2

  - Apply phonic skills and knowledge to recognise and spell an increasing number of complex words
  - Read an increasing number of high and medium frequency words independently and automatically

One of the key aspects of teaching phonics effectively is to ensure that segmenting and blending phonemes are taught explicitly and plenty of practice is provided. Segmentation means hearing the individual phonemes within a word; for instance the word 'crash' comprises four phonemes – 'c-r-a-sh'. In order to spell, a child must segment a word into its component phonemes and choose a letter or letter combination (e.g. 'sh') to represent each phoneme. Blending means saying phonemes together to pronounce a word. In order to read an unfamiliar word phonemically, a child must attribute a phoneme to each letter or letter combination in the word and then merge the phonemes together to pronounce the word (for example, /f/a/t/ = fat).

**Activity: Checking on terminology**

Review the Glossary and work with a colleague to ensure that you understand the terms. For example:

- What is the difference between a phoneme and a grapheme?
- Give examples of words containing split digraphs.
- Define the difference between blending and segmenting.

**Glossary**

| | |
|---|---|
| *Alliteration* | A sequence of words beginning with the same sound |
| *Blend* | A combination of letters where individual letters retain their sounds |
| *Blending* | To draw individual sounds together to pronounce a word, e.g. /c/l/a/p/,blended together reads 'clap' |
| *Digraph* | Two letters which combine to make a new sound |
| *Grapheme* | A letter or combinations of letters that represent a phoneme |
| *Initial consonant blend* | The consonants retain their original sounds but are blended together as in '**sl**ip' |
| *Long vowel sounds* | The long vowel sounds as in 'feel' or 'cold' |
| *Mnemonic* | A device for remembering something, such as 'ee/ee/ feel the tree' |
| *Phoneme* | The smallest single identifiable sound, e.g. the letters 'ch' representing one sound |
| *Rhyme* | Words that sound the same but do not necessarily share the same spelling |
| *Segmenting* | Splitting up a word into its individual phonemes in order to spell it, i.e. the word 'pat' has three phonemes: /p/a/t/ |
| *Split digraph* | Two letters, making one sound, e.g. a-e as in 'cake' |
| *Syllable* | A unit of pronunciation having one vowel sound |
| *Trigraph* | Three letters which combine to make a new sound |

*Approaches to teaching phonics*

There are a number of approaches to teaching phonics. What is important is that the programme adopted by a school should be adhered to 'with fidelity' (DfES 2006a: para 55), that is applied consistently, and the programme should be used regularly. The key aspects of effective programmes, identified in the Rose Report (DfES 2006a), emphasise the importance of being systematic; include teaching of blending phonemes and segmenting words into phonemes; provide regular assessment; be multisensory in approach and be manageable within a broad and rich early years curriculum.

One programme that is clearly multisensory is Jolly Phonics (see Lloyd 1998). This programme introduces actions for each phoneme and is recommended to be taught quickly and early. However, it does not introduce all forty-four phonemes, nor deal with the issue of different ways of spelling the same sound.

The Teaching Handwriting Reading and Spelling Skills (THRASS) approach (Davies and Ritchie 1998) introduces children to both lower-case and upper-case letters by name and involves teaching of all phonemes using correct terminology such as graph, digraph, trigraph, grapheme and phoneme. The THRASS charts, which are fundamental to its operation, provide a visual representation of the English sound system. Each of the forty-four boxes on each chart provides a range of alternative spellings for phonemes. For example:

**c**at **k**itten du**ck** s**ch**ool **q**ueen for the 'k' sound

This approach does not provide a systematic programme of teaching the phonemes however, nor does it teach children to blend phonemes.

The *Success for All* (SFA) approach to teaching phonics (Slavin and Madden 2005) provides an element of multisensory work and highlights the use of blending and segmenting phonemes using a puppet who can talk only in phonemes. It also provides help with the most difficult aspect, learning the long vowel phonemes with a rap and clearly links the reading and writing of phonemes. However, it does not include all forty-four phonemes, and teaches only some of the spelling choices for phonemes.

One of us has attempted to address the shortcomings of the above approaches by writing a programme (Jolliffe 2006a) that contains three stages:

- Stage 1: Identifying sounds.
- Stage 2: Teaching consonant and short vowel phonemes.
- Stage 3: Teaching long vowel and schwa phonemes.

This programme teaches the necessary elements of phonological awareness, followed by all forty-four phonemes with their most common spelling choices. It contains actions, a rap to teach the long vowel sounds, constant over-learning, diagnostic assessment throughout and emphasises partner work.

## Teaching comprehension skills

The Primary National Strategy has provided new guidance on teaching comprehension skills in response to the Rose Report (DfES 2006a) and states 'Reading comprehension is a highly interactive process that takes place between a reader and a text' (DfES 2006c: 28). The key aspect to consider here is the experiences and cultural background of each child. According to the Simple View of Reading model, comprehension is the product of word recognition and listening comprehension. Once the words are recognised they can be understood as long as they are in the child's oral vocabulary, but vocabulary is also increased through reading. From an educational viewpoint this means that practitioners and teachers must encourage the development of oral language skills in order to safeguard children's reading comprehension.

The development of comprehension skills begins with listening comprehension skills (simply comprehending what you hear) which requires the skills of vocabulary knowledge, grammatical skills, pragmatic abilities (the ability to understand and use language in appropriate ways and contexts) and metalinguistic awareness (the ability to reflect on the structure of language to understand non-literal, figurative and meta-phorical use of language). Reading comprehension is a less natural act than listening comprehension and requires additional strategies. Teaching strategies that support this are identified in the report of the National Reading Panel (2000: 19), which states that 'Research on comprehension strategies has evolved dramatically over the last 2 decades'. The National Reading Panel (2000) reviewed a range of studies that showed evidence that instruction leads to improvements in comprehension and identified broad areas as follows:

- comprehension monitoring
- cooperative learning
- curriculum integration
- graphic and semantic organisers (including story maps)
- question answering
- question generation
- summarisation.

## Supporting comprehension skills

Comprehension skills can be supported by:

- Directed Activities Related to Text (DARTs), which are divided into either text analysis (locating, organising and reconstructing information in text); or text reconstruction (used with modified text, words deleted, paragraphs, reordered, group sequencing).
- Using structural or graphic organisers to reconstruct the information read will also support comprehension.
- Explicitly teaching and modelling of determining literal and inferential comprehension.
- Visual imagery training to support comprehension of fiction texts.

---

**Activity: Supporting comprehension skills**

Review some of the key strategies for supporting comprehension skills as outlined on pages 123–27 and also read the section on 'Developing Reading Comprehension' contained in the Core Position Papers for Literacy and Mathematics from the Primary National Strategy (DfES 2006c: 28–39).

Discuss the following questions with colleagues:

- How does reconstructing information for example by using graphic organisers or charts help comprehension?
- Why does reading comprehension depend on oral language skills?
- What are the advantages of encouraging children to create visual images as they read?

---

## Teaching a comprehensive reading programme

For many trainees or recently qualified teachers, the teaching of reading is clouded by the many debates about the correct methods. The following provides guidance on how to put the key findings from research and advice from the latest government reports into action. The simplest way of viewing this is to understand that teaching needs to be *text level* (centred on developing an understanding of how texts work, and deriving meaning and pleasure from them), and simultaneously *word level* (providing the necessary subskills of decoding using phonics and building a store of words in the memory, linked to their meaning). Teaching should provide for both of these in structured steps. The following provides some guidance of how to go about this.

### *Stage 1: Beginning reading*

At this stage children need a rich diet of books explored in an interactive way, relating it to their own experiences and supporting children to attend to fine details through the text and pictures, leading to imaginative play. Alongside this children need to develop their word level skills ensuring they develop and consolidate their phonological awareness (the ability to distinguish individual sounds).

### *Text level*

When working with texts, fiction or non-fiction, the following procedure should be adopted.

1   Before reading

- Activate background knowledge of the subject, i.e. talk about the book *before* opening it; what does the picture show, talk about the title, read the blurb and relate it to the children's own experiences.
- Discuss any significant new words.
- With fiction, encourage the children to predict the story.
- Give a purpose for listening by asking key questions, e.g. 'What do you think might happen to . . .?' etc. For non-fiction, have a question to explore the answer in the book.

2   During reading (at this stage this will be shared reading)

- Consider expression when reading with children: pitch, intonation, stress and patterns of language all help comprehension.
- Ensure the book (if fiction) is read through without a break, either on first or later reading, for enjoyment.
- Use props, where possible, for fiction, such as objects from the story to bring the text alive.
- Stop frequently when examining the text, and ask summative questions about the story for fiction, for non-fiction closely examine sections to answer specific questions.
- Finish by referring to original questions and predictions.

3   After reading

- Provide opportunities for a brief review of main characters and events, or what they found out if non-fiction. This is ideally done through paired talk.
- Follow up later in the same day or on a following day, a more detailed retelling. A variety of techniques can be used from paired work, small groups using props such as sequencing cards, storyboards, puppets or drama techniques such as hot-seating (see page 136) or freeze-framing. (*Freeze-framing* is a drama strategy involving children choosing a key moment, and creating a still picture to illustrate it. For example, children could freeze the moment in *Goldilocks and the Three Bears* when the three bears find Goldilocks asleep in one of their beds and act out their body language and facial expressions).
- Develop further with opportunities for imaginative play and props associated with the text provided.

*Word level*

Alongside the text level work, children need to be taught vital skills to support their development as readers.

- *Learning about print:* this can be primarily achieved by the use of enlarged texts (big books), in print or on screen, and the use of a pointer. So as the adult reads and points, children learn the direction of print, the concept of individual words and spacing in between words, identifying individual letters and the concept of a sentence and the punctuation used. This is also supported by the children being encouraged to write themselves in a range of contexts alongside play activities.
- *Phonological awareness:* the first step in ensuring children develop phonological awareness is to explicitly teach how to be a good listener and to provide additional support to those children who need it. The second aspect is to begin with larger 'units' of sounds and then work towards smaller 'units'. Use nursery rhymes and rhyming games to support children in being able to detect rhymes and then to generate rhymes themselves. Following this help children to see patterns, such as repeated words, followed by identifying syllables within words, again through fun games using clapping and tapping. The final step is to be able to distinguish individual phonemes, for example by playing 'I Spy'.
- *Alphabet awareness:* here children should be introduced to the alphabet using letter names (not sounds), for example by using alphabet songs and rhymes. They should also gradually be able to distinguish upper- and lower-case letters and not, as was felt at one time, be exposed only to lower-case letters. The prolific examples of upper-case letters in the environment (e.g. B&Q, MFI, BBC, etc.) illustrate that this is not necessary. They can then begin to identify initial letter sounds.

### Stage 2: Learning to decode

*Text level*

1 Before reading

- Continue as for beginning reading.

2 During reading

- In shared reading continue as for beginning reading, but specifically model blending phonemes to make words.
- At this stage independent reading begins. Support the child to use the strategies modelled in shared reading and from developing word level skills. In particular, blending phonemes to read words should be encouraged where possible.
- Support the child with developing vocabulary and understanding of new words.
- Encourage finger pointing to reinforce one-to-one correspondence of written to spoken word.
- Support the child to continually monitor reading for meaning by stopping them to check they understand what they have read and it makes sense.
- Provide guided reading opportunities with decodable texts.

3 After reading

- Review and summarise what they have read.
- Discuss questions and predictions raised before reading.
- Provide follow-up activities, for example writing letters to Goldilocks.

*Word level*

The emphasis is on systematic teaching of phonics at this stage with practice at blending the phonemes for reading and segmenting the words for spelling.

- Provide instruction in sound/symbol correspondences (decoding).
- Provide opportunities for children to hear, say, read and write the phonemes taught with plenty of practice and over-learning.
- Ensure that regular diagnostic assessment is undertaken to identify early any child who is not making progress.

### Stage 3: Silent reading

During this time the child moves from the reliance on decoding to develop an increasing number of words recognised automatically, through a store of word meanings and familiar words. The emphasis shifts to improving comprehension.

1 Before reading
   In shared reading

- Model activating background knowledge.
- Integrate new vocabulary by modeling new words in a sentence.

- Support developing cognitive and metacognitive strategies:

    o   using prediction before and during reading
    o   using 'think-alouds' and visualisation
    o   making inferences
    o   understanding the structure of different text types.

In individual reading encourage children to apply the above strategies.

2   During reading

- Silent reading starts for first time.
- Encourage wider reading of unknown texts.
- Develop greater fluency and appropriate expression when reading aloud.
- No need for finger pointing.
- Pronunciation and word-stress problems are main areas of difficulty.
- Provide opportunities for guided reading.

3   After reading

- Support children's questioning of the text by using higher and lower-order levels of thinking, using Bloom's (1956) Taxonomy (see pages 95 and 96).
- Encourage a personal response to text through reading journals.
- Provide opportunities for drama activities such as hot-seating to support empathy.
- Provide opportunities for construction of text related to text type read, in pairs or cooperative groups.

### Stage 4: Independent reading

At this stage the child should be encouraged to read widely and develop personal preferences. In shared reading the emphasis will be on developing children's understanding at three levels: see Figure 7.4:

1   *Literal* understanding of text.
2   *Inferential or deductive* understanding by reading between the lines and encouraging paired and group discussion.
3   *Evaluative* understanding of the text by comparing with other similar texts and specific strengths.

---

**Activity: The stages of a comprehensive reading programme**

Study the four main stages of a comprehensive reading programme carefully, as outlined on pages 124–27. Then, if possible with colleagues, discuss different age groups to which each stage might apply.

## THREE KINDS OF QUESTIONS
### Where is the answer found?

**Type 1**
**(literal)**

Right there
The answer is in the
text. It's 'right there' for you
to read.

**Type 2**
**(inferential)**

Think and search
Search for clues in the
text and think about
your answer.

**Type 3**
**(evaluative)**

On my own
The answer won't be
told by words in the text. You
must find the answer in your
head. Think: 'I have to
answer this question on my
own. The story won't be much
help.'

*Figure 7.4* Different levels of reading

## Effective shared and guided reading

The research evidence, like the national reports on Standard Assessment Tasks (SATs) performance, indicates that greater use of shared and guided reading and writing are likely to help teachers to teach literacy in a more systematic and sustained way which a daily Literacy Hour provides. National surveys suggest that these teaching approaches were not being widely used (Cato et al. 1992; Ireson et al. 1995; Wragg et al. 1998) and that explicit links between text and word level teaching were not being strategically made.

### Shared reading

Shared reading, in which teacher and pupils simultaneously read aloud to a large format text, has been especially promoted in the writing of Don Holdaway (1979, 1982) for younger pupils. Older children can interact with the text with the teacher's support in a number of ways. The guidance from the Primary National Strategy (DfES 2001b) states that in shared and guided reading sessions teachers have the opportunity to

- explicitly teach strategies for enhancing critical understanding and informed reflection
- model how to use such strategies
- support children as they practise the use of these strategies
- encourage children to become enthusiastic, autonomous and thoughtful readers.

## Guided reading

In guided reading, the teacher supports a small group of children who are at the same reading level. The children each have an individual copy of the text, which the teacher introduces to the group and presents a key aspect or question for the children to find out during reading. The children then read their own copy at their own pace with the teacher carefully monitoring pupils as they read. After the reading the group discusses the question, etc. to support their understanding. It has several advantages over hearing children read on an entirely individual basis:

- It substantially increases the time which children actually spend reading.
- It creates a supportive context for children to read.
- It supports the explicit teaching of key strategies or aspects.
- It can encourage independent reading.

# Helping children with reading problems

As teachers, we need to look for ways to assess children's reading abilities and provide remedial help which will enable the children to overcome their problems. The key factor is to diagnose the precise areas of difficulty. One of the most effective ways of doing this is through a *miscue analysis* of a child's reading (see Chapter 16 for more guidance on this).

There are several methods of support for children with reading problems.

## Reading recovery

The *reading recovery* procedure devised by Marie Clay (1993) from New Zealand has been widely used and shown to be successful for early intervention with pupils who are having difficulties with reading. This programme requires highly intensive one-to-one daily instruction for a period of twenty minutes until such time as a child shows proficiency in the key areas of

- directional movement of print
- one-to-one matching of spoken to written word
- self-monitoring of own errors
- cross-checking of reading strategies
- use of multiple cue sources, e.g. visual, meaning, phonic, grammatical
- self-correction of errors and self-correction of mistakes.

The actual reading recovery session typically takes the form of

- rereading two or more familiar books
- rereading yesterday's new book and conducting a running record (miscue analysis)
- practising letter identification using plastic letters and a magnetic board, and/or word making and breaking
- writing a story (including hearing and recording sounds in words)
- rearranging a cut-up story

- introducing a new book
- attempting the new book.

This programme, although highly effective, is highly costly and teachers are intensively trained to carry it out. The National Literacy Strategy has also developed intervention programmes for pupils who are falling behind their peers and these include: Early Literacy Support for pupils in Year 1, Additional Literacy Support for pupils in Year 4 and Further Literacy Support for pupils in Year 5.

### Paired reading

The adult reads with the child, at first at the same time, but later taking turns at a given signal from the child. It may also be appropriate to pair children of different ability for reading so they may support each other.

### Taped reading material

The child listens to taped stories and follows in the book. The tapes may be commercially produced or can be made by teachers and children.

### Prepared reading

This consists of first preparing the reading through discussion of the subject and possible reading of part of the story to the child, followed by the child reading. When the child is unable to read a word, the procedure is as follows:

- *Pause:* wait for about five seconds to see if the child can attempt the word.
- *Prompt:* prompt the child if they cannot attempt the word, for example:
  - 'Can you sound it out?'
  - 'Have a look at this part of the word.'
  - 'Something didn't make sense there, did it?'
- *Praise:* praise the child for:
  - Saying the word after prompting
  - Correcting him/herself
  - Reading parts independently.

## Dyslexia: 'difficulty with words'

Dyslexia is a specific learning disorder which is now widely recognised in schools. The symptoms are set out below, but it should not be assumed that because a child exhibits some of the symptoms he or she is dyslexic. For example, letter reversal is common among dyslexics, but many young children who are not dyslexic also reverse letters and numbers early in their school careers. A combination of symptoms needs to exist before we should seek further guidance on whether a child is dyslexic.

*Possible signs of dyslexia*

- Language processing and memory can be affected.
- Phonological processing can be a problem.
- Reading can be slow and inaccurate with frequent rereading necessary and possible physical discomfort.
- Writing can be slow with poor grammar, punctuation, sentence structure and general organisation.
- Spelling can be weak and inconsistent.
- Learning and recall may be poor.
- Sequencing may be a problem.

*How can we help dyslexic children?*

Many strategies which may help dyslexics might also be useful for other children with learning difficulties. Not all dyslexics will encounter the same problems, so it is important to identify where difficulties lie and adapt teaching methods accordingly. Above all, a sympathetic attitude and a great deal of patience and plenty of praise will help to provide a secure environment in which children can learn.

- Teach using a multisensory approach with material presented visually and orally so that you can find out which approach suits the dyslexic child. If the child learns better from visual materials, make use of charts, diagrams, maps and pictures. If he/she prefers to hear information, make use of taped books, mnemonics, rhymes and recordings of his/her own notes.
- Give instructions in written as well as spoken form. Write clearly on the board and on handouts and speak clearly.
- Break instructions into smaller units, present them in an appropriate order, and ask pupils to repeat instructions.
- Provide props such as line guides, symbols keys, number squares and word lists, and allow children to follow with their finger or using a ruler when reading if this helps them.
- Check for problems with sequencing and help children to learn days of the week, months of the year and how to tell time.
- Provide time and help with organisation. If necessary, show the child what to do.
- Use mnemonics to aid learning.

## Key points

- A range of research findings have been presented showing the importance of phonics within a meaningful encounter with texts. The importance of early intervention for children who are not making adequate progress with reading has been shown and the value of shared reading and the use of enlarged texts.
- Multiple perspectives have emerged on the teaching of reading: the psycho-linguistic emphasising the whole language approach; the cognitive-psychological perspective stressing the staged developmental process and the need for alphabetic knowledge; the socio-cultural perspective focussing on the literacy practices

in the home and community; and the socio-political perspective that emphasises the need for critical literacy for the purposes of equality.

- Models of the reading process have been reviewed, specifically the Searchlights model and the Simple view of reading model. The latter approach favoured by the Rose Report and incorporated in the renewed Primary Framework for Literacy emphasises the need for phonics fast and first alongside developing comprehension skills.
- Phonics research has shown the need for teaching and assessing phonological awareness prior to any systematic phonics teaching, and synthetic phonics has been shown by recent studies to be more effective.
- Comprehension can be significantly supported by a range of techniques including shared and guided reading.
- A suggested teaching programme has been provided which is clearly staged and provides for the teaching of word level skills alongside effective engagement with texts.
- Possible ways of supporting pupils experiencing reading problems or dyslexia has been set out.

## Further reading

Adams, M. J. (1990) *Beginning to Read: Thinking and learning about print*. Cambridge, MA: MIT Press.

Center, Y. (2005) *Beginning Reading: A balanced approach to teaching literacy during the first three years at school*. London: Continuum.

DfES (2006a) *Independent Review of the Teaching of Early Reading* (Final Report by Jim Rose). Ref: 0201/2006DOC-EN. Nottingham: DfES Publications.

Hall, K. (2003) *Listening to Stephen Read: Multiple perspectives on literacy*. Buckingham: Open University Press.

Harrison, C. and Coles, M. (2001) *The Reading for Real Handbook*. London: RoutledgeFalmer.

National Reading Panel (2000) *Report of the National Reading Panel. Teaching Children to Read: An evidence-based assessment of the scientific research literature on reading and its implications for reading instruction*. NIH Publication no. 00-4769. Washington, DC: National Institute for Child Health and Human Development.

# 8 Fiction and poetry

## Purpose of this chapter

This chapter aims to:

- Look at the role of fiction and poetry in the primary classroom.
- Discuss the link between children's literature and learning about literacy.
- Emphasise the importance of reading to children.
- Analyse the art of reading to children.
- Offer suggestions for stories and poems to read to children.
- Present ways in which stories and poems can be studied and enjoyed.

## Children's literature and learning about literacy

We will begin by looking at an extract from one of the best known children's stories, C. S. Lewis's *The Lion, the Witch and the Wardrobe* (1950), which describes the scene as winter turns to spring and the Witch loses her power over Narnia:

> And however the dwarf whipped the poor reindeer the sledge went slower and slower. There also seemed to be a curious noise all round them, but the noise of their driving and jolting and the dwarf's shouting at the reindeer prevented Edmund from hearing what it was, until suddenly the sledge stuck so fast that it wouldn't go on at all. When that happened there was a moment's silence. And in that silence Edmund could at last listen to the other noise properly. A strange, sweet, rustling, chattering noise – and yet not so strange, for he'd heard it before – if only he could remember where! Then all at once he did remember. It was the noise of running water. All round them though out of sight, there were streams chattering, murmuring, bubbling, splashing and even (in the distance) roaring. And his heart gave a great leap (though he hardly knew why) when he realized that the frost was over. And much nearer there was a drip-drip-drip from the branches of all the trees. And then, as he looked at one tree he saw a great load of snow slide off it and for the first time since he had entered Narnia he saw, the dark green of a fir tree. But he hadn't time to, listen or watch any longer, for the Witch said: 'Don't sit staring, fool! Get out and help.'
>
> (Lewis 1950: 108)

**Question**

What is the most likely situation in which children will have encountered this extract at school? Will it have been through listening to the story of *The Lion, the Witch and the Wardrobe* being read to them as a serial, or will they have seen the extract in isolation as part of a literacy hour or similar English lesson?

All too often, teachers take excerpts from children's literature and, rather than putting them in context by reading the whole book, use them to teach children about adjectives, punctuation or speech marks. There is a danger that we are creating a nation of children who can read, but for whom reading is seen as something to be done in the literacy hour, which involves analysing texts rather than enjoying them. In the extract above they might, for example, be expected to look at the use of adjectives to describe the thaw. We have even seen the extract used by a rather over-zealous teacher to demonstrate to children that they should not begin sentences with conjunctions! The children were given the task of rewriting the text without any sentences beginning with *and* or *but*. Quite apart from the dubious nature of the teacher's assertion that sentences should not begin with conjunctions, it seems almost sacrilegious to interfere with the text from one of the best loved children's novels ever written.

But is it ever justifiable to use extracts from children's novels as texts to discuss and analyse in a literacy lesson? The answer is, of course, 'Yes', but this should be a qualified 'Yes'. Children should see such excerpts in context and should ideally explore them as part of an ongoing serialisation of the story, with the teacher reading to them regularly for pleasure. Alternatively, they might be told about the events which lead up to the excerpt, and then have the opportunity to read on independently. The excerpt might also be used to whet children's appetites for reading the whole book, in the way that cinemas and TV stations show excerpts from films in order to encourage us to want to watch them.

## The importance of reading to children

For some children, it is only in the literacy hour that they ever hear any part of a story being read to them. For some teachers, reading to the class was seen as a luxury which could be sacrificed as the pressure to teach a full curriculum and personal, social and health education (PSHE) grew. So why should teachers read to children? Is this merely an entertainment which has no place in the modern primary school, or does it have both an intrinsic worth and a value to work across the curriculum? Loughrey (1989) sums up its importance succinctly:

> reading stories to children whets their appetites and encourages self-initiated exploration of books . . . it introduces the language of books and helps bridge gaps between varied language styles . . . it enhances listening skills . . . and is a basic learning medium through which we make sense of the world.
>
> (Loughrey 1989: 46)

It is vital that children hear stories being read by skilled readers if they are to know how a book should 'sound'. The teacher provides a model for expressive reading and indirectly demonstrates to the children how to bring text to life. It could be argued that this is the function of shared reading within the literacy hour, but such reading is necessarily short and focused on only part of a story, whereas the sustained reading of chapters can engage children's interest much more effectively. For those teachers who feel the need to justify to others, or even to themselves, reading to their classes on a regular basis, the following might be considered:

- Children's listening skills can be developed through prolonged exposure to engaging stories.
- Vocabulary can be improved where teachers discuss the words and phrases which authors use.
- Scenarios from stories can provide starting points for discussions about moral issues and can help children to consider how they would act in different situations. This can lead into valuable work in PSHE.
- Children's written and oral work will improve if they have more ideas about phrasing and style derived from hearing good quality literature.
- Children often lack imaginative ideas for their own writing. By exploring a range of stories they can be helped to develop their own ideas.
- By reading to children, teachers demonstrate that they value reading and show that it is important.
- An interest in fantasy can be encouraged and may lead to children exploring this genre.
- Listening to stories can help make them aware of their own and others' cultural heritage.
- Class reading of a story presents children with a valuable shared experience. The whole class comes together with a common purpose and a pleasant atmosphere can be created.

## The art of reading to children

Of course, none of the above may be achieved if the teacher does not read to the children in a way which engages their interest. Besides being fluent readers, there are other attributes which teachers need if they are to read books to their classes successfully. Some of these are described in this section.

### Voice, expression, intonation – accents

While it is not necessary to be able to assume accents with the skill of Rory Bremner, it certainly helps children to follow a story if they can tell which person is speaking from the way in which characters' words are said. Radio plays almost invariably have characters with a range of accents to help listeners tell them apart. Teachers who are not confident about using different accents can still use softer and louder or deeper and higher voices for characters. A variety of voices also helps the reader, who may be able to miss out 'he said', 'Jane asked' etc. in dialogue, since the voice changes will make it clear who is speaking and if questions are being asked. More importantly, we all need to put expression into our voices when reading aloud so that the listener becomes engaged and senses the enthusiasm of the reader. To develop reading aloud skills, you might try recording yourself and then listening to the tape to discover if you are expressive and if you find listening to yourself engaging.

---

**Activity: Reading aloud**

Choose a favourite story and record yourself reading a passage of dialogue. Play the recording a few days later and ask yourself:

- Can I tell from simply listening which person is speaking when?
- Can I forget that it is me reading and enjoy hearing the passage?

---

### Class management

Class management problems might arise when teachers read to children, if the children are not interested in the story or if the teacher does not make use of the skills described above. There are some simple strategies to limit opportunities for disruption and to give children incentives to behave well and listen carefully (see Chapter 2 on 'Classroom management'). A key strategy is to involve the children as much as possible. This might be done by providing additional copies of the book for some children to follow the text and to contribute to the telling of the story by reading the words spoken by different characters. Not only does this engage them with the text and help them to understand the punctuation of dialogue, but also it provides the teacher with some of the different voices discussed in the previous section.

Other strategies could include:

- Providing cards with the names of characters for some children to hold while the story is being read. This helps listeners to distinguish between characters and provides a useful resource for word level work which might follow.
- Hot-seating: tell the children beforehand who will be asked to assume the role of different characters in the story to answer questions about their actions after the reading session.
- Reading logs: ask the children to make brief notes on what has happened and to compare these with others. The notes can be used to bring absent children up to date on the events in the story when they return.

### Reading beforehand

Before reading a story, the teacher should read it first to become familiar with the text, to check whether any material might prove sensitive for some children, and to decide where there are ideal places for stopping which will leave children in suspense and eager to hear the next part of the story. Just as TV producers ensure that their audiences are left wanting more at the end of an episode of a soap opera or drama, so teachers can leave children in suspense as they anticipate what might happen next. Indeed, children may use their reading logs to write their predictions based upon inference from what they have already heard. This can lead to interesting discussions in which children draw upon their knowledge of genres to talk about typical themes, scenarios and endings. Such engagement with texts is far more likely to help children meet literacy objectives for fiction than being shown an extract and having a teacher explain its features.

## Choosing stories and poems to read to children

One of the most useful resources a teacher can easily maintain is a children's literature portfolio in which copies of poems and interesting extracts from books may be kept, along with brief synopses of books read and children's reactions to them. The notes can be accompanied by ideas for classroom activities which might be developed as a result of reading. These can stretch across the curriculum.

---

### Activity: Listing your favourite stories

Before reading the next section, which identifies ten children's stories we especially like, make a list of ten of your favourite children's stories.

- Think about why you like them.
- How might you introduce them to the children you teach?

---

Some teachers' knowledge of children's literature may be limited and restricted to stories and poems they read or heard as a child. However, there is a rich abundance of children's literature which engages and entertains not only children but also adults. By increasing our own knowledge of children's literature, we are better able to guide children's choices and make them aware of what is available. It will also be possible to discuss different types of story, from fantasy to comedy, classic to modern, and adventure to thought-provoking. While it would be wrong to be prescriptive about what children should read, it may be helpful to look at a few well-known children's stories which are well written, stimulating, and which represent a range of styles, and to look at how these stories might be enjoyed by children and used to stimulate a range of study across the curriculum. The stories are presented in an order which might equate with their appeal to different age groups, although it is often difficult to ascribe books to age groups since some continue to be enjoyed by adults, while younger children sometimes struggle through very challenging texts (for example the Harry Potter books) because they are so fond of the stories.

## Ten favourite children's stories

For each story, a brief synopsis of the plot is presented, followed by notes on possible classroom activities which could be linked to it. Of course, it is perfectly acceptable, indeed desirable, simply to read the story to children without following it up in any way other than through discussion.

## Not Now, Bernard: *David McKee*

This book, which the publishers recommend for reading together for children 3 years and over, has brief but repetitive text and attractive illustrations. Its recurrent theme is Bernard's parents shunning his approaches and saying 'Not now, Bernard'. The accompanying pictures, especially of Bernard's father, are often comical and stimulate discussion among children. Even when Bernard is 'eaten' by a monster, which replaces him in his house, his parents continue to ignore him.

*Possible activities*

- Discussions could be held about adults and their relationship with children. Do the children ever feel that they are ignored? Do they understand why this might be?
- The story can be read to children and then with them joining in, especially with the refrain, 'Not now, Bernard'.
- Children could discuss whether or not Bernard is actually eaten by the monster. Could it be that the author uses this device to show that adults sometimes don't even notice children?

## The Bear Under the Stairs: *Helen Cooper*

This beautifully illustrated story is well written and uses language which, while occasionally it may challenge Key Stage 1 children, is always engaging and readily understood within the context of the story. William imagines there is a bear living under the stairs in his house and worries about this. He decides to feed the bear and puts food under the stairs, quickly slamming the door before the bear can get him.

*Possible activities*

- The story focuses on a child's fear and this might provoke children to talk about their own fears of shadows, ghosts etc. These could be discussed and children might be reassured to know that such fears are common and almost always unfounded.
- The story has several rhymes for *stair* and *stairs*, including *bear*, *there*, *lair* and *everywhere*, each of which has a different spelling of the same phoneme. This could promote discussion about spelling and about rhyme, and might lead to shared writing of a poem about the bear, followed by independent and guided writing.
- Each time William slams the door under the stairs he does so with a 'wham, bang, thump'. The concept of onomatopoeia could be discussed and other examples listed (splash, crash, squelch, crunch, slap, hiss, clang), perhaps as a prelude to writing.

- The book includes a cross-section picture of William's house at night. Children could look at this and at dolls' houses and might go on to draw their own houses' cross-sections.

## The Worst Witch: *Jill Murphy*

The author was only 19 when she wrote and illustrated this humorous and entertaining story: the first in a series. It tells of Mildred Hubble's exploits at Miss Cackle's Academy for Witches.

*Possible activities*

- Witches appear in many children's stories, usually as forces of evil such as in *The Lion, the Witch and the Wardrobe*. Children could compare and contrast witches in different stories, making character studies and deciding on the attributes which authors give to witches, both physical and social, in order to convey their characters to the reader.
- Children who enjoy this series will almost certainly enjoy the *Harry Potter* series. Some will have read these or seen the films, so discussions could be held about similarities and differences between the books.

## Clever Polly and the Stupid Wolf: *Catherine Storr*

Polly consistently outwits a rather dim but articulate wolf who wants to eat her. The series of books is engaging and promotes discussion. Once children have understood the basic premise of the stories, they can read chapters as stories in their own right as it is not necessary to read the books from beginning to end. 'Monday's Child' is based upon the familiar rhyme about the day of one's birth and is especially recommended.

*Possible activities*

- Children could learn the well-known rhyme and the names and spellings of the days of the week, perhaps going on to look at the origins of the names and their equivalents in other languages.
- Children could retell the story in poetry form, after an initial shared writing activity and a word level session on rhyme.
- The story could be retold in strip cartoon format, with speech bubbles.
- The story could be re-enacted as a play, with children planning this and then performing it for their classmates.
- New words could be put to a well-known song to tell the story. Again, this might begin as a shared writing activity.
- Improvised musical instruments could be used to provide sound effects for a 'radio' version of the story.

(For a literacy hour plan for the two versions of the poem, see Waugh et al. 1999.)

## Bill's New Frock: *Anne Fine*

A boy wakes up one morning to discover that he is a girl. The author does not attempt to explain the gender change, but uses it to explore the ways in which boys and girls are treated. Bill finds that his teachers and friends behave differently towards him and he begins to have sympathy with the girls whose play areas are restricted by the boys' domination of the playground. The story is both amusing and poignant.

*Possible activities*

- Discussions might be held about the ways in which boys and girls feel they are treated differently in school, perhaps preparing for a debate on the subject.
- Children could imagine themselves in a similar situation to Bill and write a story.
- Groups could devise pieces of drama, either derived directly from the story or depicting experiences which they have had.

## Danny the Champion of the World: *Roald Dahl*

This children's novel is based upon a short story Dahl wrote in 1960. The children's version replaces two friends as central characters with a father and son, who respond to persecution by an unpleasant local landowner by poaching his pheasants. Although the tension and excitement of the poaching expeditions have readers on the edges of their seats, it is the loving relationship between father and son which captivates and inspires discussion.

After waking in the middle of the night and discovering his father has not returned from a poaching expedition, and fearing that he may be in danger, Danny drives an old car along country lanes to rescue him. Dahl's description of the night drive is beautifully constructed, with skilful use of punctuation, short clauses and sentences, to give the reader an impression of rapidly changing events and rapidly building tension, culminating in Danny coming face to face with a police car.

*Possible activities*

- The punctuation of the passage could be discussed to illustrate the value of using commas and full stops carefully to indicate speed.
- Children could go on to write their own paragraphs describing exciting events, at first as a shared writing activity with discussion and then as guided or independent work.
- In PSHE, discussions could be held about whether Danny was right to take the car and drive it when this was clearly against the law. Children might be reminded of the dangers of driving when unqualified and too young to pass a test, but there could also be discussions about famous instances of law-breaking which are now celebrated, such as Rosa Parks' refusal to give up her bus seat to a white man in Alabama, USA in 1955.

**The Midnight Fox:** *Betsy Byars*

A boy stays on a farm for the summer holidays and sees an unusual fox. He writes to his friend regularly and the two speculate on various topics. The daydream about discovering a new colour (Byars 1981: 48–50) is beautifully written and could lead to some interesting work from children.

*Possible activities*

- Children could imagine they had discovered a new colour and tell of the discovery in a news item similar to that in the book.
- Children could try to make and name new colours in a painting lesson.
- Songs and poems about colours could be learned and sung or recited.
- Children could try to describe colours to partners.
- The activity could be linked to reading the poem *Mimi's Fingers*, which appears later in this chapter and in which a blind girl asks about colour.
- Atlases could be consulted to locate the part of the United States where the story is set.

**Harry Potter and the Philosopher's Stone:** *J. K. Rowling*

Orphaned Harry goes to Hogwarts, a school for sorcery, which is reached via Platform $9\frac{3}{4}$ at King's Cross Station. As in all the Harry Potter stories, Harry and his friends have to overcome dark forces to triumph. The stories follow traditional patterns and have much in common with Greek myths in their structure and cast of characters.

*Possible activities*

- Comparisons could be made between Hogwarts and boarding schools in other stories, for example *The Worst Witch*.
- Children might listen to and read children's versions of Greek myths and discuss similarities and differences between their style and that of Harry Potter stories.
- Children could write their own versions of key events.
- Rules for Quidditch could be written and compared with rules for sports children have played.
- Children could write their own Harry Potter stories, using existing characters but also, perhaps, inventing new ones.

**Kensuke's Kingdom:** *Michael Morpurgo*

This beautifully constructed story tells of a boy marooned on a desert island who discovers there is another occupant: a former Japanese soldier who does not know that the war is over. At first their relationship is strained, but gradually they come to know and like each other and to work together for survival. Kensuke teaches the boy to paint, and they become so close that Kensuke begins to fear his friend's rescue.

*Possible activities*

- The story is told in the first person. This could lead to discussions about possible bias in the way events are related. Does the author portray himself in a constantly good light or is he honest enough to describe his errors?
- The opening line instantly captures the imagination of the reader ('I disappeared on the night before my twelfth birthday, July 28 1988'). Other stories' opening lines could be studied and this could lead to shared writing of opening lines and eventually to independent work. A collection of opening lines could be displayed alongside copies of books.
- The book provides maps of the island and a map of the world showing Michael's voyage. Children could find out more about the places visited and could use GoogleEarth™ to look more closely.

## Goodnight Mr Tom: *Michelle Magorian*

Will is evacuated from London to stay with Tom Oakley, an old man who is initially reluctant to take him but who proves to be an excellent carer. As the story unfolds, it emerges that Will was abused by his mother and that this has had an effect upon him. The story describes life in wartime England with superb attention to detail, and the relationships between Tom and Will, and Will and his friend Zach, are portrayed beautifully and, at times, movingly.

- There are obvious areas for discussion about relationships and about Will's experiences at home, which may need to be handled delicately.
- Children could find out more about evacuation and children's lives during wartime. They might also look at other novels which feature evacuees, including *Carrie's War* by Nina Bawden (1974) and C. S. Lewis's *The Lion, the Witch and the Wardrobe*.

---

### Activity: Devising activities for a favourite book

Now that you have read about the ten books above, consider how you could devise worthwhile activities for one of the favourite children's books you chose for the previous activity, which would engage children's interest and enhance their enjoyment of the story.

---

### *Enid Blyton*

Anyone with a knowledge and love of children's literature would easily be able to suggest ten quite different books to represent genres which would be equally captivating for young and old readers alike. Our selection is not intended to represent a top ten. Indeed, as soon as prescriptive lists appear, as they did in prequels to the National Curriculum in 1990, lovers of literature become indignant about omissions. However, one author whose absence from such lists has provoked little outcry, but who was the best-selling writer of the twentieth century and whose books continue to sell in huge numbers, is Enid Blyton.

There is a strange and now predictable response from trainee teachers when they are asked what they read as children, if Blyton was their favourite. With chin moving towards chest they often, almost shamefully, mumble something like: 'Enid Blyton, but I think that's frowned upon now, isn't it?' In some quarters, Blyton's books are regarded as unchallenging and not especially well written, but they continue to sell in huge numbers and have been, for many children, the first books which they read eagerly from cover to cover. They are page-turners in which the stories rattle along at a pace, leaving the reader eager to know what happens next. The problems that some critics have with Blyton's work revolve around issues such as sexism, racism, class distinction and use of language. It is not difficult to find examples of the first three in some of her stories, although it should be remembered that she was born in 1897 and wrote in a different era, when most people were less conscious of political correctness. Recent editions of her books have been 'sanitised' and the names of the golliwogs are now Wiggie, Waggie and Wollie rather than Golly, Woggie and Nigger; 'I say' has been replaced by 'Hey', 'queer' by 'odd'; Dame Slap became Dame Snap, and now scolds naughty children rather than smacking them, and Fannie and Dick have been changed to Frannie and Rick.

An excerpt from *The Three Golliwogs* may make uncomfortable reading, perhaps moving some of those who speak of changes to the books as 'political correctness gone mad' to think again:

> Once the three bold golliwogs, Golly, Woggie, and Nigger, decided to go for a walk to Bumble-Bee Common. Golly wasn't quite ready so Woggie and Nigger said they would start off without him, and Golly would catch them up as soon as he could. So off went Woggie and Nigger, arm-in-arm, singing merrily their favourite song – which, as you may guess, was *Ten Little Nigger Boys*.
>
> (Blyton 1968: 51)

Of course, anyone who wishes to be critical of Blyton can easily focus upon extracts which appear to condemn her whole output, but it should be remembered that these are not typical of all of her work. It should also be borne in mind that Blyton is far from the only author from the past to have written in a way which now seems offensive and anachronistic: try looking at Hugh Lofting's *Dr Doolittle* (1968), in which the Sleeping Beauty will not marry the black prince until he becomes white.

---

**Activity: Choosing suitable books for children**

In considering our choices of books to present to children, it may be helpful to focus upon the following questions:

- Is it acceptable to leave some books off classroom shelves because teachers are offended by their content? If so, which would be omitted?
- Should literature be modified to bring it in line with current thinking? If so, what would you change?
- Are children capable of seeing authors' work as products of the times in which they wrote?
- How do we know what children might enjoy?

## Helping children to choose books

If children have a limited knowledge of literature and have explored few different genres, they will, when faced with choices, be rather like people faced with a menu in a foreign restaurant. Will they choose something exotic and take a risk, or will they stick to what they know? It is the teacher's job to ensure that their knowledge of the literature menu is broad enough for them to be able to make informed choices and not to be afraid of the unknown or unfamiliar. We should, therefore, ensure that we introduce them to a wide range of texts, including both modern and classic stories.

It is very tempting to choose only those stories which will make children laugh – after all, as teachers we all want to see our pupils happy. However, children also enjoy stories with moral dilemmas, adventure stories, and stories which make them afraid for the characters.

Stories set in the distant past, especially when the period described is one children are studying, will not only engage their interest but also add to their knowledge and give them an insight into how people actually lived. For Romans, try *The Eagle of the Ninth* by Rosemary Sutcliff, or Caroline Lawrence's series of Ostia Mysteries; for Vikings, Terry Jones' excellent *Erik the Viking* will both inform and entertain. Topics on the Victorians can be brought to life through reading stories by Joan Aiken, whose books are often set in a period similar to the Victorian era but in which there is a different monarch, and by reading *The Elephant War* by Gillian Avery, which is based upon a real event from 1882 when Jumbo the Elephant was to be taken from Regent's Park Zoo to work for Barnum's Circus in America. For the Second World War there are several excellent books written by people who were alive at the time, for example, *Carrie's War* by Nina Bawden and *Goodnight Mr Tom* by Michelle Magorian.

Stories from different cultures and countries will expand children's understanding of how other people live and how they solve problems. For example, *Handa's Surprise* by Eileen Browne, *We're Going on a Lion Hunt* by David Axtell, and *Dragon Mountain* by Tim Vyner.

Books which extend thinking and challenge ideas are plentiful and include many by Anne Fine, including *The Tulip Touch*, in which a popular girl befriends an unpopular one. Stories by Jacqueline Wilson and Judy Blume are equally thought-provoking and can be linked to PSHE discussions.

We hope that these suggestions will encourage you to explore children's fiction more widely, both for your own enjoyment and for that of your pupils, many of whom might be unlikely to experience a wide range of literature without guidance from an experienced reader.

## Poetry

'Hands up if you like poetry!' A question aimed not at a class of children but at a class of trainee teachers, and one which traditionally produces a disappointingly small number of raised hands. For many, poetry at school was limited in range and at secondary school had been studied, analysed and learned to enable students to pass exams. This legacy of negative attitudes to poetry is perpetuated by some teachers who see poetry either as something to be avoided or as a genre which they must explore with their pupils in order to meet literacy objectives, but not one which they will dwell upon for any longer than is absolutely necessary.

---

**Activity: Thinking about poetry**

- Can you recite any poems by heart?
- Did you enjoy poetry at school?
- Do you ever read poetry now?
- Do you ever write poetry?

---

If our responses to the above questions are largely negative, how can we encourage children and teachers to enjoy poetry and discover its significance as a literary genre and as a vehicle for developing a love and understanding of language? A good starting point is to ensure that teachers are aware of a range of poems of different types and have heard these read aloud and understand their features. Just as a portfolio of children's literature is a valuable career-long resource, so a burgeoning anthology of poetry will prove invaluable, both as a resource for literacy lessons and for sharing with children purely for pleasure. These might be drawn from some of the popular anthologies which are available cheaply, including the excellent *The Works* series (Cookson 2000; Moses and Corbett 2002). The poems in the Cookson anthology are divided into genres to cover the types described in the old Literacy Strategy, while Moses and Corbett (2002) have sections for each subject in the primary curriculum. While this may seem rather functional, the anthologies can of course be enjoyed in their own right without teachers feeling that they are merely vehicles for learning about language.

Having built a collection of varied and interesting poems, teachers need to reflect upon the value of sharing these with children. This will be considerably enhanced if they learn to read the poems well, with expression and intonation and without falling into some of the traps which inexperienced readers succumb to, such as pausing at the end of each line of a narrative poem after the rhyme, rather than reading on to sustain momentum and help listeners understand what is being read to them. BBC Radio 4's excellent *Poetry Please* programme, usually broadcast on Sunday afternoons, features high quality readings of well-loved poems and provides a good model for anyone wishing to read poetry to others. Read well, poetry will engage children and encourage them to want to talk about what they have heard. Read poorly, poetry will arouse the same negative feelings described earlier.

### Exploring poetry with children

In this section we will look at examples of poems and ways in which they might lead to discussion, literacy work and cross-curricular study, as well as giving pleasure to readers. The poems have been chosen partly because they are short enough to be looked at as a whole on a screen, and so might be studied within a single lesson such as a literacy hour, but mainly because of the quality of the language used, their imagery, and the way in which the poets capture the imagination of the reader.

Mimi's Fingers: *Mary O'Neill*

*Mimi's Fingers* begins by informing the reader that the narrator is blind, and then proceeds to describe how she manages to understand her environment through other senses, particularly touch (see Sweeney 1999). The description is simple yet clear and the poem ends with a twist which is thought-provoking. Only colour cannot be understood through touch, and Mimi does not have a clear idea of the concept of colour.

> I know a snowflake as a melting star,
> The sticky-thick honey and of tar.
> Colour alone my fingers cannot do.
> Could you, could you, tell me about blue?

Having listened to the poem and read it with the teacher, children could be asked to consider how they would describe colour to a blind person. The importance of clear descriptions can be emphasised, and the need to be aware that someone who had never been able to see would not understand descriptions which relied upon any prior knowledge of what things looked like. Study of the poem can be linked to reading Betsy Byars' *The Midnight Fox* (1981), with Tom's discovery of a new colour being discussed as well. An obvious cross-curricular follow-up would be in art where colour-mixing could lead to descriptions of the colours created, and a study of a paint chart might prompt children to invent names for their colours which could be used in their own poems and prose about colour.

November: *Thomas Hood*

*November* by Thomas Hood has a regular pattern, with each line beginning with 'No' and telling the reader about things which cannot be seen, before the final line is simply November, so that the reader discovers only at the end what the poem is about (http://www.learnenglish.org.uk/stories/poem.asp?poem=55). This poem is best introduced with the title and final line concealed, as children always enjoy the twist at the end and this promotes discussion. *November* was written in 1844 so some of the vocabulary may be unfamiliar to children and may require some explanation, although children should be encouraged to use the context of unfamiliar words to attempt to understand their meanings. Reading the poem could ultimately lead to discussions on the use of apostrophes for omission, a device used by poets to ensure their words scan and fit in with the rhythm of the poem. Children might look at *t'other* and *'em* and could discuss what the full versions might be and go on to examine wasn't, couldn't, shan't, won't etc. The poem also offers scope for writing in a similar style, perhaps on the subject of November or, alternatively, using a different prefix or word opening such as 'De' for December (delightful, delicious, deep snow, depart), or even 'Uni' for United.

November

No sun – no moon!
No morn – no noon –

No dawn – no dusk – no proper time of day.
No sky – no earthly view –
No distance looking blue –
No road – no street – no 't'other side the way' –
No end to any Row –
No indications where the Crescents go –
No top to any steeple –
No recognitions of familiar people –
No courtesies for showing 'em –
No knowing 'em –
No travelling at all – no locomotion,
No inkling of the way – no notion –
'No go' – by land or ocean –
No mail – no post –
No news from any foreign coast –
No Park – no Ring – no afternoon gentility –
No company – no nobility –
No warmth, no cheerfulness, no healthful ease
No comfortable feel in any member –
No shade, no shine, no butterflies, no bees,
No fruits, no flowers, no leaves, no birds –
November!

*Thomas Hood*

## Jabberwocky: *Lewis Carroll*

Lewis Carroll's *Jabberwocky* offers great scope for creativity and for language study, since it is replete with invented words which can be interpreted by readers. We have seen classes write their own versions, both with accepted English words replacing Carroll's inventions, and with invented words. In deciding which words to use, children have discussed the functions of the words, identifying parts of speech in order to determine appropriate substitutions. The poem also lends itself extremely well to performance, with children's interpretation of the text being linked to actions. We once saw 130 Year 6 children perform *Jabberwocky* under the guidance of an English teacher during a day's pre-visit to their secondary school!

### Jabberwocky

'Twas brillig, and the slithy toves
Did gyre and gimble in the wabe;
All mimsy were the borogoves,
And the mome raths outgrabe.

'Beware the Jabberwock, my son!
The jaws that bite, the claws that catch!
Beware the Jubjub bird, and shun
The Frumious Bandersnatch!'

He took his vorpal sword in hand:
Long time the manxome foe he sought –
So he rested by the Tumtum tree,
And stood a while in thought.

And as in uffish thought he stood,
The Jabberwock, with eyes of flame,
Came whiffling through the tulgey wood,
And burbled as it came!

One, two! One, two! And through and through
The vorpal blade went snicker-snack!
He left it dead, and with its head
He went galumphing back.

'And hast thou slain the Jabberwock?
Come to my arms, my beamish boy!
O frabjous day! Callooh! Callay!'
He chortled in his joy.

'Twas brillig, and the slithy toves
Did gyre and gimble in the wabe;
All mimsy were the borogoves,
And the mome raths outgrabe.

*Lewis Carroll*

The invented words should promote discussion about pronunciation and thus consideration of phonemes and graphemes. Words might be related to more familiar words as children debate how to say them and what they might mean, with dictionaries referred to as they justify their ideas. For example:

- Should *gyre* be pronounced with a soft g as in *gyrate* or a hard g as in *gate*?
- Is *raths* pronounced as *baths* with a short a as in most northern English accents, or a long a as in southern England?
- Does *tulgey* have a hard or soft g?

Most of the invented words seem to be phonically regular and accessible to young readers, ensuring that they should be able to make a good attempt at reading the poem even before they have begun to decide what it might be about.

Autumn Song: *Ted Hughes*

Ted Hughes' *Autumn Song* is rich in imagery and tells the story of the end of summer and the beginning of winter (Hughes 1968). It opens with:

> There came a day that caught the summer
> Wrung its neck
> Plucked it
> And ate it.

and has a final verse which likens the period to an animal:

> There came this day and he was autumn.
> His mouth was wide
> And red as sunset.
> His tail was an icicle.

The poem has a repetitive structure which can be replicated by children, and each verse has a rhyming couplet with rhyming words which could induce discussion about different ways in which phonemes can be represented (bare/there, worth/earth), as well as rhymes with the same graphemes (small/all, pie/die). The first and last verses have no rhymes. Children could discuss the effect this has upon the reader and the benefits or otherwise of rhyming and non-rhyming poetry.

## More activities using poetry

Of course, a study of poetry does not have to be restricted to classic poems. Children might explore the following:

- Rhymes are used to remember things (mnemonics), such as '30 days hath September' to remember the number of days in each month, and 'Never Eat Shredded Wheat' to remember the points of the compass.
- Nursery rhymes can be looked at by young children and learned by heart as well as by older children who might explore the hidden meanings behind some of them, for example, 'Ring o' Roses' and the Plague.
- The lyrics of songs, including hymns, which can sometimes be difficult for children to understand.
- Jingles used in advertising: children could go on to write their own to advertise school and local events.
- Rhymes in greetings cards: many tend to be trite and children could be asked to try to improve upon existing ones.
- Short comic verse such as Spike Milligan wrote.
- Longer comic verse, for example Roald Dahl's *Revolting Rhymes* (2001), and poems by Pam Ayres, Allan Ahlberg, Michael Rosen, Roger McGough and Kit Wright.
- Ballads and narrative poems.
- Structured poems with a clear syllable pattern such as limericks, haiku, cinquains and triolets.
- Free verse without rhyme.
- 'Nonsense' poems.
- Poems written by children.
- Extracts from descriptive 'adult' poetry, such as *Ode to Autumn* by John Keats, the Witches' Brew in *Macbeth* by Shakespeare and *Daffodils* by William Wordsworth.
- Poems from different cultures.

Children should be encouraged to perform and even record poems to develop their oral and presentational skills. They might do this individually or in pairs, but may also work in groups to devise performances, perhaps including choral speaking.

Finally, one reason for reading poetry to children and discussing it with them is to help enable them to write their own poetry. This can be done initially through shared reading, followed by shared writing, with the teacher modelling poetry writing. Discussion can take place about making the poem scan and about rhymes. Teachers can show how they explore possibilities for rhymes, perhaps by taking a key word which they wish to use and then making a list of possible rhymes. The resulting word banks will not only help children with their own rhymes, but also support their phonic understanding and can provide opportunities for them to explore words, using dictionaries to check if the words they create actually exist, and if so what they mean.

---

### Activity: Writing structured poems

Look at the examples of structured poems below, try to work out their pattern, and then replicate it by writing a poem of your own in each style. Not only will this help you to remember the features of the poems, but also it will help you to see some of the challenges children face when asked to write poetry.

#### Haiku

Watching the moon rise,
Seeing the western sun fade,
My worries lie down.

Beautiful feline,
Stalk your unsuspecting prey.
So quiet, deadly.
(see Waugh with McGuinn 1996)

#### Triolets

David Dean read lots of books
His friends all gave him funny looks
He couldn't put them down
David Dean read lots of books
He brought them home in a fleet of trucks
From the library in town.
David Dean read lots of books
His friends all gave him funny looks.

Louise McCarthy sits in front of me
She's the kind of girl I'd like to be
She has long hair
Louise McCarthy sits in front of me
I'd really like to ask her home for tea.
I wouldn't dare.
Louise McCarthy sits in front of me
She's the kind of girl I'd like to be.

*continued on facing page*

*Cinquains*

| | |
|---|---|
| Never | I love |
| Keep your shoes on | To hear the sound |
| When you get into bed | Of happy young children |
| Because you will make the clean | Dashing around the school |
|     sheets |     playground |
| Dirty | Yelling. |

(see Waugh 2000b)

In this chapter we have looked at the importance of fiction and poetry in the class-room and at the importance of reading both stories and poems to children, as well as at some of the skills which teachers will require to be able to do this successfully. We have also examined a range of stories and poems and have considered some of the ways in which curriculum-related work might be linked to sharing them with children. In addition, we have looked at some issues related to choosing literature to share with children.

## Key points

- Stories and poems are an important part of the primary curriculum and should be shared with children regularly.
- Reading aloud to children is a skill which requires development and it is important that teachers hone their skills if they are to engage their pupils' interest.
- Stories and poems can be starting points for activities both in literacy lessons and in other areas of the curriculum, but these activities should be meaningful and should enhance rather than detract from children's enjoyment of the texts.
- Teachers should build up a knowledge of children's literature and should think carefully about the choices of texts they make for sharing with their classes.

## Further reading

Carter, D. (2000) *Teaching Fiction in the Primary School*. London: David Fulton.
Gamble, N. and Yates, S. (2002) *Exploring Children's Literature*. London: Paul Chapman.

## Children's books

Aiken, J. (1962) *The Wolves of Willoughby Chase*. London: Jonathan Cape.
Aiken, J. (1964) *Black Hearts in Battersea*. London: Jonathan Cape.
Aiken, J. (1968) *The Whispering Mountain*. London: Jonathan Cape.
Avery, G. (1960) *The Elephant War*. London: Collins.
Axtell, D. (2000) *We're Going on a Lion Hunt*. London: Macmillan Children's Books.
Bawden, N. (1974) *Carries War*. London: Puffin.
Blume, J. (1988) *Just as Long as We're Together*. London: Pan Macmillan.
Blume, J. (2003 [1972]) *Tales of a Fourth Grade Nothing*. London: Macmillan Children's Books.
Blume, J. (2006 [1974]) *Blubber*. London: Macmillan Children's Books.
Blyton, E. (1968) *The Three Golliwogs*. London: Dean & Son.
Browne, E. (1995) *Handa's Surprise*. London: Walker.

Byars, B. (1981) *The Midnight Fox*. London: Puffin.

Carroll, L. (1972 [1871]) *Jabberwocky*, in *Through the Looking-Glass and What Alice Found There*. London: Macmillan.

Cookson, P. (ed.) (2000) *The Works*. London: Pan Macmillan.

Cooper, H. (1993) *The Bear Under the Stairs*. London: Picture Corgi Books.

Dahl, R. (1977) *Danny the Champion of the World*. London: Puffin.

Dahl, R. (2001) *Revolting Rhymes*. London: Puffin.

Fine, A. (1992) *Bill's New Frock*. London: Longman.

Fine, A. (1997) *The Tulip Touch*. London: Puffin.

Jones, T. (1989) *Erik the Viking*. London: Robson.

Lawrence, C. (2001) *Thieves of Ostia*. London: Orion Children's Books.

Lewis, C. S. (1950) *The Lion, the Witch and the Wardrobe*. Harmondsworth: Penguin.

Lofting, H. (1968) *Doctor Doolittle Stories*. London: Cape.

McKee, D. (1980) *Not Now, Bernard*. London: Red Fox.

Magorian, M. (1998) *Goodnight Mr Tom*. Harmondsworth: Penguin.

Morpurgo, M. (1999) *Kensuke's Kingdom*. London: Egmont.

Moses, B. and Corbett, P. (2002) *Works 2: Poems for Every Subject and Occasion*. London: Pan Macmillan.

Murphy, J. (1974) *The Worst Witch*. London: Young Puffin.

Rowling, J. K. (1997) *Harry Potter and the Philosopher's Stone*. London: Bloomsbury.

Storr, C. (1967) *Clever Polly and the Stupid Wolf*. London: Puffin.

Sutcliff, R. (2004 [1954]) *The Eagle of the Ninth*. Oxford: Oxford University Press.

Vyner, T. (1996) *Dragon Mountain*. London: Collins.

Wilson, J. (1993) *The Suitcase Kid*. London: Corgi Yearling.

Wilson, J. (2004) *Midnight*. London: Corgi Yearling.

Wilson, J. (2006) *Clean Break*. London: Corgi Yearling.

# 9 Reading and writing for information

## Purpose of this chapter

This chapter aims to:

- Explore reading and writing of non-fiction.
- Give examples of using everyday texts.
- Describe various genres of texts.
- Provide strategies for effective interaction with texts.
- Suggest activities in the classroom for each year group.

The chapter provides possible activities in the classroom and explains how programmes of study can be devised to incorporate a range of genres and a diversity of activities which will develop children's skills and engage their interest.

## Non-fiction literature

Many of children's early experiences of reading often focus on fiction, with stories and poems, including nursery rhymes and songs, figuring strongly. However, as they learn about the world around them they become increasingly curious about plants, animals, transport and natural phenomena. They also find that the literature in their environments is predominantly non-fiction. For example, they will see notices, signs, advertisements, letters and timetables. We are surrounded by text when we walk down the street, turn on the TV or computer, and even when we look around our homes. Children need to make sense of all of this text, need to understand how it can be useful, and know what it tells us. As they develop as readers they then need a broad diet of texts which reflect the real world as well as fantasy. Boys, in particular, often prefer non-fiction texts. Look, for example, at the popularity of Top Trumps cards and at the way they extract information from them.

Even quite young children often have access to the internet, which provides them with the potential to find out almost anything they want to know. However, it also provides a wealth of unedited material which reflects the opinions of the authors and which has not been scrutinised by editors in the way that printed material often is. Given this mass of available 'information', it is vital that children understand that what they read may not necessarily be true and that they need to explore information about topics from a number of sources. Thus, the National Curriculum for English at Key Stage 1 states that children should 'understand that texts about the same topic may contain different information or present similar information in different ways' (DfEE 1999: 46).

Even at this early stage, children should also 'use the organisational features of non-fiction texts, including captions, illustrations, contents, index and chapters, to find information' (DfEE 1999: 46). There are, inevitably, implications for the Key Stage 1 classroom, which might have reference areas equipped with dictionaries, thesauruses, encyclopedias, directories and databases. Children can begin to appreciate the value of such materials if they become part of a 'literate' home corner. This might include writing materials, a telephone directory, catalogues and timetables.

The National Curriculum Programme of Study for Key Stage 2 maintains that pupils should be taught to

> scan to find information; skim for gist and overall impression; obtain specific information through detailed reading; draw on different features of texts, including print, sound and image, to obtain meaning; use organisational features and systems to find texts and information; distinguish between fact and opinion; and consider an argument critically.
>
> (DfEE 1999: 53)

Children are, then, expected to develop quite sophisticated study skills, not only to enable them to meet the requirements of the National Curriculum and the Primary National Strategy, but also to enable them to find and make use of information from a range of sources, which has grown considerably as information technology and paper publications have expanded and become increasingly accessible.

### Focusing on the Victorians

To illustrate ways in which texts may be used with children to develop their understanding of the features of different genres and their ability to extract information and produce their own texts, let us look at a series of possible lessons for a Year 2 class. (Similar lessons can be found in Waugh 2005: 174–91.)

The starting point for the lessons, which are linked to work in history on Victorians, could be some pictures of children in a Victorian classroom. By introducing the topic with pictures, the teacher can make it accessible to children whose reading skills might prevent them from being engaged from the outset. This technique also enables children to draw upon prior knowledge and to bring their own ideas to discussions. They can look at the pictures and comment upon similarities and differences between the Victorian classroom and their own classroom, while posing questions about things which they do not recognise or understand. Initially, the discussions might be held in pairs, with partners sharing ideas in preparation for whole-class discussions.

Having encouraged children to look closely at the pictures, the teacher can ask for their ideas and write these on the board in note form, for example, high windows, rows of desks, big stick. The teacher can go on to model writing by asking the children to suggest how the notes might be turned into sentences. This initial activity can be used both to stimulate interest in a topic and to set the agenda for future study, including independent research by children using books, the internet and

*Table 9.1* The Know, Want, Learned grid

| What do I **know** about this topic? | What do I **want** to know about this topic? | What have I **learned** about this topic? |
|---|---|---|
| | | |

other resources, both at school and at home. Indeed, the teacher might at this stage introduce a *Know, Want, Learned grid* as shown in Table 9.1 (Wray 2004: 41).

In the left-hand column of the grid, the teacher should write a list of things the children already claim to know about Victorians, while in the central column the teacher should write a list of questions children would like answered during their study of the topic. The list can be added to in future lessons, and can be prominently displayed so that children are encouraged to find possible answers to the questions in the central column.

In the next lesson, children can be introduced to simple text which provides information about aspects of school life in Victorian times. Before reading the text to the children, the teacher should ask them to scan it and discuss what information might be contained, justifying their ideas by talking about titles and subtitles and any key words they notice. After reading the text to the children and then with them, the content should be discussed before focusing on unfamiliar vocabulary and spellings. As discussed elsewhere in this book, it is important that children see texts as meaningful and worth studying in their own right, and not simply as vehicles for learning about spelling, grammar and punctuation. However, this should not prevent teachers from looking for opportunities to explore aspects of word and sentence level within the context of whole texts.

Independent, paired or group work, which might follow the shared whole-class work, could involve children in finding out more about Victorian school life, writing their own versions of parts of the text, or making up questions for each other which could be answered by reading the text carefully.

A further lesson might focus upon fact, fiction and opinion, with children looking as a class at some statements prepared by the teacher. For example:

- Some Victorian teachers hit children with canes when they were naughty.
- Children wrote on slates in Victorian schools.
- Victorian schools were better than modern schools.
- Victorian schools had computers.

After reading the sentences to and then with the children, the teacher could ask them which of the sentences they think are true and which are untrue. The sentence 'Victorian schools were better than modern schools' should be looked at carefully and children should be asked if they agree with it, based upon what they have found out so far. They can be asked to justify their opinions. The teacher can then go on to write further sentences with the children's help, with children supplying ideas for ones which are fact, fiction and opinion.

Further lessons might focus on other aspects of Victorian children's lives such as games, toys, clothes and work. Once again, children's interest might be aroused through the use of pictures, simple texts, websites and artefacts.

The method of working described above enables children to make links between subjects and allows teachers to use texts associated with foundation subjects within English lessons. This cross-curricular approach chimes well with the Primary National Strategy's emphasis on making links between curriculum subjects and areas of learning (DfES 2006c: 13).

## Using everyday texts

Although books of lesson plans and texts for use in literacy hours and English lessons are available, it is important that the texts used in the classroom are, wherever possible, real texts of the type children might meet in everyday life. Teachers should make collections of suitable texts, and these might include timetables, advertisements, television programme listings, information leaflets, programmes for plays or sports events, tickets, letters, forms, lists and notices. Such texts make good starting points for discussion about textual style, vocabulary and presentation.

Another excellent resource is newspapers. Although a variety should be available, teachers may wish to consider the contents carefully before making some of the national tabloids available in the classroom. Local papers tend to have the advantage that they are generally well written and their style tends to be accessible for able readers at Key Stage 2, with fewer examples of esoteric phrasing and hyperbole than many national papers. In addition, their contents are related to the children's local area. Within a newspaper there are examples of a range of non-fiction genres including

- report writing
- persuasive writing (editorials and advertisements)
- instructions (recipes)
- recount.

A display of the anatomy of a newspaper with extracts enlarged for easy reading can form a useful interactive resource which groups children may work at independently or as part of guided work. A natural progression from reading newspapers is for children to produce their own. There are several computer programs which can enable them to produce text with a professional appearance (examples) and these can not only be printed for distribution but also be sent to readers as email attachments. This is a particularly good idea where a class has a partner school, perhaps in another country.

## Genres of texts

The range of texts which children should work with as part of the Primary National Strategy is wide and reflects the kinds of texts which adults meet in everyday life. Six main non-fiction text types were described by the National Literacy Strategy (DfES 2001b), as set out below.

## *Recount texts*

Purpose: to retell events for information or entertainment.
Text structure

- orientation – scene setting, opening
- events – recount the events as they occurred
- reorientation – a closing statement.

Language features

- written in past tense
- in chronological order.

Example

- A biography of William Wilberforce.

## *Instruction or procedural texts*

Purpose: to instruct how something should be done through a series of graded steps.
Text structure

- goal – a statement of what is to be achieved
- materials/equipment needed
- sequenced steps to achieve the goal
- often a diagram or illustration.

Language features

- written in the imperative (e.g. 'mix the ingredients')
- in chronological order
- impersonal rather than named individuals.

Example

- A recipe for a cake.

## *Report texts*

Purpose: to describe the way things are.
Text structure

- an opening, general classification
- more technical information
- a description of the phenomenon.

Language features

- present tense
- non-chronological
- focus on generic participants (e.g. sparrows in general).

Example

- A report on Victorian schooling.

## Explanation texts

Purpose: to explain the processes involved in natural or social phenomena or to explain how something works.
Text structure

- general statement to introduce the topic
- a series of logical steps explaining how or why something occurs
- these steps continue until the final state is produced and the explanation is complete.

Language features

- simple present tense
- uses time connectives, e.g. then, next
- uses causal connectives, e.g. because, so.

Example

- An explanation of the rain cycle.

## Persuasion texts

Purpose: to argue the case for a point of view.
Text structure

- thesis – an opening statement, e.g. 'vegetables are good for you'
- arguments – often in the form of elaboration
- reiteration – summary and restatement of opening position.

Language features

- simple present tense
- focus mainly on generic participants
- mainly logical rather than time connectives, e.g. this shows, however, because.

Example

- An essay on why we should recycle waste.

## Discussion texts

Purpose: to present arguments and information from differing viewpoints.
Text structure

- statement of the issue – a preview of the main argument
- arguments for and supporting evidence
- arguments against and supporting evidence
- recommendation – summary and conclusion.

Language features

- simple present tense
- generic participants
- logical connectives, e.g. therefore, however.

Example

- A discussion of the arguments for and against building a new by-pass.

(based upon table in DfEE 1998b: 4)

---

**Activity: Using different text types**

If they are to develop an understanding of these text types, children will need
to explore them through shared reading and writing, and will also require
strategies for reading them and extracting information.

- Look at the different text types described above and try to think of examples
  of writing which you have used or seen used in the classroom for each one.

---

## Reading and interacting with texts

### Finding information and making notes

With computers available in virtually every primary classroom, children do not
necessarily need to make notes by hand when reading texts. They might, for
example, use highlighting or cut and paste to select key words or phrases. However,
they will still need strategies for selecting relevant information. Teacher modelling
can help them to see how skilled readers skim texts for key words or key information, for example by looking down a timetable to find a particular train, looking at
TV listings for a programme, or using an alphabetical list such as an index to find

a word. If the teacher models this and talks about it drawing the children into discussions about techniques, this will demonstrate to the children ways in which they may work independently.

Another approach is to preview a text, gaining an overview by looking at pictures, charts, maps, headings and subheadings. This alerts the children to prior knowledge and provides a 'big picture' which enables them to put details into context.

Note-making can be seen as part of the drafting process which is now well developed in many schools. Although children should be encouraged to be accurate, they should also realise that notes do not have to be written in 'best writing', as their purpose is to inform future writing and they are not an end in themselves.

Children should be encouraged to discuss their notes with others as well as co-operating in research. For example, a group of children might be given the task of finding out about early flying machines. They could first determine what they already know and identify questions which they would like to answer. They could then discuss where the relevant information might be found and divide up the task of reading about the subject. A wall display showing different parts of books and their functions (title page, contents page, index, etc.) would be a useful reference point. Information can be presented to the rest of the class in a variety of forms, including:

- telling or taping
- radio or TV presentations
- newspaper articles
- posters and brochures
- plays
- charts and diagrams
- booklets and books
- instructions, question sheets for others
- letters.

### Library skills

Many schools organise libraries along Dewey lines so that children see a progression from primary school library use to the use of public libraries and those in secondary schools. Whichever method is used to organise books, children need to be shown how it works and there should be discussion about the probable location of books on different subjects. Children will need to learn how to use the alphabet to help in their research and should be shown as soon as possible how to find subjects by using their second, third or even fourth letters.

### Gaining access to non-fiction texts

Inevitably, some children will experience problems when working with non-fiction texts, particularly if their previous reading experiences have revolved mainly around narrative texts. Key questions can be asked about the text and strategies devised which will help children to gain access to texts. Four questions about texts which children find difficult are suggested in a core position paper (DfES 2006c: 39):

- Is it too dense?
- Are there too many unknown or difficult words?
- Is the author's style accessible?
- Is the genre familiar?

We have used these questions to offer suggestions for strategies to support children.

*Is it too dense?*

A lot of information may be presented in a short piece of text and it can be difficult for readers to extract key points or even to know what to look for. Supportive strategies could include:

- discussing the subject with the children before they look at the text
- asking them to think of questions they would like to answer by reading it
- discussing what they already know about the topic
- talking about the way in which the text is set out, including the use of maps, charts and pictures
- encouraging children to survey the text before attempting to read it in detail, to see what it might be about and to look for some of the items discussed previously.

*Are there too many unknown or difficult words?*

Information texts often contain unfamiliar vocabulary which can frustrate children as they attempt to read and extract information. Before reading teachers might

- produce a word bank, discuss it with the children and display it
- ask more able children to partner others to turn the word bank into a glossary
- encourage the children to read on beyond any difficult words and then use the context to try to work out what the words might mean.

*Is the author's style accessible?*

Often non-fiction books may appear attractive and well presented, but a closer look often reveals that the authors may know more about their subjects than they do about presenting information in an accessible way. If we use information texts which are not written specifically for children, the problem inevitably increases. Before reading such texts:

- read the text aloud to the children
- work with the children in shared writing to produce non-fiction text and to discuss phrasing and style
- spend time talking about layout
- use shared reading to show how headings and subheadings can be used to guide readers to what they want to find out
- discuss key words which often feature in non-fiction but which may be unfamiliar, such as 'however' and 'therefore'.

*Is the genre familiar?*

It is not only authors' styles which may challenge children, but also the nature of the genre they are reading. Many non-fiction texts are written in the present tense, yet stories are written in the past. Often styles change within a text, with information being presented in prose and then in charts or in lists, or sections being presented in a different genre such as instructional (this is a feature of this chapter, with bullet points beginning with imperative verbs).

### Supporting children when using non-fiction texts

- Ensure that they often read a variety of genres in shared reading.
- Display a range of genres in the classroom.
- Use a highlighter and an overhead projector or whiteboard to show children how key points can be identified and used as signposts for re-presenting information.
- Make use of graphic organisers to present information extracted from texts and work with children to show them examples. For example, they might use a Venn diagram with two overlapping circles to present information about two contrasting environments, with the area of overlap representing similarities. A web chart or spider chart can be used to identify key points about a topic, with further information placed around each point. This also helps children to plan for writing about a topic and, if they might work together before dividing the task, allocating a key area to each subgroup.

Readers need to understand, above all, that non-fiction texts are usually read in a quite different way from narratives, which are read from beginning to end. Often, we skim non-fiction texts for information or use reference devices such as contents pages or an index to find what we want to know. We often refer to the same book many times over a long period without ever reading it from cover to cover. If children are to develop the ability to use non-fiction texts effectively, they will need to have lots of opportunity to see a range of genres and discuss their features, as well as developing the ability to use their knowledge of alphabetical order and reference devices to locate information quickly.

### The Primary National Strategy

The Primary National Strategy makes specific demands upon teachers to develop children's abilities to use information texts effectively.

> In order to read for meaning, children must both understand the purpose of the activity and the goals of the author. If not they will become confused. They must have a positive attitude towards reading and be motivated to read.
>
> (DfES 2006c: 34)

The literacy hour lends itself to working with whole classes and groups looking at the structure of texts and the analysis what it is that we can find out by using them. There should be opportunities to talk about the features of non-fiction texts and the ways in which they differ from fiction and poetry texts. The next section explores some activities which could be used in the classroom with different year groups, either as part of literacy hours or as part of cross-curricular work focused upon non-fiction texts.

## Foundation Stage: activities in the classroom

At this stage, children will be curious about the world around them and may be unfamiliar with written texts. Some will have looked at books and may already be able to read, but for some school will be virtually the only place in which they have the opportunity to share texts. The Primary National Strategy (DfES 2006c: 23) states that most will learn 'how information can be found in non-fiction texts to answer questions about where, who, why and how'. Activities might focus on notices and signs around the classroom, with attention being drawn to those which will help them to find things or to know whose drawer is whose. They might be asked, in turn, to go and find notices, copies of which are held up by the teacher. This might be followed by a hunt for print walk (see Jolliffe et al. 2005) in which they first read notices in the classroom and then go and look for some of them around the school with the help of the teacher or a classroom assistant. The activity can then lead to children attempting to write their own notices.

Lists are a key element of early reading and writing and might focus initially on children's names and then on items in the classroom. When non-fiction texts, particularly in big book format, are shared, children might help the teacher to make a list of things they have learned or key points form the text. They may go on to write their own lists, using simple texts to find names of animals, types of transport and so on.

## Year 1: activities in the classroom

In Year 1 children should begin to 'distinguish fiction and non-fiction texts and the different purposes for reading them' (DfES 2006c: 25), and should be familiar with the anatomy of a book. By using big books, teachers can draw attention to features such as blurbs, contents pages, indexes, titles, subtitles, authors and illustrators. Children can look at such features to help them to decide what a book might be about and if it might contain information they are looking for. The words fiction and non-fiction can be used and children can be shown examples of each to promote discussion about genres. There are many excellent non-fiction books available which possess all the features one would expect in textbooks written for adults.

Children can be shown different books on the same topic and this can lead to discussion about the level of detail provided, the different ways in which information is presented and the relative quality of the books. They should be shown examples of charts, diagrams and illustrations as they learn about different ways of presenting information. Labelling activities may be differentiated so that all children are challenged, and children can go on to produce their own charts and diagrams. This work can be linked to other subjects, with geography work involving labelling maps and creating simple diagrams with lists of the features of contrasting environments. In history, they might sequence events, using arrows, numbering or other devices. In converting lists and diagrams of sequential events into prose, children can be introduced to words such as first, then, next, finally, which will also be useful to them in story writing. For all of these activities, the provision of word banks will not only support the children but will also offer opportunities for word level study and the development of increased phonic knowledge.

## Year 2: activities in the classroom

Although they may have used them in Year 1, children should be introduced, in greater depth, to ordered texts such as dictionaries, encyclopedias, indexes, registers and glossaries as part of literacy work in Year 2. An understanding of alphabetical order will be vital and they can also be shown how to use the second, third and so on letters of words to place them in lists. Most children in Year 2 learn to 'Explain organisational features of texts, including alphabetical order, layout, diagrams, captions, hyperlinks and bullet points' (DfES 2006c: 27).

Many of the concepts met in Year 1 should be revisited, with concepts such as fiction and non-fiction reinforced through discussion about different types of texts. Displays of a variety of texts will provide stimuli for discussion and for independent and group work.

Year 2 children should be working towards being able to make simple notes about the information they have discovered, perhaps noting in brackets the page of a book or the source where they found it.

Instructions and directions feature strongly in Year 2, so work on recipes and map work in which journeys are plotted between places can be useful. Instructions and directions should be part of shared writing, with children talking about the use of imperative (or 'bossy') verbs as well as left, right and words which denote a sequence of events such as first, next, then and finally.

A class book on an historical or geographical topic might be produced, both as shared and independent writing, with children learning how to use captions, headings and subheadings. This might be produced electronically, using an interactive whiteboard or a wordprocessing or desktop publishing package. This can be linked to the children's work in ICT with teachers modelling techniques such as importing pictures and diagrams and changing fonts and layout so that material is presented in an interesting way which will attract readers' attentions.

## Year 3: activities in the classroom

In Year 3 many children begin to read with some fluency and to enjoy finding books to read independently. They need to be made aware of the huge range of literature available to them and, perhaps, to be guided towards texts which they will find accessible but not frustrating so that they gain satisfaction from their reading. An exploration of their hobbies and interests could be a good starting point for putting together a display of books which can be discussed and be available for children to borrow. These might be divided into fiction and non-fiction or children could be given the task of sorting them into these two categories, drawing upon their growing understanding of different genres.

The concept of alphabetical order will need to be revisited and reinforced as children begin to make greater use of reference books. The classroom should have a plentiful supply of reference texts such as dictionaries, thesauruses, encyclopedias, atlases and directories. It is important that the reference materials they encounter at this stage are attractive and stimulating. A greater understanding of reference texts will be gained if children also have the experience of creating their own as a shared writing activity. A glossary of key terms for a topic could be a starting point with children looking at examples of glossaries and dictionary definitions in shared reading before producing their own. More able children might look at a range of definitions of the same word or term in a variety of sources before agreeing upon their own version.

Reading aloud by the teacher should not be restricted to fiction, but should include poetry and non-fiction. Extracts from different non-fiction texts can be read to children to whet their appetites for independent reading as well as to foster discussion of the differences between fiction and non-fiction. The extracts could also be displayed alongside complete copies of books so that children can try to identify which book which extract was taken from, using scanning to look at subject matter, style and presentation.

The texts which are discussed, even in the literacy hour, might include maps, diagrams, charts and lists. In looking at the place names on a map, children will need to work out how they might be pronounced, drawing upon their growing phonic knowledge. While most British towns and cities have names which are sufficiently phonically regular that children should be able to find a place after listening to an initial phoneme or cluster of phonemes, others with irregular pronunciations, such as Belvoir (pronounced 'Beaver'), Alnwick (Anik), Hawick (Hoik), and Woolfardisworthy (pronounced 'Woolsery'), can be used to provoke discussion. After all, many common children's names seem to defy common phonic knowledge (e.g. Chloe, Siobhan, Stephen etc), so encounters with other examples should not surprise them.

To emphasise the concepts of fact and fiction, children can be given statements and asked to find out if they are true or false. The Primary National Strategy states that most Year 3 children 'identify and make notes of the main points of sections of text' and 'Explain process or present information, ensuring that items are clearly sequenced, relevant details are included and accounts are ended effectively' (DfES 2006c: 28). Activities providing opportunities for them to extract information and present it include the following.

## Rainbowing

After working on a topic, each member of each group is allocated a number, letter or colour and then meets with all the others with the same number, letter or colour to share ideas and compare what each group discovered from their texts. Children are provided with a real audience for their speaking and will be able to listen and respond to a range of people. They will also be able to share ideas, insights and opinions.

## Jigsawing

The class is organised into groups with each member of each group being given an aspect of the topic on which to become expert. The experts from each group meet to share ideas and then report back to their groups. Many of the benefits which are derived from rainbowing may be found here, but children will also have the opportunity to show their own 'expertise' and to explore develop and explain ideas. Simple computer databases can be devised so that children develop skills in recording and research. One which records children's height, weight and so forth and which may be amended throughout the year can provide a good starting point.

### Character quiz

Children might write statements about an historical character, based upon research from the internet, and then display or read the statements and ask the rest of the class to try to identify the characters and the books.

### Fact or fiction?

Reference books and the internet might be used to produce statements which may or may not be true. Others have to conduct their own research to check the veracity of the statements. Initially, teachers may wish to provide some statements and ask the whole class or group to check their veracity. This could be a useful guided reading activity for a group of children, which focuses on locating information.

### Dictionaries and thesauruses

Dictionaries should be appropriate for pupils but there should always be a large and more comprehensive version available for looking up words which do not feature in the children's dictionaries. If they are to be able to use reference books successfully and without frustration, it is important that children understand alphabetical order as early as possible.

Literacy hour activities on non-fiction should focus on note-making, recording information, identifying key words, locating information from different sources and presenting it using devices such as flow charts. Make use of information technology to enable children to 'publish' their work.

## Year 4: activities in the classroom

Most children in Year 4 will, according to the Primary National Strategy, 'learn to use knowledge of different organisational features of texts to find information effectively' and will be able to 'Summarise and shape material and ideas from different sources to write convincing and informative non-narrative texts' (DfES 2006c: 30). Children's interests and hobbies can provide useful starting points for developing their reference skills if books for the classroom are chosen carefully. Such texts should include features such as contents pages, indexes, glossaries, maps, charts, illustrations and diagrams.

Children should be able to 'offer reasons and evidence for their views, considering alternative opinions' (DfES 2006c: 30). They may, for example, be asked to work with others to identify key points from an historical story and then dramatise the story and perform it for the rest of the class. The different versions could be compared with those of other groups and children could be asked to explain their interpretations.

## Persuasive writing

In order to see the power of writing as a tool for persuasion, children might look at a range of advertisements, noting the kinds of words used, the presentation, including varied font sizes, illustrations and the use of adjectives and adverbs. A real writing activity could follow, with children preparing advertisements for school events such as sports fixtures, class assemblies, plays, fetes or fairs. They should be encouraged to plan and discuss their advertisements, working in small groups to determine font sizes, vocabulary choices, illustrations etc. The computer might be used to enable them to import pictures and make use of colour and varied fonts.

Wray (1995: 76–7) provides an example of the way in which the same event can be interpreted differently by different authors, and such examples might be used to show children how their use of language can be important in the way they provide messages to their readers. Children could compare reports on the same event from different newspapers before producing their own reports, either written or presented as TV or radio news items. A class newspaper could then be produced using a desktop publishing package.

Historical artefacts may be used as an alternative to texts and as a stimulus to using texts to find out information about the artefacts. Children might make notes about the item's appearance, smell and feel, before turning their notes into a presentation, perhaps using Powerpoint. This can lead to discussions about descriptions, presentation and interpretation, with other children being asked to research the artefacts to find out more about them.

In Year 4, children will 'Organise text into paragraphs to distinguish between different information, events or processes' (DfES 2006c: 31), and so will need to explore and discuss ways in which texts are organised. Follow-up activities might include writing sections of a textbook as part of a group, with the authors of each section then having a real incentive to read other people's work in order to avoid repetition and ensure comprehensive coverage of issues.

## Educational visits

Educational visits, which may range from residential to short walks in the school's locality, offer a rich source of material to stimulate both reading and writing. For a journey, children might prepare by looking at atlases, road maps and websites such as Multimap to find out possible routes and could go on to use Google to find out about some of the places they will pass through as well as those they will visit. They may produce an itinerary for the journey and perhaps create a sheet of 'Things to look out for' for classmates. Reports about the visit need not necessarily be set out in prose form and could involve lists, diagrams or charts. For example, if they visit a factory or an industrial museum they could record the production processes using flow charts, while a visit to a supermarket could be recorded on a floor plan with brief descriptions of places of particular interest. For all visits, the provision of information in advance will help alert children to what they might see as well as to aspects which may be of particular interest.

## Year 5: activities in the classroom

In Year 5 most children learn to 'Make notes on and use evidence from across a text to explain events or ideas' and to 'Compare different types of narrative and information texts and identify how they are structured' (DfES 2006c: 32). The range of material which children have the opportunity to read should be wide, and they should be introduced to texts which are not necessarily written for children, such as newspapers and reference books. They may also make use of the internet to seek out information or may be given access to CD-ROMs which feature databases and encyclopedias.

### Historical events

In order to gain a strong insight into the sequence of events which lead to a particular conclusion, children might make use of their reading and research to re-enact historical events to perform for classmates. Their interpretations can then be discussed and this may lead to revisions and additions. In working in this way, children tend to retain a knowledge of events and this is helpful if they go on to write about them. It also opens up their interpretations to a wider audience and encourages the sharing of ideas and knowledge.

### A range of texts

In order to help children acquire the ability to compare texts and to understand the different ways in which they are structured, teachers need to provide a range of materials including reference books, catalogues, timetables, newspapers, magazines, programmes for sports or drama events, brochures, pamphlets, printouts of computer texts, as well as access to CD-ROMs and the internet. Besides comparing and contrasting different text types, children might also look at different versions of the same text types, perhaps examining timetables to determine which are most user-friendly, or comparing pamphlets from tourist information offices to decide which present places most appealingly. The logical progression from such activities is for children to produce their own texts, often using computers to produce attractive and professional looking work.

### Gift shopping

Catalogue shops, which can be found in most towns and cities, usually provide customers with free catalogues, which can be a rich source of material for literacy development. Activities might begin with work on alphabetical order, with children using the index to find different items, and dictionaries to find alternative names for items which do not appear to be listed. For example, they might discover that *spoons* would be found under *cutlery* and *plates* under *crockery*.

A further activity could be linked to mathematics, with children being given an (imaginary) amount of money to spend on gifts and being challenged to spend as much of it as possible without exceeding their budget. In attempting this, they would need to use reference skills, read descriptions of items, make choices and record them, as well as doing a lot of addition and subtraction.

*Information skills*

Central to children's development of research skills is a sound understanding of alphabetical order. Without this, searching for information becomes a tedious or random activity. Besides singing the alphabet to help them memorise it, children should be given lots of opportunities to study alphabetical texts. These could include pages from dictionaries which can be enlarged using a projector. In looking at a single page children will see that words which begin with the same letter are arranged according to their second, third and fourth letters etc. They can also be shown other features of dictionaries including:

- the first and last word on each page is usually printed at the top of the page to make for easy reference
- phonetic spellings are given to aid pronunciation
- plurals and adaptations into different parts of speech are provided
- alternative definitions are given.

They might go on to look at examples of different dictionaries, ranging from simple picture dictionaries to adult dictionaries and dictionaries related to particular topics. Comparisons between presentations could be made, and they could look up the same word in each dictionary to see how it is defined at different levels.

The class could go on to make its own dictionary, drawing upon definitions from a range of published works. This could be a wall dictionary, with each word presented on a separate piece of paper and arranged in alphabetical order. As words are added, children will need to place them correctly and this will reinforce their understanding of alphabetical order. A light-hearted stimulus for this could be showing children an excerpt from *Blackadder 3* in which Baldrick accidentally burns Samuel Johnson's dictionary and he, Blackadder and the Prince Regent set about making a replacement. A further activity could revolve around definitions (perhaps not Baldrick's 'big wobbly thing with fish in it' for sea!), with children taking turns to give the definition of a word and its initial letter or letters and asking others to use dictionaries to find the mystery words, for example, 'It begins with E-L and means *first born*, what is it?'

*Reorganising text*

A piece of information text can be divided into paragraphs or sentences and cut up for children to work in pairs or small groups to organise it logically. They will need to discuss the concepts of introduction and conclusion and use semantic skills to determine an appropriate order. In addition, they will need to look for words which provide clues about the order such as finally, secondly and however.

*Diagrams and charts*

Examples of diagrams and charts from newspapers and magazines can be displayed to stimulate discussion about different forms of presentation, and so that children have models for producing their own diagrams and charts.

## *Encouraging close reading*

Children can be given pieces of text to read as the teacher reads the same text but with errors and amendments. As they listen to the teacher reading the text, they should mark the places where the teacher's version differs from theirs. This encourages both careful listening and close reading. A possible activity is to include several antonyms (for example, irregular instead of regular, possible instead of impossible, and mistrust instead of trust). This can lead to discussion about the ways in which prefixes can be used to modify words and to change their meanings (for Year 5 the Primary National Strategy states that most children learn 'less common prefixes and suffixes such as im-, ir, and -cian').

## *Cloze work*

Cloze work involves removing words from text and replacing them with lines, and asking children to read the text and use semantic and syntactic clues to decide the most appropriate words to fill the gaps. Words might be removed at regular intervals, such as every tenth word, or a particular part of speech such as nouns, verbs or adjectives might be removed. The best cloze exercises do not have only one possible solution for each missing word, as these provoke discussion and debate and allow children to interpret and justify choices.

## *Posing questions*

Rather than being asked questions by the teacher when they have read a piece of information text, children might write their own questions for the teacher and others to answer. They should be encouraged to think of both closed and open questions, with some requiring simple factual answers and others demanding inference and interpretation.

## Year 6: activities in the classroom

Children should, at this stage, be able to 'appraise a text quickly, deciding on its value, quality or usefulness' (DfES 2006c: 34) and be able to skim and scan to seek out key points or particular details. Activities should be challenging, purposeful and related, wherever possible, to the world outside school. Year 6 children are likely to 'participate in whole-class debate' (DfES 2006c: 34) too, and this section includes a focus on different types of texts including those which might promote discussion and debate, while encouraging children to 'recognise rhetorical devices used to argue, persuade, mislead and sway the reader' (DfES 2006c: 34).

## *Environmental issues*

This activity might be linked to work on 'The Town' described in Chapter 11 on 'Developing writing'. A map of the locality or of an imaginary area could be the initial text, with children being told about certain scenarios which have been chosen by you to fit in with issues of importance to the children. Perhaps a new bypass might be proposed and children have to discuss the best route or perhaps whether the bypass is desirable at all. Alternatively, you could tell them exactly where the bypass is to be built and let them begin their discussions from that point. They might research bypasses and debates about their construction on the internet to find out typical arguments for and against. The work could be linked to other work in science on protection of wildlife, as well as to geographical work on land features.

A debate or discussion could involve children taking on different roles, with some being planners and builders who have an interest in ensuring the bypass is built; some being local councillors in favour of the bypass or opposed to it; some could be local residents, and someone, perhaps the teacher, acting as chairperson of an inquiry into whether the bypass is needed and where it should go.

In preparation for the debate, children should be encouraged to research carefully and be able to justify their views. It may be a good idea to 'plant' some key questions or issues by asking some children to focus on these. For example, someone may be a shop owner who is concerned that the bypass will take away trade from her shop because there will be fewer passing cars, while someone else may be a parent concerned about road safety who feels the bypass will make the town's roads safer for his children. Ideally, the debate might be based upon a real local issue, but in any case it may provide an opportunity to invite in a local councillor so that children can ask questions and find out more about how such issues are decided.

The debate might take place over several days and children could prepare campaign literature, write letters to a class newspaper, and even record a phone-in to their own 'radio station', which could be recorded and played as part of an assembly.

### Reference area

A Year 6 class reference area will include encyclopedias, atlases, spelling dictionaries, timetables for local transport services and for school. Other information sources might be changed regularly to take into account the particular topic which the class is studying or to reflect children's interests. Timetables of television programmes as provided in Sunday colour supplements of newspapers such as the *Observer* and *The Independent on Sunday* or the TV guides provided by the *Telegraph* and *Guardian* on Saturdays could be included, and children could use these as a starting point for writing their own synopses of programmes and films they have watched. They might use sources such as *Halliwell's Film Guide* to find out more about programmes. Since many newspaper TV reviewers make extensive use of film guides when describing films, this could lead to discussion about précis and paraphrasing. Children may also discover similarities between comments about films in different newspapers, since many of these are provided by the Press Agency and are sold to newspapers.

Sports fixture lists and league tables for football teams including (if one exists) the school team can arouse a great deal of interest, as can soccer reference books such as *The Rothmans Book of Football* or the much cheaper *Playfair Football Annual*. Similar reference sources for other sports, including cricket, rugby, athletics, tennis and American Football can be found, often in discount bookshops. *The British Book of Hit Singles*, which details all records which have appeared in the top seventy-five best-sellers list since the inception of the charts, offers lots of scope for developing reference skills, and children may be interested to find how many of their current favourites were first recorded when their teachers were children! Ideally, a computer will be available as an additional source of information and a tool for recording findings.

If children are given 'ownership' of the reference area, with opportunities to add their own texts, write texts and display them, as well as making extensive use of the area, this will add status to the use of reference sources and will make using them a natural part of school life. Visits to local libraries can show children how reference sources can be organised and displayed and may introduce them to types of texts they have not previously encountered.

### Précis

If children are to produce class newspapers which offer limited space for reports, they will need to develop the art of writing concisely. A task which can help them to develop this ability might use, as a starting point, a story, newspaper article or a section from a text book. Set the children a target of say 100 words and ask them to rewrite the passage using exactly that number. Encourage them to think carefully about unnecessary words and about choosing phrasing which is economical with words without destroying the message. They might also discover that they are a few words short and so have the opportunity to add more description or might make use of some words which are often superfluous such as 'got', or 'in spite of' instead of 'despite' (see Chapter 5 on 'Knowledge about language' for examples).

### Desert Island Discs

The popular BBC Radio 4 programme has been running since 1942 and involves celebrities being interviewed about their lives and choosing eight pieces of music, a luxury and a book they would take with them if they were to be marooned on a desert island. Children can draw upon research skills and knowledge of literature to write about their own choices, with some being recorded or performed for the class. They would need to explain the reasons for their choices and perhaps how particular pieces of music remind them of events from their lives. This could be linked to the following activity on 'Memories'.

### Memories

Year 6 is usually the children's final year before transferring to secondary school. They might be asked to write about their school careers so far, including their happiest day, school trips, plays, assemblies, sports matches, and people who have left an impression on them. Examples of autobiographies and memoirs could be read or shown to children and they might listen to an edition of *Desert Island Discs* or watch *This is Your Life*. The final versions of the children's memories could be produced as books, including photographs, and might be printed as treasured souvenirs of the children's primary education and early childhood. An end of year presentation to the rest of the school and to parents could allow them to share these memories and may enable them to end their primary school education on a high note by demonstrating many of the skills and abilities they have acquired.

## The wider curriculum

The Primary National Strategy makes demands upon teachers and pupils which will require close scrutiny of the whole curriculum, as well as that for English. There is a natural link with subjects such as history and geography, given the emphasis on non-fiction texts throughout the strategy.

Texts from across the curriculum can be used to provide the range of literature which is demanded by the National Literacy Strategy and teachers can use these to model approaches to non-fiction. Children's understanding of devices such as captions, labels, headings, subheadings, indexes, contents pages, charts and diagrams should no longer be left to chance, but should be developed explicitly through direct teaching and through children's own writing.

---

**Activity: Developing children's use of non-fiction texts**

Consider your response to each of the following questions:

- What do you consider to be essential features of a Key Stage 1 classroom in which children are able to develop their understanding of non-fiction texts?
- What do you consider to be essential features of a Key Stage 2 classroom in which children are able to develop their understanding of non-fiction texts?
- How can computers be used effectively to promote reading for information?
- What factors will teachers need to take into account when planning for children to use computers to find information?

---

## Key points

- Children need to encounter a range of different types of non-fiction texts and develop strategies for extracting information from them.
- There are many simple classroom activities which can help children to engage with texts in stimulating and interesting ways.
- Classrooms should be well stocked with all kinds of reference materials and children should be guided in their use.

## Further reading

Wray, D. (2006) *Teaching Literacy across the Primary Curriculum*. Exeter: Learning Matters, Chapters 4 and 5.

## Resources for teaching

Head, C. and Waugh, D. (2007) *50 Shared Non-fiction Texts for Year 1*. Leamington Spa, UK: Scholastic.
Jolliffe, W., Head, C. and Waugh, D. (2004) *50 Shared Texts for Year 1*. Leamington Spa, UK: Scholastic.
Jolliffe, W., Waugh, D. and Taylor, K. (2005) *All New 100 Literacy Hours, Year R*. Leamington Spa, UK: Scholastic.

# 10 Learning and teaching in a multilingual classroom

*Claire Head*

## Purpose of this chapter

This chapter aims to:

- Differentiate terminology and discuss the problems of pupils for whom English is an additional language.
- Show the important role that language plays in children's lives at home and at school.
- Describe how teachers can create a multilingual literacy environment and use this as the springboard for learning and teaching.
- Provide a range of teaching strategies that can be employed to support learning across the curriculum.

This chapter will discuss how teachers can support pupils who are in the process of learning English as an Additional Language (EAL). Language is intrinsically linked to a person's sense of home, culture and self-esteem and this should be valued and respected. Pupils who are new to English will encounter some difficulties in school settings but teachers can adopt a range of effective strategies that will help to positively engage all pupils in active learning.

> Language makes accessible culture, culture includes the bilingual pupils' experience, and experience shapes knowledge . . . if teaching strategies encourage, value and support the use of bilingual pupils' home language, the children are more likely to share their language and culture freely without feeling that they are the centre of attention.
>
> (Blackledge 1994: 58, cited in Devereux and Miller 2003: 74)

By taking a broad and flexible approach to 'literacy' in the classroom, teachers can extend and enhance children's understanding of the role language plays at home, at school and in the wider world. This chapter explores how teachers can ensure that bilingual learners have access to the whole curriculum by building on their existing linguistic skills and by using a range of practical strategies which will help children to improve their knowledge about language in meaningful contexts.

Approximately 700,000 pupils, more than 10 per cent of the UK school population, speak English as an Additional Language. Over 300 languages are spoken in UK schools by pupils who are in various stages of adding English to their language repertoire. Inevitably, most teachers will work alongside some of these children at some point in their career. Remembering that language is acquired by interaction is the first step teachers must make in preparing to meet pupils' specific individual needs.

## Terminology

This section explains several terms.

### Bilingual

Pupils who are bilingual can function in two languages. This ability positively enhances cognitive development and bilingual speakers are able to switch back and forth between two languages (some more competently than others). Some teachers feel that the term 'bilingual' can be misleading as it does not indicate the help that children who are learning a new language alongside their first language will inevitably need. Gregory (1997: 8) suggests a more appropriate term for these children is 'emergent bilinguals'.

### Multilingual

This term describes people who are able to converse in and control three or more languages (there is controversy regarding how proficiently 'multilingual' people should be able to do this).

### English as a second language

This is not an accurate term because for many children English is the third or fourth language they are becoming familiar with. Some children speak one language at home, a different language with their grandparents and another language to teachers at school.

### English as an Additional Language

This term is used to describe children who are in the process of learning English on entry to school. It implies that children are learning English in addition to their existing linguistic skills. This is the terminology used most frequently in Literacy Strategy publications although some educators feel that 'EAL learners' implies that these children have a weakness to surmount. They argue that 'bilingual' learners is a much more positive term for children who are developing new language skills by building on existing strengths (Brent Language Service 1999).

### Mother tongue

This term describes the language most commonly used in a child's home. It is also referred to as a child's *home language* or *first language*.

## Supporting minority language pupils

The difficulties children encounter when learning a new language, especially when that language is the main language of instruction in the classroom, must not be underestimated or ignored by teachers but that does not mean that these pupils have learning difficulties. Assessment in the child's home language would access prior learning and check if the child has any special educational needs. Pupils often understand and know much more than they are able to express in a new language. Teachers should view a child's multilingual or bilingual talents as an asset in the classroom: it is often the monolingual teacher who faces the challenge!

Jim Cummins' (1996) theoretical framework for minority student intervention and empowerment suggests that minority language pupils are 'empowered' or 'disabled' by four characteristics of schools:

- *The extent to which a child's home language and culture is incorporated into the school curriculum:* do children feel their home culture is valued or rejected? Schools may celebrate different festivals and consequently demonstrate knowledge about these beliefs and respect for them. Faith assemblies may be lead by religious leaders from the local community who work in partnership with the school. Successful schools create a curriculum which values and reflects pupils' identities and cultures.
- *Community participation:* how are children's parents and extended families encouraged to participate in their child's education, e.g. family literacy programmes, book fairs, library visits, help with translating?
- *Encouragement of children to become active seekers of knowledge:* using interactive teaching strategies such as reciprocal teaching with bilingual support teachers.
- *Assessment and diagnosis:* with a view to evaluating how the curriculum can best serve the child, rather than focussing on how the child can fit in with the system. It is important to consider work from across the whole curriculum when assessing language competence. In order to raise standards of achievement levels for minority ethnic groups it is essential for schools to use assessment data to proactively target specific groups and individuals.

Ofsted (1999) evidence indicates that the following ethnic groups consistently underachieve compared to white counterparts: Bangladeshi, Pakistani, Traveller pupils, and African Caribbean boys. Strong leadership from head teachers to raise awareness about equal opportunities is crucial (Teacher Training Agency (TTA) 2000).

Schools need to develop policies and whole-school approaches that cultivate these empowering characteristics in order to nurture the development of all their pupils and to celebrate linguistic and cultural diversity.

### Bilingualism as an aid to children's learning

The Welsh Language Board (1999) advertises the benefits of bilingualism in education in their pamphlets for parents entitled *Two Languages: Twice the choice* (cited in Kenner 2000: 15). They argue that some of the positive skills bilingual learners develop include:

- more creative and flexible thinking
- increased curricular achievement
- ease in learning a third language
- twice the enjoyment of reading and writing
- access to two cultures and worlds of experience
- enhanced economic and employment benefits.

Researchers such as Charmian Kenner (2000) and Jim Cummins (1996) argue that children's self-esteem can be positively developed if their home language, which is part of their cultural identity, is valued and welcomed in the classroom. This means allowing children to actively engage with their home language and English as part of everyday teaching and learning in school. Activating children's prior knowledge about language is the first step in creating a learning environment which fosters a positive curiosity in all pupils about language and how it can be used to enrich our lives.

Studies that compare approaches to the education of bilingual children highlight the importance of allowing children to learn a new language alongside their home language, integrating the two together. Thomas and Collier (1997, cited in Edwards 1998) investigated the impact that different intervention programmes had on a large number of children who started primary school with little or no English. The aim of the study was to compare children who attended two-way bilingual programmes, where they studied both English and their home language in equal proportions, with children who were withdrawn from some lessons to devote more time to focus exclusively on the sounds and structures of English in special classes for second language learners. Research findings indicated that there was little difference in the academic performance of children in these two groups by the end of Key Stage 1; however, results in the next four years showed that the children in the two-way language programme consistently performed better than the 'withdrawal' group and attained a higher level compared to the level achieved by average mono-lingual English speakers. This evidence supports an approach to teaching and learning that advocates drawing upon what children already know about language to help them in their acquisition of another language.

Theories surrounding the process of second language acquisition highlight the following common principles that teachers need to build on in their classrooms.

- It is based on and impelled by a desire to communicate.
- They must be treated as communicators from the start.
- Emphasis should be on meaning rather than on form.
- Language learning takes place with and through other learning.
- It requires models of natural speech in a range of normal settings.
- It is extended and developed through exposure to a range of environments and language models.
- Learning a language is a creative process that involves making errors and formulating rules.
- It is a risk-taking process so a supportive environment is important.
- It is not a linear process.

- Experience of listening is part of language learning.
- Bilingual learners already have at least one other language to build on.

(Gravelle 2000: 4)

Pupils for whom English is an additional language have particular language and learning needs which must be taken into account if the literacy development of these pupils is to be effectively supported. How can teachers ensure that their planning is effective for all pupils – including those children who have differing and continually changing needs? The best starting place is to find out as much as possible about each child's home language and culture.

### Finding out about home literacy

Teachers need to acknowledge and value each child's home language as this is essentially tied up with who that child is and who he/she has the potential to become. The suggestions summarised below are based on research conducted in a South London nursery class by Charmian Kenner (2000).

- If possible enlist the help of bilingual teachers or assistants and home–school liaison officers who have knowledge about the local community.
- Display multilingual 'welcome' posters around the school to signal to parents your appreciation and recognition of the different languages that are part of the community. This can act as the starting point for further communication with parents or carers.
- Communicate your interest in children's literacy at home by asking parents about bilingual literacy activities, such as videos, TV stations, tapes, books, magazines. Ask parents if children can bring some of these into school so you can talk about them with their child and the rest of the class, e.g. a Gujarati newspaper, a Chinese calendar, an Arabic alphabet chart. Inclusion of these materials as part of the classroom environment may encourage parents and children to enter into a dialogue with you about family literacy at home. This will be a useful springboard from which you can continue discussions during parent–teacher conferences.
- Listen to the children in your class as they interact with the home literacy resources in different areas of the classroom. Children may explain to their friends how their family uses specific items.
- Take time to build up your relationships with parents and children – you are not checking up on the sorts of books children read at home or if children practise their handwriting. You are demonstrating a genuine interest in what children already know about language so that you can celebrate and build on this experience, with the help of parents, in school.

### Language surveys

One of the ways that teachers can find out about the linguistic diversity in their class and demonstrate that they are interested in their pupils' culture and language skills is by conducting a language survey. Ideally this should be a whole school survey so that teachers can collate information which will help them to meet the needs of all pupils. This could include structuring learning groups, informing planning, devising assessment tasks, recruiting bilingual support staff and organising family literacy activities and parents' meetings.

The following questions were devised by a group of Year 4 pupils from Larkrise First School, Oxford.

- Which languages do you speak?
- Do you know quite a lot of that language?
- Which country does that language come from?
- Which language do you speak at home?
- Which language do you speak the most?

(Edwards 1998: 12)

Teachers can use a simple set of questions like this to interview each child in their class at the start of the academic year. Questions should be adapted to suit different age groups and may need translating into the child's home language.

### Children who are new to English

Some of the children who are new to English may also be new to the United Kingdom. Children who are refugees or asylum seekers could also be suffering from the trauma of having to leave their familiar home and belongings and may also have been separated from members of their family. A new school is a bewildering environment for these children and their emotional needs must be taken into account as class teachers help them to settle in to a new life. Teachers can help these children feel welcome and more confident in school by

- teaching them names of key adults who can help them at school
- taking individuals on a tour of the school and showing children how to get to the toilet, dinner hall and main entrance
- spending some time in the classroom with the pupil showing where materials and books are kept
- naming objects around the room (this could be done one playtime as it is less daunting for the child if he/she can spend a little time with the teacher without interruptions from other children in the class)
- helping the child to learn numbers, body parts, colours, clothes, shapes, days of the week and appropriate answers to simple questions (key words and 'survival' language)
- showing how to form the letters in his or her name.

It helps to involve other children in this process: you could develop a buddy system so that the child's peers can help by acting as mentors as well as friends. It is also important to establish a good relationship with the child's parents or carers so that you can reassure them about progress and begin to build links between home and school.

## Links between home and school

Teachers and schools can create a positive, multicultural atmosphere which nurtures and values language and cultural diversity by

- translating literature that goes home for parents to read into their children's home languages, e.g. school booklets, letters, reading records
- offering regular parents' meetings to inform and update parents on new school initiatives, e.g. reading at home, preparation for assessment tasks
- letting parents know that bilingual staff will be on hand to translate the information and to discuss issues with parents
- learning how to greet parents in their home language
- encouraging parents to explain concepts and themes to children in their home language.

Parents and carers and members of the local community can be encouraged to become part of school life by helping with many aspects of the curriculum. The following ideas can be put into practice with any age group:

- *Translating:* labels, class books, making dual textbooks, instructions for games, children's stories, number lines for display
- *Storytelling:* telling stories to children, tape recording versions of stories in different languages, helping children to write stories in their home language
- *Cooking:* preparing food with children and talking about the ingredients and the process in their home language, naming fruit and vegetables in English and in the child's home language, finding out about food from different countries, visit a greengrocer's and name the foods on display (talk about the environmental print)
- *Songs and rhymes:* teaching these to children in different languages and helping children to learn about different cultural traditions.

## Creating a multilingual literacy environment

The learning environment that teachers create for children needs to stimulate and feed their interest in learning about literacy. The print that teachers surround their pupils with should reflect their own enthusiasm about language and how it can be used. It should also send a clear message to everyone about the value of reading and writing – in all its guises. When setting up your language-friendly classroom try to do the following:

- Ensure reading areas contain dual language texts.
- Include taped stories, rhymes and songs in children's home languages in the listening corner.
- Display meaningful labels that the children have helped to make.
- Encourage children to use and take notice of a messages board: messages need to be relevant and real so that children recognise the vital importance of communicating in this way.

- Display writing in English and in children's home languages: this could include writing volunteered by family members.
- Encourage children to bring home literacy materials into school and display these carefully in the classroom.
- Support and encourage children's experiments with multilingual writing in the mark-making and role-play areas. Encourage Key Stage 2 children to write in their home language and talk about the composition and transcription of the piece with their peers.
- Seize opportunities to compare differences and similarities between languages, e.g. when reading a dual language text: this helps children to understand how writing works.
- Invite parents and carers into the classroom to look at how home literacy materials have been used and to show parents their children's writing.
- Display alphabets and scripts in the children's home languages.

## Teaching strategies that foster successful learning

It should be remembered that there is no evidence that language is acquired just by listening; language is acquired by interaction with other language users in meaningful social contexts.

(Morris and Collins 2002: 4)

Teachers need to be reflective and to recognise that their own teaching styles can be varied and matched to the learning styles of the pupils in their care. When choosing resources, teachers must be sensitive to the cultural value systems that will affect children (e.g. 'The Three Little Pigs' would not be appropriate as a shared reading text for Muslim pupils as pigs are regarded as unclean by Muslims). Establishing a positive relationship between teachers and their pupils is the vital component of any successful learning environment. It is through this dynamic rapport that teachers can raise their pupils' self-esteem which goes hand in hand with their ability to achieve. The teaching strategies outlined below are aimed at English as an Additional Language learners but teachers will recognise that the 'good practice' described will enhance the quality of learning and teaching for all children.

- Teach children how to record their ideas and information in a range of ways, e.g. charts, drawings, diagrams.
- Try to include visual resources to explain new concepts and activities e.g. story maps, mind webs, picture prompts (referred to as 'key visuals' by Brent Language Service 1999).
- Make good use of the pictures in big books by drawing children's attention to the image that matches the text and by asking children questions related to their own experience to establish meaningful contexts.
- Choose books that have predictable, repetitive texts with large pictures to model reading strategies to EAL learners. It is also helpful to use story props or sequencing pictures to help children retell familiar texts.
- If possible, plan shared delivery of whole-class activities through partnership teaching, when a bilingual teacher and a monolingual teacher work together to

introduce new concepts and activities (this sort of double act needs a little rehearsal to work effectively).

- Ensure you give the children opportunities and (time) for active listening.
- Provide scaffolded writing tasks: writing frames with visual prompts if possible – large versions of these need to be modelled before the children use them independently.
- Focus on, praise and reinforce children's growing ability to use language to communicate rather than being overly concerned with sentence construction, vocabulary choices and pronunciation until children grow in confidence.
- Encourage children to consult a bilingual dictionary, a thesaurus, glossaries and key word lists.
- Allow plenty of time for repetition, revision and revisiting as children spiral through the curriculum and assimilate and accommodate new knowledge and skills.
- Ensure you allow children to engage in different learning styles and incorporate practical and manipulative tasks into lessons so that children do not become too tired through the constant challenge of working in words alone.
- Identify key vocabulary and the language challenges for the children involved in each lesson at the planning stage.
- Be aware of the complications caused by the use of figurative and idiomatic language and develop a range of strategies to tackle this with the children, e.g. 'rich scripting', 'shared imaging' and 'word-weaving' are excellent strategies devised by McWilliam (1998). (See explanations later in this section.)
- Plan activities that encourage peer interaction and collaborative learning (use cooperative learning techniques and activities that demand real communication, e.g. jigsaw exercises, barrier games).
- Place a special emphasis on speaking and listening and ensure this has been built into your planning for every activity.
- Look for opportunities to make cross-curricular links.
- Build in time for pre-tutoring and post-tutoring around the literacy hour: time for a teacher or bilingual support teacher to introduce a new text to give children a 'way in' to the lesson before shared reading begins and again, at the end of a lesson time could be built in to talk to a bilingual child or a group about key points to allow time to revisit and reflect *and* to remedy misconceptions.

### Language diversity across the curriculum

Topic work related to a particular theme can be the starting point for children (and their teachers) to learn about different languages and cultures. The following themes can act as the springboard for this type of valuable cross-curricular work:

- food
- ourselves
- celebrations
- light
- homes
- weddings

- communication
- the history of writing
- newspapers from around the world.

---

**Activity: Working on cross-curricular themes**

- Work in pairs to brainstorm ideas about a cross-curricular theme.
- Identify activities that link to different curriculum areas and suggest an inspirational starting point to stimulate pupils' interest.

---

### Words and their meanings

The use of metaphors, clichés and idiomatic phrases enriches our language and is embedded in the shared culture of the language users. Mastering and understanding this sort of subtlety contributes to the emotional and social aspects of communication as well as aiding children's understanding. Teachers often attempt to simplify their explanations and instructions when talking to English as an Additional Language learners but avoiding figurative language is almost impossible as it is enmeshed into every aspect of written and verbal communication (McWilliam 1998). Instead, teachers need to embrace the opportunities to engage children in exploration of language and how it is used in order to extend pupils' vocabulary and to arrive at shared meanings. Fitzpatrick (1996) argues that accepting figurative language is part of everyday life in the multilingual classroom means recognising:

- It is what we take for granted.
- It is often the key to understanding.
- It is often the trigger for misunderstanding.
- We cannot avoid figurative language so we have to 'manage' the meaning.
- Anticipate multi-meanings of words which are key words in the topic or in the way you intend to talk about the topic.
- Use analogies or extended metaphors which relate to children's experience.
- When multi-meaning words occur, explore them in a wide variety of senses but particularly those which make semantic connections with the focal new meaning.
- Use the children's understandings of possible meanings as the baseline wherever you can.
- Create a classroom 'consciously curious' about the meanings of words.

(Fitzpatrick 1996, cited in McWilliam 1998, 86)

Norah McWilliam (1998) in her practical and inspirational book *What's in a Word?* suggests three strategies that teachers can use to encourage children to become 'consciously curious' about words and their multiple meanings: rich scripting, shared imaging and word-weaving.

*Rich scripting*

Rich scripting is a technique that allows teachers to check pupils' comprehension of key words and phrases associated with a new topic or activity. It is more than simply defining key words and technical vocabulary, because 'rich scripting' encourages children to seek the meaning of these words in a variety of contexts. Investigating how words can change their meaning depending on how they are used allows children to draw on their own cultural knowledge as they interpret new words. For example:

> Topic: Water
> Meaning-seeking strategies: use of thesaurus/dictionaries/paired consultation in home languages/use of overhead projector to share findings/examples of multiple meanings, idiomatic phrases etc.
>     Sample of evidence children could collate:
> *Water:* liquid, body of water, water course, seas, rivers, channel, stream, beck, pool, pond, lake, mere, tarn, loch, creek, fiord, strait, spring, spa, my eyes are watering, water the garden, you can take a horse to water . . . wet, saturated, soaked, sodden, drenched, like a drowned rat.
>     (More examples of this process, a 'rich scripting' proforma and a very useful checklist can be found in Chapter 3 of *What's in a Word?*)

---

**Activity: Rich scripting**

Try rich scripting a suitable word from your cross-curricular theme, e.g. 'home'.

---

*Shared imaging*

Shared imaging is about establishing a common framework in the classroom and recognising that because we all have different life experiences, and perhaps different cultural experiences, we may imagine different images or meanings when we hear the same words. We need to help children to match meanings and images to the words we share and as teachers we need to remember that this process is one of negotiation. McWilliam (1998) cites the example of a secondary school pupil who says he does not understand subtraction but knows how to do take-aways. When talking to a Year 2 class of children (whose families came from India and Pakistan), one of us made the mistake of assuming that our 'images' of woodland creatures (squirrels, foxes, badgers) would be the same as the children's. This was clearly not the case as the question, 'What sort of animal do you think might live in a forest?' was met by answers such as monkeys, snakes and tigers. Our images may be fuelled by memories of trips to English woods to collect conkers and stories of 'Farthing Wood' and 'Winnie-the-Pooh'. Many of the children in this class had visited very different forest areas and had heard stories steeped in a different cultural tradition. Similarly, teachers should not be surprised by children's literal response to idiomatic expressions that are culturally acquired, e.g. 'pull your socks up!' The process of shared imaging actively promotes collaborative meaning-seeking and creates a positive atmosphere where children feel they can share their ideas and have fun with words.

*Word-weaving*

Word-weaving is a strategy associated with rich scripting which helps children to 'extend their semantic investigation across their home languages' (McWilliam 1998: 173). The class are given a target word and they have to work together to investigate it (using dictionaries, thesauruses, glossaries, putting the word into different sentences, looking for synonyms, metaphors etc.). The aim of this activity is to collect information about the target word and to present it on strips of paper which are woven together in a 'loom' on display in the classroom. Children can be encouraged to ask adults at home to help them by translating the target word and by identifying words and phrases with the same meaning as the target word. Once the loom is complete it can be used as the starting point for other activities (shared imaging discussions or as a resource for shared writing).

## Key points

- English as an Additional Language learners may spiral through the curriculum as they encounter language in meaningful contexts.
- Assessment plays a vital role in helping teachers to identify and respond to individual needs.
- Learning a new language involves taking risks, making mistakes and being creative. Teachers need to ensure that they promote this sort of climate in a supportive school environment.
- The opportunity to work and learn alongside people from different cultures and with different languages reminds us that there are lots of different ways of living life and communicating with each other. One of the important lessons we learn (at school and at home) is that we can benefit from sharing our experiences and cooperating with others.

## Further reading

Conteh, J. (2003) *Succeeding in Diversity: Culture, language and learning in primary classrooms.* Stoke-on-Trent, UK: Trentham Books.
Kenner, C. (2004) *Becoming Biliterate: Young children learning different writing systems.* Stoke-on-Trent, UK: Trentham Books.
Siraj-Blatchford, I. (1994) *The Early Years: Laying the foundations for racial equality.* Stoke-on-Trent, UK: Trentham Books.

## Resources for teaching

Ethnic Minority Achievement: Aiming High Strategy and general information about standards of achievement. Available at http://www.standards.dfes.gov.uk/ethnicminorities/raising_achievement
Mantra Lingua offers resources for primary classrooms such as posters and dual language texts. Available at http://www.mantralingua.com

Multiverse: Exploring Diversity and Achievement. This is a national Initial Teacher Education professional resource network designed to help teachers to raise the achievement of pupils from diverse backgrounds. Available at http://www.multiverse.ac.uk

National Association for Language Development in the Curriculum (NALDIC): working for pupils with English as an additional language. Offers support material and teaching resources. Available at http://www.naldic.org.uk/ITTSEAL2

Reading Differences: Introducing children to world literature. This material has been devised as a result of feedback from English 21 research which reported that most people felt that the books children were encouraged to read should reflect the culturally diverse world we live in. Available at http://www.qca.org.uk/english

# 11 Developing writing

## Purpose of this chapter

This chapter aims to:

- Describe how to develop early writing.
- Examine the role of the teacher in modelling and discussing writing.
- Discuss ways of developing children's ability to work independently.
- Describe how to create a writing classroom.
- Suggest practical activities for the classroom.

## The development of early writing

In this chapter we will look at the development of writing from early stages to the more sophisticated writing which many children in Key Stage 2 are capable of producing. Many factors associated with developing early writing continue to be important in later years as children develop their writing skills. We will consider the changing nature of written communication and think about how this might affect the ways in which we teach children about writing.

Writing begins with speech and reading, and the following are crucial in developing early writing:

- a rich oral experience of telling and retelling texts in preparation for writing
- frequent rehearsal of sentences orally.

Many children arrive at school having heard stories and poems being read or told to them. They have a good understanding of the concept of a story with a beginning, middle and an end. Others, however, are less fortunate and have not benefited from a key stage in their development as both readers and writers. Children who have experienced a rich diet of literature in their early years are more likely to understand the purpose of writing and to know that we write to convey meaning, share ideas, communicate and entertain. It is vital that the oral experience continues (or is initiated) in early years school education, with teachers devoting considerable time to reading to and with their pupils, and discussing what they have read with the children.

## Writing and the Primary National Strategy

The National Literacy Strategy and subsequently the Primary National Strategy responded to common difficulties found in many primary schools, which showed that the teaching of reading was far more systematic and better structured than the teaching of writing. Although the National Curriculum English Order sets out a model of the writing process (children should learn to plan, draft, revise, edit, present and evaluate their writing) it is easy to misinterpret this by treating it as a simple linear process which can result in a sequence whereby:

The teacher prepares and stimulates ideas of writing with the class

↓

The children write independently

↓

The teacher responds, discusses, marks, etc.

This shows that the teaching of writing can be reduced to teaching by correction, i.e. teaching after the event, instead of teaching at the point of writing. *Teaching at the point of writing* focuses on demonstrating and exploring the decisions that writers make in the process of composition. The writing process therefore becomes not linear at all, but iterative. Drafting, revising and sometimes the presentation of the text are all aspects of a common process involving constant rereading and improvement. This shows why shared writing was given such a prominent place in the literacy hour.

## The role of the teacher in modelling and discussing writing

### Shared writing

Shared writing is a powerful teaching strategy and is much more than merely scribing for pupils. It enables teachers to model how a skilled writer works at the point of writing, demonstrating the compositional process. It shows how links are made between reading and writing and how to use similar techniques to achieve particular effects. It *scaffolds* some of the transcriptional aspects of writing, as well as the style and construction of sentences, and can demonstrate particular aspects, such as how to plan, draft and edit text. Scaffolding, in writing, involves building up a framework which children can use to write around, perhaps using headings, titles for paragraphs, or key phrases such as *Firstly* . . ., *After that* . . ., *Next* and *In the end* . . . For the key features of shared writing, see *National Literacy Strategy: Grammar for Writing* (DfES 2000: 14).

There are three broad teaching techniques which can be used during shared writing sessions: teacher demonstration, teacher scribing and supported composition.

### Teacher demonstration

The teacher demonstrates how to write a text, how to use a particular feature, or compose a text type, maintaining a clear focus on the objective(s). The teacher thinks the process aloud, rehearsing the sentence orally before writing it, and shows how changes are often made to the construction or word choice. At least two sentences are demonstrated in this way, and the teacher does not at this point take contributions from the children.

*Teacher scribing*

Here pupils make contributions building upon the teacher's initial demonstration. The teacher focuses the pupils' suggestions to the objective(s) and challenges them in order to refine their understanding and compositional skills.

*Supported composition*

The focus here is on children's composition. Children might use dry-wipe boards or notebooks to write in pairs, or individually, a limited amount of text, sharply focused upon a specific objective. This is a quick activity and once sentences are complete they are held up for the teacher to make an immediate assessment. The aim is to practise until the large majority of the class has mastered the objective to the point where children can apply it.

## Guided writing

Guided writing sessions should be scheduled to take place with different groups in a class. The principles of shared writing also apply to guided writing, the main difference being that guided writing is an additional supported step towards independent writing. Guided writing should be planned with three major purposes in mind:

- to support children in planning and drafting their work based on the model provided in a shared writing session
- to revise and edit work in progress through a group discussion
- to provide differentiated support for particular groups.

## Independent writing

Because of the constraints of time, guided writing cannot always be used as a stepping stone into independent writing. However, most children should be able to manage the transition from shared writing into independent writing, as long as the shared writing provides the necessary support. Shared writing can be used to scaffold independent writing sessions by providing, for example:

- a worked plan for children to write to
- writing for children to complete
- an outline for children to expand
- a clear narrative ending or punch line, with known steps towards it, to be retold to create particular effects, e.g. tension.

## Developing children's ability to work independently

The techniques described above support children's writing during the writing process and not merely before or after the event. A typical sequence which leads from hearing a story to participating in writing one might be as follows.

### The Tiger Who Came to Tea

The teacher tells the children she is going to read them a story about, say, a tiger who comes to someone's house and asks for something to eat and drink (*The Tiger Who Came to Tea*: Kerr 1968). Before showing the book cover, questions can be asked to draw out children's prior knowledge and to engage their interest:

- What do you know about tigers?
- Has anyone ever seen a tiger in a zoo?
- Where do tigers usually live?
- What do they eat?

By being shown pictures and talking about tigers, children can begin to acquire an interest in the unusual theme of the story. Next, the children can be shown the cover of the book and asked what they think might happen in the story. Is the girl frightened of the tiger? Does the tiger look fierce?

Having set the scene for the story, the teacher can now read it to the children, perhaps involving some children, either simply by giving them labels to hold or wear with the names of different characters, or, where there are strong readers, asking them to read some of the lines spoken by their characters.

While reading the story there will be opportunities to pause to discuss what has happened and to predict what might happen on the next page. Children could be asked to discuss these things in pairs, before sharing their ideas with the class.

At the end of the story, after discussions and comments, a shared writing activity could involve children imagining that a tiger came to their house and asked for tea. In pairs, they could think of opening lines, before sharing these and the teacher choosing one to write on the board. As she writes, the teacher will talk about what she is doing, think aloud about spelling, and model clear handwriting. When the sentence has been written, it can be read and re-read with the children, and their suggestions for modification invited and included. In modelling writing in this way, teachers demonstrate how writers work and show how the spoken word can be recorded in writing.

As children develop as writers, they can be given dry-wipe whiteboards on which to write their ideas during shared writing sessions, before sharing them with the class. Not only does this foster participation and cooperation, but it also enables the teacher to monitor and assess children's knowledge and understanding of writing.

---

**Activity: Planning a children's writing activity**

How would you plan a lesson for Year 3 which would lead to children being able to write a story with a beginning, middle and end?
  Think about:

- examples of texts you would share with them
- modelling and demonstration
- supported composition and scaffolding
- guided writing activities
- independent writing.

---

### Stimulating children's writing

Good teachers of writing constantly seek new and interesting contexts and experiences for their pupils to stimulate their writing, as well as modelling writing in different genres. For example, for a foundation stage or Year 1 class the writing might centre around an incident in the play area or could focus on stories about a soft toy's adventures. A particularly successful activity involves the introduction of a teddy bear which the children discover in their classroom one morning with a name tag around its neck (a phonically regular name such as Ben or Sam might be used). On subsequent days there are postcards from the bear, which can be read to the children and replies written. Occasionally, the bear may reappear with souvenirs from his travels, including books, postcards, maps and pamphlets, all of which can be shared with the children. These may be authentic or created by the teacher to make them easy to read.

  Eventually, the shared writing activities may lead to guided writing, with children attempting to produce their own postcards to send to the bear. At this stage, many children's writing will be 'emergent' and may not obviously resemble normal graphics. There is considerable value in such writing, both because the children feel able to communicate through writing, and because it enables the teacher to see what the children know about writing and what they need to learn to take them to the next stage. Thus, there may be evidence of some phoneme–grapheme correspondence in parts of the words written but not in others, or the child may show evidence of understanding that writing begins at the top left-hand corner of the page and moves to the right and down the page. Pencil grip can be observed and letter formation noted. Sometimes these might be corrected during writing, but more often teachers will leave this for a more opportune moment, perhaps in a class lesson, rather than stopping the flow of the child's writing at the point of composition.

### Creating a literate environment

Allied to children's development of writing through shared and guided sessions will be a systematic teaching of phonics, a discussion of new words, and regular teaching of handwriting with daily practice and modelling by the teacher. In addition, teachers will want to create a literate environment for their pupils, with displays of children's writing and of writing for children. Where there is a play area, writing can become part of it, with different themes offering different opportunities. For example:

- A café could have children acting as waiters and writing down orders for their 'customers'.
- Shopping lists could be made for visits to the class shop.
- Tickets could be made for a station ticket office, as well as timetables, place names and notices. Children could write and record station announcements (apologies for the late arrival of the 11.30 train).
 (See Chapter 1 on pedagogy for further ideas.)

As children's confidence in writing develops and as they move into Year 2 and then into Key Stage 2, the principles upon which early writing development are founded will continue to be important. The stimuli for writing will still involve oral rehearsal, shared reading and shared writing. Teachers' modelling of sentences may be at an increasingly sophisticated level, but it will still be important for children to see and engage with different idioms and styles of writing, as well as with varied sentence structures. The tools for writing will continue to include sound phonic knowledge, confidence in spelling or attempting to spell the words they need, and a comfortable, legible style of handwriting. Increasingly, children will make use of wordprocessing as well as handwriting, and drafting, editing and revising will grow in importance as they move towards producing polished pieces of writing which can be shared with classmates and with other classes, teachers, parents and other audiences.

## Creating a writing classroom

Chapter 2 on 'Classroom management' includes extensive guidance on managing writing sessions and you could read that section in conjunction with the section which follows. There are some key principles which need to be considered when planning not only for individual lessons or phases of lessons, but also for the class throughout the year. A key element is to create an environment in which writing is celebrated and in which children feel confident and comfortable and able to write without distraction. The latter is probably the greatest challenge.

Although we want to encourage children to think of themselves as real writers and authors, the typical model for independent writing in school is hardly the way in which published authors write. Many great works of children's literature would probably not have been created had authors had to sit at tables surrounded by perhaps twenty-nine other authors, maybe vying for the use of resources such as rubbers, dictionaries and thesauruses! Roald Dahl, for example, did most of his writing in a draughty summerhouse in his garden well away from distractions, although J. K. Rowling did write some of the early Harry Potter stories sitting in a café with her daughter sleeping in a pram next to her.

In the classroom, there will be times when children will need to discuss their ideas for writing and write these cooperatively with a small group or with a writing partner. Even when writing independently and individually, discussion, sharing of ideas and sharing of work will still be important. Periods of quiet work followed by discussion enable children to concentrate for manageable sessions, while still allowing them a break from composition and an opportunity to talk about their work. By building these into planning, teachers make class management easier for themselves, whereas setting lengthy periods of silent working not only is unrealistic for most classes, but also creates a discipline problem which would hardly exist if children knew they would be given the chance to talk at regular intervals. Also consider what the rest of the class will be doing if all groups are not writing at the same time. If a writing group is placed adjacent to a group holding a lively discussion or planning a piece of drama, the likely distraction will inevitably lead to a reduction in concentration and quality, as well as to frustration for writers.

Regular intervention by the teacher to highlight good work and good working practices also creates a positive atmosphere in which success is celebrated, and children's attention is drawn to what they should be doing and what they might strive to achieve, rather than to what they are doing wrong. These interventions also enable teachers to monitor progress and to draw attention at suitable times to misconceptions, common spelling errors, and interesting use of vocabulary and phrasing. However, while errors should be noted, it is vital that children are not afraid of making mistakes. The following section may be read as a cautionary tale for anyone planning a writing lesson.

### How not to teach writing

Making children fearful before they put pen to paper seldom leads to good, creative, imaginative writing. This method was capably illustrated by a student whose lesson was witnessed many years ago.

On the chalkboard was a list of dos and don'ts:

- Draw a neat margin.
- Put the date at the top left-hand side of your page.
- Do not cross out.
- Do not use a rubber.
- Use capital letters at the beginnings of sentences and full stops at the ends.
- Do not misspell any of these words – because, their, there, once . . .

The student went through the list with the class of 8 and 9 year olds in a stern and rather hostile manner, before telling them that they were to write a story about life in a Victorian factory.

Within five minutes of starting work, two children were crying because they had incurred the student's wrath by putting the date on the wrong side of the page, and several others, having surmounted that hurdle, had gone on to sit chattering or chewing pencils as they tried to think about what they might write. An atmosphere of trepidation pervaded the classroom, and children, afraid of making mistakes, left their seats clutching blue spelling dictionaries to ask for words which they almost invariably knew how to spell. The lesson gradually fell apart and little was achieved.

The student, during the post-lesson discussion, blamed the children and stated that they were a dreadful class, full of lazy boys and chatty girls. He would prefer to teach older children, he said, who could do more and needed less help. In fact, the problem had been the student's attitude to the task and the animosity which he conveyed to the pupils. There had been little discussion about what life in a

Victorian factory might be like, and he had not read any stories or poems to them to provide ideas. Instead of showing the children that he was interested in what they would write, he gave the impression that it was only the secretarial aspects of the writing with which he was concerned. The wrong atmosphere was created and the task was depicted as a chore rather than as a pleasant activity.

---

**Activity: Advising a trainee teacher**

- Consider what advice you would give to the trainee teacher (apart from give up teaching and become a prison officer) to help him improve his writing lessons?

---

Course tutors had tried to convey to students in lectures the importance of making writing an enjoyable act. They had told the students that children's spelling was more likely to improve if they were encouraged to attempt words which were new to their written vocabulary, safe in the knowledge that their teacher would help them to spell the words correctly rather than penalise them for making mistakes. They had talked to students about the importance of children being encouraged to experiment with language. This is not to suggest that spelling and accurate writing are unimportant: far from it. Accuracy is vital if readers are to be able to enjoy what they read, but there are times when real writers concentrate on ideas rather than presentation, leaving editing and revising until later. We will see, in the examples later in this chapter, how the writing process can be developed to foster an increasing concentration on accuracy as a piece of writing develops.

---

**Activity: Considering how pupils perceive writing**

Before moving on to other aspects of writing, it is worthwhile considering a classroom in which you work or have worked to assess how writing might be perceived by pupils. How would you answer the following questions?

- Are quiet writing areas available?
- Are vocabulary lists and word banks available and easy to use?
- Does the teacher have time to help children?
- Do the children ever see the teacher writing?
- Is children's writing displayed and regularly shared with the class and others outside the class?
- How often do the children write for people other than the teacher?
- Do children always know why they are being asked to write?
- Do children have opportunities to work with others as well as individually?
- Do children often use the wordprocessor?
- What do the children think that the teacher is looking for when responding to their work?

## Responding to children's writing

As we have seen, teachers' response to children's work can have a profound effect upon their pupils' attitudes to writing. Teachers' responses will, of course, be largely focused upon the learning outcomes determined for the lesson, but this does not mean that in a lesson in which the word level focus is use of speech marks, teachers should only check children's work for accurate punctuation of dialogue, ignoring content. As a general rule, it is best to comment upon content before presentation. If children feel that the only reason they are writing is to demonstrate proficiency in word or sentence level skills, writing ceases to be regarded as a purposeful activity and a means of communication. Central to ensuring that writing is valued in its own right is ensuring that children have an 'audience' for their writing, and that this audience is not always only their teacher. As Andrew Lambirth (2005) has argued:

> Real writing – writing for real audiences – is a struggle, but the labour becomes worthwhile when the author knows that his/her work will be read, respected and valued as a genuine and authentic attempt at meaning-making.
>
> (Lambirth 2005: 58)

Knowing whom one is writing for should help dictate style, use of vocabulary and idiom, as well as content, so that Year 6 children writing for Year 2 pupils will write differently from when they write their own versions of, say, a Joan Aiken story.

Marking a child's work should, ideally, take place with the child present. However, this is not always possible and inevitably teachers find themselves taking home piles of exercise books. Inevitably, too, this can lead to inattentive marking and a focus purely on secretarial aspects of work. How much easier it is to skim through a story, pick out and underline three spelling errors and write 'a good try' at the foot of the page than it is to read the story properly, comment upon events and structure, and then draw attention to errors and misconceptions, concluding with a meaningful comment which shows the child that the teacher has really read his or her work.

A strategy which many teachers use to encourage accuracy is to ask children to check their work before handing it in for marking. This often results in children returning to their seats, adding a full stop or two and then returning. If checking or proof-reading is to be done effectively, children need to know what they are look-ing for. A solution is to provide a checklist for children to look at when rereading their work (see Chapter 5 on 'Knowledge about language' for another example). This might include some items as standard, but others will be focused upon the par-ticular learning objectives for the activity. For example, if a piece of story writing had followed work on dialogue, the checklist might be as follows:

PLEASE CHECK THE FOLLOWING BEFORE SHOWING YOUR WRITING
1  Does each sentence begin with a capital letter?
2  Does each sentence end with a full stop, question mark or exclamation mark?
3  Is every word legible?
4  Does each person's speech begin on a new line?
5  Have you opened and closed speech marks?
6  Have you varied the verbs you have used to show how people spoke (e.g. whispered, called, muttered)?

The first three items might be common to all checklists, but the others would vary according to learning objectives, with the total not exceeding six items.

The response to children's writing should not be restricted to the teacher. Where a healthy atmosphere of constructive criticism is developed, children can listen to and read each other's writing and offer suggestions and comment on secretarial errors. This might be done in class or group sessions, or through writing partners with whom children regularly discuss and share writing.

### Providing a varied diet

The Primary National Strategy and the Literacy Framework provide a wide range of writing tasks with interesting and varied starting points offered in exemplified materials. With such a wealth of ideas and activities also available through published resources and websites, no teacher need be short of stimulating ideas for children's writing. We are now, thankfully, past the stage where children equated quantity with success in writing, and one beneficial side-effect of the limited time available for independent writing within the literacy hour has been an increased emphasis upon shorter, structured writing, such as reports, opening paragraphs, definitions, and various types of poetry including haiku, cinquains, limericks and triolets. Of course, teachers did not always expect completed, polished pieces of work within a twenty-minute period, but used the literacy hour as a starting point for extended and more adventurous writing.

If the literacy hour is used in this way, perhaps once a week, the requirements of the National Curriculum can be met as well as those of the Primary National Strategy. The starting point for many writing activities should be whole-class shared writing in which the teacher models writing for the children, drawing upon their ideas and showing them how these can be presented. This can be followed by an exploration of the features of different text types, such as style, phrasing, presentation and vocabulary. Children can then work independently individually, in pairs or in groups to produce short pieces of writing during the literacy hour. Subsequently, these short pieces may be starting points for more extended writing.

What is essential is that the teacher shares a range of genres with the class and models each one that the children are expected to attempt to reproduce, discussing all the time the features of the genre and inviting the children to put forward their ideas for replication through shared writing.

### Supporting children's spelling

We have seen in Chapter 2 on 'Classroom management' some strategies for overcoming what, for some teachers, is a constant problem: children's repeated requests for help with spelling. In Chapter 12 on 'Spelling', we can see that spelling needs to be taught and learned through a range of activities, some of which involve investigation and trial and error, while earlier in this chapter we saw how an overemphasis upon correct spelling at what should be a drafting stage can stifle creativity and inhibit young writers. During writing sessions, teachers need to achieve a balance between supporting those children whose progress would be seriously hampered without help with spelling, and encouraging children to behave as real writers and to use the strategies they use when faced with a problem spelling. If children are to succeed and teachers are to be able to guide and support them, then teachers need to do more than spend writing lessons writing spellings into little blue books.

Pre-emptive methods are an obvious tactic for preventing children from becoming over-reliant upon the teacher. Before writing begins, teachers and children can work together to produce word banks to provide, displayed for all to see, lists of words which they anticipate might be needed. Once these have been made, teachers should read them with pupils, perhaps arranging them, on cards, in alphabetical order for easy reference. As children are writing and need to spell other unfamiliar words, they should first attempt to spell them independently, drawing upon their phonic knowledge and perhaps using a reference chart such as THRASS (Davies and Ritchie 1998) for spelling choices. Good attempts at independent spelling should be praised before discussions with individuals, groups and perhaps the whole class take place to determine how a word should be spelled. At this point, reference to an etymological dictionary could help the teacher to explain an unusual spelling or a particular prefix, suffix or root word. For example, a child wishing to spell 'petrified' could discover that this means literally 'turned to stone', while he may find that 'decimated' means 'reduced by a tenth'. There are obvious follow-up teaching points which could then be made, for example talking with children about other words which begin with *dec* which relate to the number ten, including decagon, decimal, decade and December (once the tenth month).

The provision of dictionaries at different levels, as well as thesauruses, will help children to find the spellings they need, as well as introducing them to new words which they might use.

## Children's perceptions of writing

The National Writing Project's fascinating booklet *Children's Perceptions of Writing* (1990) records children's comments about writing, which include some thought-provoking, as well as amusing, views. Typical attitudes found in the book can be summed up by the following:

> Writing is for you to be able to know more words and to do neater writing. Writing shows your teacher how you are progressing.

> The thing you need mostly for writing is that you should concentrate. You should not start talking. Then you will not be a good writer.

> People who have got pensions write because it will give them something to do before they die.

We would like to think that writing in schools has evolved since 1990, but experience suggests that this is not always the case. It is likely that anyone reading this chapter has seen, experienced, or even given writing tasks as punishments. Writing out lines (*I must learn not to give writing tasks as punishments*) or one-page 'essays' (*Why it is a bad idea to give writing tasks as punishments*) and other writing tasks were traditional punishments in many schools, and sadly continue to be in some. We need to consider how children's perceptions of writing will be affected if they see that teachers often use it as a punishment. Of course, writing is not the only aspect of the curriculum which is used in this way. We have seen games lessons abandoned when teachers were unhappy with children's behaviour and children given arithmetic to do instead, and we have frequently seen art, design technology or PE curtailed and replaced by silent reading when pupil conduct fell below teachers' expected standards. Strangely, we have never seen maths abandoned in favour of PE, or silent reading replaced by games or art in similar circumstances.

What do we convey to children when we use some subjects as punishments? We tell them that these activities are unpleasant or at least less pleasant than other aspects of the curriculum. A tutor was once summoned to a school to talk to an irate headteacher, who felt that students had undermined the school's policy of developing positive attitudes to writing by keeping several children in at lunchtime to write lines. He was quite right! If children are to succeed in writing, they need to perceive an intrinsic value in what they are asked to do. They need to see writing as:

- a means of communication and something which can be enjoyed both by the writer and the reader
- having a purpose and an audience
- an activity which teachers value and celebrate through reading examples aloud to the class, sharing with other teachers, and displaying so that others can see.

Teachers can elevate the status of writing considerably by showing that they too are writers. This can be done in different ways. For example:

- Before asking children to write in a particular genre (e.g. haiku, limerick, report, story opening), teachers might attempt the activity themselves at home. Not only will this help teachers to understand the challenges their class might face, but also it will provide an example which the children can see and perhaps model their own writing upon.
- As children begin work on a piece of writing, the teacher might do the same, using the opportunity to demonstrate discreetly how writers behave and the working conditions which they need in order to be able to concentrate. (Is anyone else finding it difficult to work when some people are chatting?)
- Shared writing may usefully be very teacher-centred occasionally, with teachers composing a short piece of writing while narrating the thought processes which they are using, and showing that they edit and revise as they write and after reflection.

It is not only the teacher who can model writing. Classroom assistants, other adult helpers, and professional writers might also demonstrate their writing skills and discuss the writing process with pupils. In addition, older children might have younger pupils as writing partners, producing shared pieces, drawing upon the ideas of both while the older children act as scribes.

## Practical activities for the classroom

Children in the same class should be given regular opportunities to write cooperatively, sharing and discussing ideas and developing both content and presentation.

This is a practice which adults make use of too, with jointly produced reports, co-written songs (Lennon and McCartney, George and Ira Gershwin, Gilbert and Sullivan) and co-written novels (Nicci French, who writes thrillers for adults, is a husband and wife team).

### A drafting activity

We need, as teachers, to consider whether writing can be good only if it is neat. While legibility, like accurate spelling and good use of grammar, is important when we write for others, we also need to consider writing as having stages. When children are preparing a piece of writing they may need to begin by making rough notes, just as real writers do. At this stage, they will chiefly be writing for themselves and presentation will be low on their list of priorities. 'The Fog' was a drafting activity which illustrates this process.

# The Fog

~~1. Hair damp~~
1. Going out Fog very thick ✓
2. Standing at edge of feeld can only see shadows. ✓
3. Going into fog ✓
~~4.~~ 5. The grass ✓
~~5.~~ 4. The air ✓
6. Everything invisiable ✓
7. Finger in air ✓
8. The Trees ✓
9. Bird flying ✓
~~15. Fog lifting~~
10. Traffic nosey (NO FOG)
11. Traffic not nosey (FOG)
~~13.~~ No speeding when fogy
14. Hair not damp any more

10. TRAFFIC NOISY (NO FOG) ✓
11. TRAFFIC NOISY (FOG) ✓
12. NO SPEEDING WHEN FOG ✓
13. FOG LIFTING ✓

# The Fog

Wet, ~~cold~~ cold, my hair is damp
out in the ~~fog~~

All you can see is shadow of trees,
fences, houses in the fog.

Going deeper and deeper into the
fog. Soon we'll be on ~~a~~ ~~a~~ a different
Planets

The grass ~~is~~ is squelchy with
cobwebs and wormcasts.

Toadstools grow up up in the grass

The air is fresh and clean. When
you breathes you can see your
breath.

The trees are still, not a single
bit of movement.

Birds ~~are~~ flying, seagull, sparrow
~~are~~ making it ~~will like~~ you ~~at~~ at the
sea side. But of cause ~~could~~ ~~you~~ ~~are~~ not

Traffic beeping ~~their~~ horn, going
over the speed level, When it's not
foggy. But when it foggy you can
hardly hear the ~~~~ cars or lorries

~~So is~~ So if you are out on a fog
~~day do~~ not speed because you
could have a accident.

# The Fog

Wet, cold, my hair is damp out in the fog.
All you can see is shadows of trees, fences, houses in the fog.
Going deeper and deeper into the fog.
Soon we'll be on a different planet.
The grass is squelchy with cobwebs and wormcast's.
Toadstools grow up up in the grass.
The air is fresh and clean.
When you breathe you can see your breath.
The trees are still, not a single bit of movement.
Birds flying, seagull, sparrow, making it look like you are at the seaside.
But of course you are not.
Traffic beebing their horns, going over the speed level, when it's not foggy.
But when it is foggy you can hardly hear the cars or lorries.
The fog was lifting a bit because I could see some blue sky.
When we go inside my hair is suddenly dry.

This piece of writing was undertaken by a Year 5–6 class and the stimulus was a few minutes spent on a foggy school field at the beginning of the day. Children were asked to look, smell, touch and listen and to make notes about what their senses told them. In the classroom, they were asked to 'splatter' their ideas onto drafting paper, using short phrases and clauses, and to keep writing for two minutes as they put their ideas down on paper before they were forgotten. They were told that, at this stage, neatness and accuracy was not as important as their ideas and that they need not worry about making mistakes or about untidy handwriting.

The next stage was to take the ideas and sort them into an order in which they might be used in a finished piece of writing. Ideas could be discarded or added to, but again presentation was a low priority. In the example, it can be seen that Claire circled and numbered items and then wrote them in a list on a second piece of paper.

The third stage was to develop the ideas into sentences, and the draft shows that Claire behaved as a real writer by crossing out ideas she did not wish to use and reordering others. The final draft is neat and accurate, and followed discussion with the teacher and some marking. The description conveys an image of a foggy morning which would probably not have been achieved had Claire been asked to write neatly and accurately as soon as she returned to the classroom from the foggy field. If we look at the Primary National Strategy core learning in literacy for Year 6 (DfES 2006b: 34–5), we can see that Claire has addressed several aspects including the following:

- Use a range of appropriate strategies to edit, proofread and correct spelling.
- Understand how writers use different structures to create coherence and impact.
- Integrate words, images and sounds imaginatively for different purposes.
- Use varied structures to shape and organise text coherently.
- Use different styles of handwriting for different purposes.

### Cooperative writing using pictures

In this section and the next one, two writing activities will be explored in order to demonstrate how some of the principles discussed earlier can be applied. The activities have been chosen because they could be attempted at different levels and with different year groups, with the degree of teacher support and the scope of the activities varying according to children's abilities. The first activity is described in greater detail than the second, which is followed by a challenge for the reader to consider, in the light of experience in the classroom and what has been read in this chapter, to devise appropriate activities for a chosen year group.

This first activity is based upon a collection of stimulating pictures. For a general lesson, these can be taken from magazines and colour supplements. Simply cut out a selection of pictures (adverts are particularly good and you can leave out references to products if you like) and then attach them to pieces of A3 paper. The activity has clear stages, but for younger or less able children, you may need to give a higher level of teacher modelling than for others. The possible stages are set out below, but some could be left out depending upon children's abilities.

1 Mount two large pictures on the board and explain to the children that you have written a short description of one of them. Ask them to listen carefully as you read your description and to wait until you have finished before deciding which of the two pictures you are describing, supporting their judgement by referring to what you wrote. Display the description so that they can refer to it.

2 Leave the other large picture in the centre of the board (or use an interactive whiteboard with a picture in the centre, if available). Explain that you would like the children to help you to produce a description of the picture so that if it were displayed along with several others, anyone reading the description would be able to identify the picture. Look at it with the children and ask them to suggest short phrases to describe various features. For example, for a beach scene: clear, blue sky; white, sandy beach; crashing, white waves; bright, orange sun. Write the children's suggestions in the space around the picture and continue to add to these as they have more ideas.

3 Having produced notes as the basis for a more refined piece of writing, ask children to discuss how they might turn some of the phrases into sentences, perhaps combining phrases or adding further adjectives and adverbs.

4 With the children's help, compose a short piece of descriptive writing to describe the picture. This could be prose, perhaps with a word limit of fifty, or a poem with or without rhyme.

5 Provide each pair of children with a picture mounted on A3 paper and ask them to work together to make notes on the paper around the picture with descriptive phrases. These could include feelings generated by the picture, as well as descriptions of what can be seen.

6 After a few minutes, ask each pair to pass their picture and notes on to another pair, but not to discuss what they have written or to draw attention to errors. Ask the new pairs to look at what has already been written and then to add their own ideas.

7 Pass the pictures and notes on once more after a few minutes for further additions from another pair of children.

8 Ask the children to return the pictures to their original owners, and allow some discussion between all of the six authors involved.

9 Explain that the original writers can now draw upon everyone's ideas to help them to produce a short descriptive piece of writing. Tell them that you will be displaying all of the pictures and all of the pieces of writing, but not next to each other. The writers need to make their descriptions good enough for readers to be able to match them to the appropriate pictures.

This activity can be done as part of work in a range of subjects. For example, for history a selection of pictures related to a period about to be studied can serve to alert children to prior knowledge, as well as to raise questions about the period. The pictures used could be prints of famous paintings or paintings by a particular artist (these can be found cheaply in books in discount bookshops) and the activity might be linked to art appreciation.

There are several points in the process at which teacher intervention might take place to make points about various aspects of writing. The extent to which this is done will depend upon the abilities of the children, but there can be opportunities

for discussing vocabulary, talking about spellings, and about punctuation and presentation. Modelling of text types could feature and the activity could be linked to
a genre which had recently been studied.

The pictures activity, then, features shared reading and writing, note-making,
cooperative work, drafting, editing and revising, with many opportunities for word
and sentence level study, as well as writing in different genres, and leads to accurate
and careful presentation.

### The Town

This second activity is, again, potentially cross-curricular and offers opportunities for
a wide range of writing in different genres. Again, the activity is suitable for a range
of year groups and can be tailored to the learning objectives needed for a particular
class. It focuses on a map or plan of a town which can be designed by the teacher or
by children, or may be taken from a published source (Waugh 2000b). The map
should include shops, key facilities such as police and fire stations, a medical
centre, religious buildings for different faiths, schools, recreation areas, housing,
and industry. The programme, which could extend over several weeks and which
might cover a range of learning objectives, could include the following:

1   A shared reading activity at the beginning of the programme looking at the plan
    and reading labels and, if one is provided, a key. Any new or unfamiliar words
    can be discussed in terms of their etymology, with prefixes and suffixes and
    root words studied, as well as phoneme–grapheme correspondence.
2   Instructional shared writing asking children to give directions for travel between
    different points, using left and right as well as points of the compass. There can
    be discussion about imperative (sometimes referred to as 'bossy') verbs, and
    other sources of instructional writing might be examined.
3   Discussion about the use of capital letters for names, with a focus on when, for
    example, 'street' and 'road' have capitals and when they do not.
4   Letter writing between characters from the town.
5   Drama and speaking and listening work involving children in role as characters
    from the town.
6   Fiction writing about events in the town.
7   Persuasive writing about campaigns for improvements to the town or about con-
    troversial issues such as building a new road in a conservation area, building a
    power station or factory.

**Activity: Creating a programme of work**

Look again at the suggested activities for work on The Town and make notes on ways in which you could adapt these and add others to create an engaging and worthwhile programme of work for a year group of your choice. In doing so, consider the following:

- How will you engage and sustain children's interest?
- Which aspects of the Primary National Strategy will you cover?
- Which different genres of writing and reading will children encounter and how will you model these for them?
- How can you make the activity 'real' by relating to other aspects of the curriculum and to their own environments?
- Which different 'audiences' will be available for children's work?
- How will you create a suitable classroom environment for children to work in?

If, when you attempt this activity, you find you have lots of ideas for answering these questions, then you are either a skilled teacher of writing or this chapter has been successful in promoting thinking about writing (or both!).

## Writing in the twenty-first century

For some adults, writing is an onerous task and one to be undertaken only when absolutely necessary. Yet for others it is a pleasure and an integral part of daily life. People probably write more now than ever before, with texting an almost constant activity for some, and extensive use of email having replaced letter-writing for many. Millions of people, who might not previously have put pen to paper, now communicate electronically. Radio and TV programmes often feature emails and texts as instant audience reactions to topics, and these are shared with millions, while many people have their own websites or 'blogs' which are used to express their opinions.

Within the constraints of space for this chapter, the focus has inevitably fallen upon pen and paper writing, but as teachers we need to embrace and understand the electronic age which children are growing up in and exploit their interest in communication as we develop their writing skills. Chapter 13 on ICT will explore some of these methods of writing in greater detail, but it is worthwhile pondering upon this new age of communication before moving on.

**Activity: Embracing electronic communication**

- How will you take into account children's experiences of electronic communication when devising activities to develop their writing skills?

## Key points

- It is important to create the right environment for writing, with the nature of the classroom, the attitude of the teacher, and the topics chosen for writing being central.
- The role of the teacher in modelling and discussing writing is central to children experiencing a range of texts and genres and understanding how to produce their own.
- Children need to develop the ability to work independently, both for their own benefit and for the teacher, who needs to be able to spend time supporting and guiding writers, rather than simply giving help with spellings.
- Children need to write for different audiences and purposes and to know that what they write will be read by others.
- The nature of writing outside the classroom is constantly changing as technology advances, and this has implications for how we approach writing in the classroom.

## Further reading

DfES (2000) *National Literacy Strategy: Grammar for writing.* London: DfES.
DfES (2001b) *National Literacy Strategy: Developing early writing.* London: DfES.

# 12 Spelling

## Purpose of this chapter

This chapter aims to:

- Discuss problems in the English spelling system.
- Describe phonic approaches to teaching spelling.
- Examine the place of word lists in teaching and learning spelling.
- Discuss the teaching of spelling rules and spelling principles.
- Develop strategies for teaching and learning spelling.
- Describe ways of finding out what children know about spelling.
- Suggest classroom activities to develop good spelling.

## Problems in the English spelling system

> Shakespeare himself did not spell the name the same way twice in any of his six known signatures and even spelled it two ways on one document, his will, which he signed Shakspere in one place and Shakspeare in another. Curiously the one spelling he never seemed to use himself was Shakespeare.
>
> (Bryson 1990: 116)

Whilst poor spellers may take some comfort from the efforts at spelling of England's most revered playwright, in the twentieth century, poor spelling is viewed by many as a sign of lack of intellect or carelessness and can certainly damage people's career prospects. Many employers discard badly spelled application forms.

By the time they reach Year 6, most children, according to the Primary National Strategy, should be able to 'spell familiar words correctly and employ a range of strategies to spell difficult and unfamiliar words' (DfES 2006b: 51). This chapter will explore a range of methods of helping them to achieve this, while drawing attention to some of the problems inherent in our spelling system and the obstacles these may place in the way of children's spelling development.

The lexicon of the English language has developed over hundreds of years from a variety of languages including French, Norse, Latin and Greek. This means that there are inconsistencies in the pronunciation of letters and clusters of letters, because many words have retained a pronunciation similar to that used in the language from which they are derived. Thus, we have *ch*, which teachers have tended to teach makes the sound *ch* as in *chip*, also making a *k* sound in words with Greek origins such as *chemistry, charisma, school* and *character*, as well as in names like *Chloe*, and a *sh* sound in words with a French origin such as *chef, charade* and *chute*, as well as in names like *Charlotte*.

As Raymond Williams (1965: 244) argues, when spellings were first compiled in dictionaries, many spellings were altered 'by men ignorant of their origins, confident of false origins'. 'Island', 'scissors', 'scythe', 'could' and 'anchor' replaced 'iland', 'sissors', 'sithe', 'coud' and 'ancor' without affecting pronunciation. However, similar false alterations such as 'fault', 'vault' and 'assault' (which needed no *l*s) have perpetuated their errors into both spelling and pronunciation.

## Phonic approaches to teaching spelling

The challenge for teachers and pupils is significant, even at Foundation Stage, where the Primary National Strategy (DfES 2006b: 50) expects most children to learn to 'use phonic knowledge to write simple regular words and make phonetically plausible attempts at more complex words'. Let us take one simple consonant-vowel-consonant (CVC) word and explore the spelling possibilities in order to see the problems children face.

*Fox:* the initial sound could be represented by *f* or *ph*. *Ff* is another alternative, although this is not found at the beginnings of words other than names (e.g. *Ffion*); the vowel sound will probably present few problems, although many words in children's early vocabularies have the *o* sound represented by *a* (*was, what, want*); the final sound is problematical and often leads to interesting spelling choices such as *foks, focs* or *focks*. This is because *x* usually has two phonemes (try sounding *fox, box* and *fix* and notice how your mouth shape changes), except in a few words such as *xylophone*.

---

**Activity: Teaching spelling**

- Try looking at other simple words and consider how you would teach their spellings to children by anticipating possible misconceptions.

---

Table 12.1 provides examples of different ways in which the same letters may be pronounced and illustrates the challenges we face when using a one-letter-makes-one-sound approach to spelling. Although some, like *c* having a *ch* sound (as in chip) in ciabatta result from recent word imports and are uncommon, many letters are frequently pronounced in different ways in different words.

A similar chart of spelling choices could be produced for the classroom, perhaps involving children in its construction. Alternatively, THRASS (Davies and Ritchie 1998) produces charts with pictures and words, words, and graphemes to show possible spelling choices for the forty-four sounds in English.

*Table 12.1* Problems with one letter makes one sound

| a | apple, woman, snake, car |
| b | big, thumb |
| c | cat, city, ciabatta |
| d | dog, dune |
| e | end, the, women, café |
| f | fit, of |
| g | go, huge, gnome |
| h | hit, hotel, oh |
| i | ink, fir |
| j | jam |
| k | kick, knot |
| l | log, calm |
| m | mop, mnemonic |
| n | nip, hymn |
| o | on, go, woman |
| p | pig, pneumonia |
| q | queen, Iraq |
| r | run, bar |
| s | salt, sugar, rose |
| t | tiger, debut |
| u | up, tube |
| v | vase |
| w | wall, write |
| x | fox, xylophone |
| y | you, by, hymn |
| z | zip, azure |

There is little wonder, then, that when Peters (1970) asked a thousand 10 year olds to spell *saucer* fewer than half of them did so correctly, and that those who wrote it incorrectly gave 209 different spellings.

---

**Activity: Ways of spelling 'saucer'**

Think of the word *saucer*. Spend two minutes trying to see how many different phonically plausible ways you could spell it. This should help you to see how and why children make mistakes.

Despite the many anomalies in English spelling, children still need to learn to spell accurately and they need strategies to help them to do so. Virtually every English word has some phonic regularity, as well as other clues which can help us to learn how to spell it successfully. Look, for example, at some simple words which often present problems because they include sound symbol correspondences which do not necessarily conform to those many children learn when sounding out the alphabet: was, of, once, your, would.

For *was* there are two problems: the medial *a* is commonly taught as *a* sounds in *bag*, and the final *s* as in *sit*. Here, however, the *a* has the sound of *o* in *hop*, and the *s* the sound of *z* in *zip*. Not surprisingly, children often write *wos* or even *woz* (Kilroy woz 'ere!). Do we simply teach *was* as a whole word or does it provide an opportunity to look at some other words in which *a* has an *o* sound as in *hop* and *s* a *z* sound? We looked at *want* and *what* earlier and there are other examples (often beginning with *w* such as *wander, wasp* and *warrior*), while *s* is frequently pronounced as *z* in, for example, as, is, has, please, revise and phrase. Learning how to spell *was* can, then, provide an opportunity to extrapolate and to enhance children's phonic awareness.

Similarly, *of* presents problems if children have learned only that *f* has a *fff* sound as in *fog*. Indeed, *of* is frequently misused in another way, with many adults writing *could of, would of* and *should of* instead of *could've, would've* and *should've*. This error probably emanates from the way we speak in abbreviating *could have* to *could've*, and the fact that people, perhaps subconsciously, relate the *'ve* sound to the similar sound they hear in *bag of chips, packet of nuts* etc.

*Once* is possibly the hardest word to explain, given that it begins with a *w* sound as in *wing* and this is represented by an *o*. This also occurs in *one*, which is another problematic spelling compounded by the presence of a *w* in *two*, which must be very confusing for children learning English numbers. *Once*, despite its difficult beginning, has a regular ending, *-nce*, which can be found in many words such as *dance, chance, mince* and *prance*.

*Your* and *would* present problems if children learn only that the vowel digraph *ou* is sounded as *ou* as in *about*, but at least they have phonetically regular beginnings and endings.

While the use of phonics is a key method of learning to spell, children need to know when this strategy is appropriate and when it is unlikely to work. As Norma Mudd (1994) argued,

> 'sounding out' usually only works effectively if one knows the spelling alternatives to be selected for particular words; for example, the good speller knows that 'once' may *not* be sounded out to produce the correct spelling, whereas he or she knows that 'went' may be successfully sounded out.
>
> (Mudd 1994: 138)

Usha Goswami and Peter Bryant (1990) had similar reservations, maintaining:

> Children's invented spelling is often wrong because they seem to be using a phonological code too literally when they spell. This of course is not really a surprise, because it is impossible to spell English properly just on the basis of

letter-sound relationships. No one who relies just on a phonological code will ever spell 'laugh', 'ache', or even 'have' properly.

(Goswami and Bryant 1990: 53)

The role of the teacher is to help children to develop strategies to enable them to learn spellings and be able to apply what they have learned to new words. One method is to teach words in families so that children see that there are common patterns in words. For example, for *your* they could also learn *pour* and *four*, while for *would* they could learn *should* and *could*. Therefore, the much-maligned teaching of word lists needs to be considered.

## Teaching word lists

The main reasons that some educators have questioned the value of giving children lists of words to learn are as follows:

- Children are often sent home with words to learn but without any strategies to help them to learn them.
- Sometimes teachers simply write the lists on the board on Monday morning for the children to copy into books, without discussing the words, their meanings or their spellings.
- Sometimes the words are either not relevant to children's needs or not related to each other in such a way that general 'rules' about spellings might be deduced.
- The inevitable spelling tests which follow can compound children's sense of being poor spellers and create a sense of failure for some.
- Some teachers think that they have taught spelling if they give children spellings to learn, and do little else to develop their pupils' spellings abilities.

Of all the arguments against giving children lists of words to learn, the last is probably the most important. Learning to spell involves much more than learning words by rote. In particular, it involves developing the ability to extrapolate and to apply what one learns about spelling some words to other words. In order to do this, we need to see that however irregular some words may appear, there are usually others which follow the same pattern. We also need to learn about common prefixes and suffixes and understand how these can be used to modify meanings of words. If children are to be given lists of words to learn, then it is important that teachers spend time talking with them about spellings and relating what they learn to more general principles about spelling. It should be remembered that if children were given 10 words a week to learn throughout their primary school lives they would learn only around 2700, assuming that no word was ever repeated. Jane Bouttell (1986) maintained that by the age of 12 an average child has a vocabulary of 12,000 words. The need to extrapolate and to generalise from knowledge acquired is, therefore, crucial.

Teachers should not only discuss the words which appear on the lists, but also talk about other words which may be derived from them. Teachers should differentiate the lists according to the spelling abilities and vocabulary needs of the children. However, some words may be common to all lists if they relate to a particular

*Table 12.2* Sample word lists for a Year 5 class

| Lowest ability group | Middle ability group | Highest ability group |
| --- | --- | --- |
| prefer | preference | characteristic |
| enjoy | enjoyable | rhyme |
| setting | character | dialogue |
| author | illustrate | sequence |
| verse | Carroll | metaphor |
| Lewis | Dahl | illustrator |
| blurb | describe | illustration |
| cover | description | incident |
| publish | paragraph | excerpt |
| publisher | extract | situation |

topic which all children are studying. Table 12.2 has some sample lists for a Year 5 class who are studying novels, stories and poems by significant children's writers.

All the lists can be looked at by all of the groups, with links made between words such as *prefer* and *preference, extract* and *excerpt, illustrate and illustrator*. There might be discussion about the ways in which prefixes or suffixes can be used to modify words, so that we can take the word *enjoy* and get *enjoyable, enjoying* and *enjoyed*, or *sequence* could be turned into *consequence, sequential, sequentially* and *subsequent*. As long as examples are given in sentences, children will begin to appreciate that words are often related to each other and that we can often work out what unfamiliar words mean by looking for the roots within them.

The strategy of teaching related words together is far from original. The word lists in Fred Schonell's *Essentials in Teaching and Testing Spelling* (1957 reprint) were based upon the written material of 7 to 12 year olds. Schonell maintained that homonyms and homophones should be separated to avoid confusion and so *new* and *knew, him* and *hymn* and *there* and *their* each appear in different lists. *There* would be learned in conjunction with *where* and *here*, while *new* would be linked to *few, chew* and *dew*. Schonell (1957) argued that:

> The first essential is that children should be taught words which they use frequently in their written work and that they should not waste time learning words which they seldom use.
>
> (Schonell 1957: 12)

### Developing children's fascination with words

If the weekly spelling lists are to be used to foster an interest in vocabulary, teachers need to take time to talk about words and their derivations. This will inevitably require some research in etymological dictionaries, but the benefits will be considerable both for pupils and teachers. Common prefixes could be studied through looking at words familiar to children, and then they could be encouraged to apply their knowledge of these and examples of root words to help them to understand new words. Thus they might look at the prefix *sub-*, which means under, less, lower or inferior, in words such as *subway* and *submarine* and then try to work out the meanings of *sub-aqua, submerge, substandard* and *subtract*.

Children's fascination with words can be fostered through a variety of classroom activities. Despite criticism of the use of weekly word lists for children to memorise for tests, many teachers persist with these, sometimes citing parental pressure as a reason. However, if used imaginatively, these lists can provide a valuable learning tool. Dictionaries can be used to find alternative meanings and, sometimes, alternative spellings. The lists can provide a starting point for children to make collections of, say, homonyms and antonyms both in school and at home with the help of parents.

It is the broadening of knowledge about words which will enable children to develop their spelling abilities rather than simply the memorising of lists. Teachers often complain that children could spell the words in the test, but seem unable to do so a few days later in their written work. Perhaps if they engaged children more deeply with the words and took the time to discuss their etymology and strategies for learning how to spell them, their pupils might be better able to work out how to spell them when the test is a distant memory.

## Teaching spelling rules and spelling principles

Ask any group of English speakers to tell you a spelling rule and it is almost guaranteed that they will chorus: '*i* before *e* except after *c*'. We remember this partly because it has a short, memorable rhyme, but the rule has many exceptions including *seeing, their, weigh, sleigh, neighbour* and *being*, words which children meet frequently. The rule is better amended to take into account the exceptions, and many people prefer '*i* before *e* except after *c* when the word rhymes with *me*' (think of *chief, thief, shield* etc.), which takes into account where common exceptions can be found.

What is interesting is to ask people to name another spelling rule: they usually find this difficult. Richard Gentry (1987: 31) argued that most spelling rules were of little use and maintained that the following were the only ones worth learning:

- the rules for using full stops in abbreviations
- the rules for using apostrophes to show possession
- the rules for capitalising proper names and adjectives (e.g. The Pink Panther)
- the rules for adding suffixes (changing *y* to *I*, dropping the final silent *e*, doubling the final consonant)
- the rule that English words do not end in *v*
- the rule that *q* is followed by *u* in English spelling.

Gentry goes on to argue that we should 'Teach only the rules that apply to a large number of words, not those that have lots of exceptions' (Gentry 1987: 31). Significantly he does not include '*i* before *e* except after *c*' in his short list.

However, despite the complexity of English spelling, there are some rules or general principles which are worth looking at with children. The problem with many rules is that in order to understand them we need quite a sophisticated knowledge of linguistic terminology, and it may be that by the time we have acquired this, we will already have internalised the rules through our everyday reading and writing. For example, a principle which children begin to apply is 'double the consonant when adding -ing where verbs contain short vowels': hit becomes *hitting, bat* becomes *batting, hop* becomes *hopping* and so on. The rule is widely applicable, although there are some exceptions (benefiting), but the terminology may challenge the pupils who need to learn the rule. Of course, they should learn about consonants, vowels and verbs, but combining the three terms in one rule may over-face many children.

One solution to the problem of learning the principles of spelling is to adopt an investigative approach whereby children are asked to look at lots of examples and try to work out the principles for themselves. Their ideas can then be discussed by groups or by the class, with teachers addressing misconceptions, and rules being written as a shared writing activity. Try this yourself in the activity.

---

**Activity: Making words ending in *y* into plurals**

Look at the following and then write a rule for making words ending in *y* into plurals:

*baby – babies, lady – ladies, monkey, monkeys, day – days, hobby – hobbies, body – bodies, guy – guys, boy – boys.*

(For a possible solution, see page 226.)

---

Margaret Peters (1975: 115) maintained that a generalisation of probabilities for spelling may be developed as we become increasingly familiar with the 'look of our language in writing'. For example, we might point out similarities between and within words, perhaps beginning with a child's name. Thus, *Ian* might learn that part of his name features in tri*an*gle and Mart*ian*. Peters (1975) argued that the essence of teaching children to spell lies in teaching them how to learn letter strings. While Norma Mudd (1994) sums up her experience of teaching spelling rules thus: 'I have found that, though these rules are generally of great interest to those who are already good spellers, they need very explicit teaching to be helpful to most novice spellers' (Mudd 1994: 159). She goes on to advocate the teaching of generalisations rather than rules, with exceptions being pointed out.

## Teaching children how to learn to spell

So far, we have looked at phonics, word lists and spelling rules. We now describe a range of spelling strategies in order to demonstrate that while we may use phonic knowledge as a key strategy when we first learn to spell, as we develop our understanding of our language we are able to draw upon other tactics too. The Primary National Strategy description of what most children will learn at Year 4 is interesting here, since it is at this stage that children are not only expected to 'use knowledge of phonics, morphology and etymology to spell new and unfamiliar words', but also expected to 'develop a range of personal strategies for learning new and unfamiliar words' (DfES 2006b: 51). These personal strategies might be drawn from some of the approaches described in this section.

## Look, Say, Cover, Write, Check

Margaret Peters (1975) argues that visual perception of word form is crucial to learning how to spell. Children should be presented with words used in the course of free writing, supplemented by useful variants, and be shown how to learn them by the following routine: *LOOK* at the word, *SAY* the word aloud, *COVER* the word, *WRITE* the word from memory, and *CHECK* that the word has been written correctly. If the word is misspelled the process should be repeated.

*Look, say, cover, write, check* or *look, cover, write, check* is one of the most widely known and used strategies that teachers encourage children to use when learning spellings. In order to determine how useful it can be, and to explore some other useful strategies, it would be helpful to look at them as we attempt to learn how to spell words which often challenge even the best spellers.

---

**Activity: Testing your own spelling**

Look at the words below and decide which of them you might usually struggle to spell accurately. Better still, ask a friend to test you on the spellings before you look at them.

| | | | |
|---|---|---|---|
| supersede | accommodation | liaise | correspondence |
| embarrass | raspberry | graffiti | separate |
| Wednesday | Mediterranean | harass | idiosyncrasy |
| definitely | necessary | weird | focused |

---

## Origins of words

If, as is quite likely since the words in the activity were chosen because many people find them challenging, you made some mistakes, then you are on the way to understanding the problems children face when learning to spell. Even if you got all the spellings correct first time, it is still possible to reflect upon how you did this. Let us look at some of the words and consider which strategies we might deploy when learning them.

*Supersede* is often misspelled as *supercede* by people who do not understand its etymology. *Super* means *above* or *beyond* and *sedere* means *to sit* (in Latin – think of *sedate, sedan, sedentary* and *sediment*), so *to supersede* is *to sit above* or *replace* someone. In understanding *supersede* we can apply our knowledge to other words beginning with the prefix *super* such as *supervise* (to oversee – think of *vision, visual, visor* and *visit*), *supernatural* and *superman*. In using our knowledge of word derivations, we are using a *cognitive approach to spelling*. We might also use this approach to help us to spell *definitely*, which is often misspelled as *definately*. However, if we know that the word is derived from *finite*, it is much more likely that we will spell it with an *i* rather than an *a*.

### Mnemonics and overarticulation

For some words, we may know or devise *mnemonics* to help us to remember how to spell the tricky parts. For example:

- I should be embarrassed if I put two *r*'s in harassed.
- Separate has a rat in it (sep *a rat* e).
- Accommodation has double beds (to remember the double *c* and double *m*).
- I liaise whenever I can (to help us remember to put an *i* after the *a* in liaise).
- It is necessary to have one collar and two sleeves (to help us remember that necessary has one *c* and two *s*'s).

For some words with silent letters, we may *overarticulate* by sounding the silent letters in our heads. Just think how you remember to spell *Wednesday* and you will understand what is meant by this term. We may do the same thing for *raspberry*, *February*, *gnome* and *pneumatic*.

### Phonic knowledge

The above strategies are useful both when learning the tricky parts of words and in internalising their spellings, but when we reflect on the other strategies we bring to bear, we can see that phonic knowledge is also vital. However, once we have acquired sufficient phonic understanding to cope with simple words, we need to develop strategies to help us with the more complicated. Central to learning such words is an ability to identify the parts of words which we need to pay particular attention to, such as the double letters in *accommodation*. Our phonic knowledge will help us with the rest. It may, therefore, be a useful strategy when presenting children with spellings to learn to begin by giving them a test, so that they can determine what they actually know already and what they need to learn. Providing this is done in a non-threatening way and that marks are not collected or shown to others, and that children understand the purpose of the exercise, this can be a valuable method of helping them to learn and to determine strategies for learning.

A natural development of the strategies described above is for children to investigate words themselves. While the grammar exercise books which were widely used until the 1960s seem dull and boring today, they can be a rich source of lists of similes, synonyms, homonyms, antonyms, collective nouns and so forth, which can induce a fascination for words in some readers. Such lists encourage children to think about vocabulary. They might, as one class did, devise their own collective nouns after reading and giggling over those in *The New First Aid in English* (MacIver, undated: 19–20). *A crawl of caravans* was apparently inspired by a long journey from the South of France by one pupil, while others came up with *a grumble of teachers, an irritation of younger brothers and sisters,* and *a defeat of English footballers.* In looking at the examples provided, the children explore spelling and make use of dictionaries both to look up unfamiliar words and to find new ones for their own use.

## Handwriting and spelling

Margaret Peters (1985) maintained that handwriting can be a vital factor in influen-
cing good spelling and argued that the teaching of groups of letters through joined
script reinforces the child's concept of the serial probability of letters within words.
She stated that:

> There is no question that children with swift motor control write groups of
> letters . . . in a connected form and this is the basis of knowledge about which
> letters stick together. This is the crux of spelling ability, for handwriting and
> spelling go hand in hand.
>
> (Peters 1985: 55)

Charles Cripps (1988, 1998), who based his work on Margaret Peters' research,
developed a joined handwriting scheme, *A Hand for Spelling*, in which he emphasises
the importance of free-flowing handwriting and argued that,

> Spelling is a visual skill. Good spellers look carefully at words and it is through
> this visual familiarity that they learn the possibility of certain letters occurring
> together.
>
> (Cripps 1988: 1)

## Reading and spelling

The assumption that children's spelling abilities improve as their reading improves is
challenged by Sue Carless (1989). She maintained that spelling and reading are quite
different skills and pointed out that fluent readers are sometimes very weak at
spelling:

> A fluent reader will use semantic, syntactic and graphophonic cues in order to
> read words. However, he does not need to look consciously at every word, as
> a swift reader uses only partial cues to gain meaning, and so is highly unlikely
> to use all cues available to him at once.
>
> (Carless 1989: 16)

Carless (1989) went on to quote Joyce Todd's (1982) view that 'reading allows for
intelligent guesswork from clues already on the printed page and from the child's
knowledge of language, but guesswork is of little help in spelling' (Todd 1982: 9).
Thus mistakes in reading, providing they do not alter the sense of a passage, are
relatively unimportant whilst a spelling mistake reflects the writer's skill in using
language. Uta Frith (1980) studied good readers who were poor spellers and found
that the majority of their errors were phonetic misspellings caused by a lack of close
attention to the text 'in order to assimilate serial probability' (as described by Carless
1989: 17).

Although Carless (1989) conceded that reading must have some influence upon
spelling, she argued that spelling cannot be 'caught' through reading and writing
activities alone and must, therefore, have a place in the primary school curriculum.

## Finding out what children know about spelling

The activities described in this section are designed to enable teachers to find out what the children know about spelling, and in particular about their level of phonic understanding. For example:

- Do they understand that phonemes can be represented by graphemes?
- Are they aware that some phonemes can be represented by many different graphemes and that some graphemes can represent several different phonemes?
- Can they build words using logical groups of graphemes?

Try the following, but be prepared to vary strategies as you discover the ability levels of the children with whom you are working.

### *Words containing 'ea'*

Make a set of cards with words containing the *ea* digraph (see Waugh et al. 1999: 152). Include words such as *bread, idea, break* and *early* as well as several in which *ea* makes an *ee* sound such as *each, please, treat* and *bean.*

- Ask the children which sound the letters *ea* make. Talk about the most common sound made by the digraph, but encourage them to discover that *ea* often makes other sounds, especially as in *bread, dead, head* and *dread.* You might also talk about *read* and *lead* which can both be pronounced in different ways.
- Cut out the *ea* words and ask the children to sort them according to the phoneme which *ea* represents in each.
- Look at a piece of writing which includes *ea* words and ask the children to find them and pronounce them.
- Ask children to look at a range of texts to investigate *ea* words and to decide which are the most common sounds for *ea*. This could be linked to data collection work in mathematics and to data presentation work in ICT.

### *Grapheme cards*

Make a set of cards with common graphemes. Include both the most common representations of the forty-four phonemes, including the letters of the alphabet and common vowel and consonant digraphs, and some which occur less frequently, as well as those which have been discussed in recent spelling lessons. The cards can be used over and over again so you may wish to cover them with a clear film to protect them. They can be used in a variety of ways:

- Ask children to spread them out face up and then take turns to take one. You should play too to model the activity. Explain that they are going to make words using at least three graphemes. Continue to take turns to take graphemes until each child has three. If someone is struggling to make a word, help him or ask others for suggestions. Ask if anyone can take another grapheme and make a word with four phonemes. If children misspell words, look to see if their mistakes are phonically plausible. Show them how to spell the words correctly.

- Ask children to sort the graphemes into graphs, digraphs and trigraphs, or into vowel digraphs, consonant digraphs and consonant blends.
- Work as a group cooperatively to build as many words as possible or to make the longest word possible. When a word has been made, help the children to learn its spelling.
- Ask the children to match graphemes which represent the same phonemes, e.g. *kn* and *n*; *ch*, *k*, *ck* and *c*; *ea*, *ee* and *ie*. Ask them to tell you a word which has each grapheme in it.
- Turn all the graphemes face down and ask children to take turns to turn one over and name a word which includes that grapheme.
- Ask children to take turns to turn graphemes over and place them on the table face up. The object is to use each grapheme to build a word, e.g Sam turns over *cl* and has to name a word which includes *cl*. Pam turns over *ea* and has to put it with *cl* and suggest a word which includes *cl* and *ea*. If she cannot, ask someone else. If no one can, turn the card face down again and ask the next child to choose a different one.

---

**Activity: Using grapheme cards**

We first used the grapheme cards with trainee teachers working with groups of children in an inner city school. They were a huge success and both trainees and children soon found new and more adventurous ways of using them.

- Try to devise some ideas of your own.

---

## Classroom activities to develop good spelling

Daw et al. (1997) looked at factors associated with high standards in spelling from Reception to Year 4 and found that the following were features of those classrooms and schools where spelling standards were high:

- Displays of spelling, alphabet, key words, letter strings etc. designed to promote learning being actively used by children in their writing.
- An interest in language permeating the teaching of pupils, opportunities to discuss words being taken up constantly across the curriculum.
- Clear understanding of approaches taken by other teachers throughout the school and constant use of a few key strategies.
- Early and systematic teaching of phonics, extensive use of rhymes in early years, mastery of letter names as well as sounds, and effective early reading.
- An early but systematic move through the first stages of writing, with independence always the goal but structure always sufficient to produce coherent legible text.
- A systematic approach to covering major spelling regularities, which includes teaching and discussion, learning words and assessing progress through regular testing.

- High quality teaching with regular brief instruction sessions to class, group or individuals, to maintain an interest in spelling and a fascination with words and their meanings.
- Appropriate differentiation within a context of high expectations for all pupils.
- Teaching methods and resources deployed to encourage pupils to experiment and become independent as spellers from an early age.
- Pupils' writing marked regularly with the indication of some spelling errors as part of the feedback provided to help them to improve.
- Parents involved in helping their children learn spellings at home regularly, as well as hearing reading.

Daw et al.'s (1997) conclusions resonate with much of what has already been stated in this chapter and elsewhere in this book (see Chapter 7 on 'Teaching and learning reading'). In this section, we will explore some practical activities which might be used in the classroom, or at home by parents and children, in order to ensure high standards in spelling and to make spelling interesting and enjoyable. The age group of the children for which each activity might best be suited is deliberately not suggested, since abilities vary greatly within classes and some activities normally designed for younger children might be appropriate for older strugglers while others, usually the preserve of older pupils, may be adapted for use with very able younger pupils.

### Developing an interest in letters and words

Children can create collages of letters, make pastry letters, create patterns using groups of letters, trace letters in sand or cut letters out of newspapers to make sentences (like ransom notes). One teacher encouraged the children to add to her list of what she called *silly words* (those which were irregular) and to find others which were called *easy words*. Children can make collections of foreign words seen in shops and on television and can be encouraged to look for deliberate misspellings on house-hold products and businesses (Kwikfit, Weetabix, Betabuy etc.).

### Playing games which highlight sounds and letter strings

I-spy, rhyming games, tongue-twisters and work on alliteration all emphasise word relationships. A particularly successful and amusing activity involves children in creating spoonerisms, beginning with names (*Bavid Deckham*) and moving on to other items of interest such as football teams (*Roncaster Dovers*), and TV programmes (*Storonation Creet*). They will soon realise that some names are more difficult than others because of the presence of letter and sound combinations which do not feature in English, and that words beginning with vowels are difficult to spoonerise. However, even when the spoonerisms do not work, children will be learning some-thing about combinations of letters and initial sounds which are possible and impos-sible in English spelling.

## Using 'environmental print'

Many teachers take children on *literacy walks*, encouraging them to look at signs and symbols in the environment. Alternatively, photographs, slides and websites can be used to show the proliferation of 'literature' which exists all around us. Children can follow this up by learning spellings from the environment and discussing strategies for doing so.

## Using dictionaries and thesauruses

In successful classrooms these are readily available and children are shown how to use them. Teachers select dictionaries appropriate for their pupils, and there is always a larger and more comprehensive dictionary available for looking up words which do not feature in the children's dictionaries. Many thesauruses are suitable for use in primary classrooms and children can become so absorbed in them that they go off at tangents looking up several words as their interest grows. It is important that children understand alphabetical order as early as possible if they are to be able to use reference books successfully and without frustration (see Chapter 9 on 'Reading and writing for information').

## Helping to develop drafting techniques

For some teachers, *drafting* involves the children writing a piece of work, having it marked, and then copying it out. In classrooms where children are encouraged to develop independence in drafting and see the teacher as an audience for their writing rather than merely the marker of their work, writing tends to be more adventurous and better presented. Children need to learn how to check their work. For some, being told to do this leads to confusion, while for others it is an intrinsic part of writing which fosters careful consideration of word structures and reference skills (see Chapter 11 on 'Developing writing' for a guide to checking writing).

## Using wordprocessors and spellcheckers

The wordprocessor enables the writer to amend and adapt work easily and produces print in which children often find it easier to spot their spelling mistakes than in handwriting. Spellcheckers can be useful, but children should be encouraged to use them with caution (one does not recognise *headteacher*, and offers the peculiarly apt *heartache* as an alternative). This poem by Jerry Zar (1992) might serve as a warning and stimulate an interest in homonyms and homophones:

> I have a spelling checker.
> It came with my PC.
> It plane lee marks four my revue
> Miss steaks aye can knot sea.
>
> Eye ran this poem threw it,
> Your sure reel glad two no.
> Its vary polished inn it's weigh.
> My checker tolled me sew.

## Reducing stress in writing sessions

For some teachers, a writing session is a stressful occasion in which little time is available for sitting with children discussing their work. Often, this situation could easily be avoided. For example, the excessive use of personal spelling dictionaries tends to create a dependency culture in which children become over-reliant upon their teachers for help with every word which they do not feel completely confident of spelling correctly. Some teachers encourage this by telling children that they expect accurate work first time with no spelling mistakes. Besides being an unreasonable demand to make of young children, this also negates much of what the writing process is really like for adults as well as for children. Most adults draft important pieces of writing and try out spellings by writing them down to see if they look right. Alternatively, they continue their writing and then check spellings at the end or when they reach a natural break.

Children in classes where the spelling book rules tend, in our experience, to produce stilted and unimaginative work and actually do not spell as well as those who are encouraged to attempt spellings and then check them. For some children, the spelling dictionary provides an excuse to stop work and join the queue which inevitably follows the teacher around the room. Often, children reach the front of the queue and have forgotten which word they were going to ask for, or have not opened the book at the right page.

If one argues against the use of spelling books in this way one may be accused of devaluing spelling, but this is far from the case. In one of the National Writing Project's publications, *Responding to and Assessing Writing* (1989a), a teacher describes how she refused to help children with spellings and encouraged them to *have a go*. After some initial reluctance, the children accepted the approach and the teacher reported:

> What has surprised me most is that this approach has actually led to a marked improvement in the children's spelling. I did not realise just how well they could spell without my aid. I now feel I was holding them back and not giving them the confidence they needed to attempt their own spellings. They had more experience and knowledge than they or I had realised. It is especially significant that this improvement was seen in the majority of children, representing a wide range of abilities.
>
> (National Writing Project 1989a: 15)

It is this independence, allied to a programme of teaching spelling in a systematic way, which, we are confident, serves children best and allows teachers time to spend with children discussing writing and keeping them on task. Simple guidance can be given to children to enable them to sustain the momentum of their writing when they wish to use a word they cannot spell with confidence:

- Underline the word or circle it and check spelling later or write the word in different ways and choose the one which looks right.
- Write as much as you can and fill in details later, e.g. *b---tiful*.
- Tap out syllables quietly and write the word bit by bit, e.g. *yes-ter-day*.
- Ask someone, look at a chart or word bank, use a dictionary.

Another way in which individual children's spelling might be monitored and developed is through the use of *spelling cards*. Each child has a card which is kept on the teacher's desk or in some easily accessible place. Whenever a child has a word corrected by the teacher, or asks for help with a spelling, the word is written on the card by the teacher. The child looks carefully at the word and then returns to his or her place and tries to write the word correctly. He or she then checks that the word is written correctly and, if it is not, repeats the exercise. The cards are regularly given out to the children and they spend time looking closely at the words before being tested on them by classmates. Each child builds up a store of words which he or she uses regularly and which can be referred to whenever necessary using the *Look, say, cover, write, check* method. The words may be copied, by the children, into personal dictionaries for easy reference. This method has the advantage of being an individual approach to spelling and it does not preclude the use of other spelling lists or tests. Children can achieve success at their own levels and testing is less stressful when carried out individually rather than in a whole-class situation.

---

**Activity: Thinking about spelling**

Having read the chapter, look at the questions below and *think about your views and discuss them with a colleague.*

- How would you conduct a formal spelling lesson?
- Should invented spelling be tolerated?
- When should spelling instruction begin?
- Which spelling rules should be taught?
- What is the purpose of spelling tests?
- How can phonics be taught as a basis for spelling?
- Should teachers correct every mistake in a piece of work which is to be displayed?

---

## The importance of spelling

US President Andrew Jackson, a poor speller, maintained: 'It's a damn poor mind that can think of only one way to spell a word!' While it may be true that it requires intelligence to apply a range of strategies to the problem of accurately spelling words in a language full of irregularities and exceptions, it is, nevertheless, important that children leave school able to spell accurately, and knowing strategies for attempting those words which challenge them. Even though many people have access to a wordprocessor with a spellchecker, it is still, as we have seen, quite possible to mis-spell words, particularly in a language so rich in homonyms and homophones.

This chapter has explored a range of strategies for developing children's spelling. The principal approach promoted by the Primary National Strategy is the use of phonic knowledge, and this is central to teaching and learning spelling. However, this approach needs to be allied to others as children develop as writers if they are to succeed. In many professions, application forms which include spelling errors are routinely discarded. An inability to spell accurately can, then, be both education-ally and financially costly.

## Key points

- The English spelling system is problematical because of the number of phonic irregularities, but this should not prevent teachers from making extensive use of phonics when teaching spelling.
- There are many strategies which can be used to teach and learn spelling. A key objective for teachers is to arm children with a range of strategies which will enable them to learn spellings independently.
- Teachers need to develop the sensitivity to know when it is important to use errors as teaching tools and when to show tolerance of mistakes which, if high-lighted, might deter future attempts at writing.

---

**A spelling rule for plurals of words ending in *y* (see page 216)**

If the word ends with a consonant before the *y*, take off the *y* and add -*ies*. If the word has a vowel before the *y*, add *s*. The key to remembering this is the word *key*, which we all know has the plural *keys*, and not *kies*!

---

## Further reading

Montgomery, D. (1997) *Spelling: Remedial strategies*. London: Cassell.
Topping, K. (2001) *Thinking Reading Writing*. London: Continuum, Part 4.

# 13 Using ICT to enhance the teaching of English

*Richard English*

## Purpose of this chapter

This chapter aims to:

- Define what is meant by ICT.
- Put forward arguments for using ICT.
- Describe specific ways of using ICT in the teaching of English.

Information and communications technology (ICT) is an essential component of our everyday lives and is used by most of us both at work and in leisure activities. It also features strongly in the world of education, with most primary schools now generously equipped with computers, interactive whiteboards and an increasingly widening range of other technological gadgetry. With all of this now at their finger-tips and with the need to prepare young people for a technology-rich world, the challenge for schools and teachers is to ensure that the potential offered by ICT is fully realised, so as to enhance teaching and learning, not only with regard to the English curriculum but also in all aspects of primary education. The aim of this chapter is to get you started on the road to making the best possible use of ICT in your English teaching. The chapter ends with a list of useful online resources.

## What do we mean by 'ICT'?

ICT stands for 'information and communications technology', and many people interpret ICT in a narrow way, considering it to be simply synonymous with 'computers'. Yes, computers do represent one aspect of ICT, but it is far more wide-ranging than this. Some aspects of ICT have been commonplace for many years, for example audio-cassette and CD players, radios, televisions, DVD players, electronic calculators, overhead projectors, telephones, fax machines and photo-copiers. More recent additions include digital cameras, video cameras and mobile phones. Even our understanding of the word 'computer' now includes variants such as laptops, notebooks, handhelds and tablet PCs, as well as an increasing range of peripheral equipment that can be connected to a computer, notably digital projectors and interactive whiteboards. Now add to this the high-speed internet access found in most schools and we have an environment for children which is rich in technology in the broadest sense. Not all of these things are available in every primary school, but if most of them exist only on your wish list then we suggest you ask your headteacher what has happened to your school's share of the millions of pounds which the government has pumped into funding ICT in recent years. By the spring of 2004 63 per cent of primary schools were equipped with at least one interactive whiteboard and 26 per cent had three or more (DfES 2004d). Since this survey was carried out, the current percentages have certainly grown much higher. A recent show of hands among a group of eighty primary PGCE students indicated that only a handful did not have access to an interactive whiteboard during their previous teaching practice.

Although high-quality ICT resources are becoming increasingly commonplace in primary schools, not all teachers are enthusiastic about them. The possible reasons include lack of self-confidence in the use of ICT and limited awareness of what is possible. Other teachers remain unconvinced that ICT has the potential to transform teaching and learning. The next section provides a persuasive argument for utilising ICT in all aspects of your work in primary schools, with a particular emphasis on teaching English. At every stage, you can reap the benefits offered by ICT, from preparation and planning, to teaching and learning in the classroom, through to assessment, recording and reporting to parents.

---

**Activity: Using ICT in the classroom**

- Make a list of reasons why you ought to be using ICT in your teaching, with a particular emphasis on the teaching of English.
- What are the potential benefits to you?
- What are the potential benefits to your pupils?
- Are there any particular individuals or groups of pupils who would benefit?

When you have answered these questions, compare what you have written with the discussion presented in the next section.

---

## Why use ICT?

The first point to make justifying the use of ICT relates to the nature of the high-tech world in which we live. Just think of the wealth of electronic gadgetry that we have in our homes and carry around in our pockets, as well as the technology we encounter when we go through the supermarket checkout, fill the car with petrol, withdraw money from the bank, pay for a meal out or a round of drinks in the pub, have the electricity meter read, or borrow a book or CD from the library. At work there are very few occupations that do not involve the use of ICT in some form. We need to prepare pupils to be citizens in a technology-rich world, from the earliest stages of their schooling. This alone should be sufficient justification for ensuring that all pupils experience ICT in a positive way, not just in English but in all areas of the curriculum.

Computers are fast and powerful and can therefore carry out low-level mechanical chores very efficiently, thus freeing up time for the user to spend on higher-level skills. One example is when a teacher employs a spreadsheet to analyse pupils' marks; another is when a pupil uses a wordprocessor to cut and paste text, or to check spellings or to count the number of words in a document. The computer does the donkey work so that the user can concentrate on things such as analysis and interpretation in the case of the teacher, and creative writing in the case of the pupil. Computers can also store and retrieve huge quantities of information, both locally, for example using hard disks, CDs and memory sticks, and also remotely via networks, intranets and the internet. Consequently, teachers, pupils and parents are able to access rich and varied resources that were simply not available a few years ago, all at the click of a few buttons.

Technology allows the information to be presented more accurately and more attractively than by traditional means so that it engages the attention of the user. Why rely on a scruffy, hurriedly written piece of text on the blackboard when you can produce a more effective visual aid with a computer? Technology is also inclusive, in that the information can be presented in a variety of ways according to the size of the audience and the special needs of particular individuals. Another feature of the information being presented is that it can comprise various media such as text, graphics, sounds, animations and video: hence the expression *multimedia*. This, together with the often interactive nature of the materials being presented, captures the interest of the user and motivates him or her to want to learn.

### Benefits of ICT for pupils

It would be easy to get into a discussion of learning theories, behaviourism, constructivism, Piaget and other psychologists, but instead let us consider one simple fact: children learn what they choose to learn. We cannot force pupils to learn, and this requires us to inspire, to motivate, to open doors and to make children want to learn. ICT can play a key part in achieving this. Many of us have anecdotal evidence of how children are motivated by ICT, and there is a growing body of research literature to support these beliefs (Becta 2003a). This evidence suggests that ICT can have a positive impact on pupils' levels of concentration, self-confidence, self-esteem, independence and behaviour. There are particular benefits for those who are reluctant learners or have special educational needs. When using ICT the pupil is required to employ different skills from those needed when using pens, pencils, sheets of writing paper, dictionaries and other paper-based materials. These pupils usually adapt to the ICT approach more readily than the traditional one and their much-needed success raises their self-esteem (Becta 2003a). In terms of presentation, their story or poem will look just as impressive as those produced by the rest of the class, and can be displayed on the wall along with everyone else's. One specific target group that could benefit from these sort of ICT approaches is boys, who typically are reluctant to engage in the writing process or read fiction (Becta 2003a).

ICT can provide access to the curriculum for children with a special educational need of a physical nature, for example those with poor motor-control who find it difficult to produce legible work by hand can use a keyboard or other input device. Speech-recognition software means that those with severe physical disabilities can simply speak and see their words appearing on the screen. Visually impaired pupils can increase the font size or zoom factor when viewing text on the screen, and dyslexic pupils can change the font and background colours to improve their ability to read text accurately.

ICT can benefit pupils with special educational needs in other ways. First, computer-based learning materials often break down the skills and content being taught into small, achievable steps, thus allowing the learner to demonstrate measurable progress. Second, there are major advantages in terms of the learning taking place 'in private'. The child can work at his or her own pace without fear of appearing slow or holding back the rest of the class. If a mistake is made then the child does not have to worry about looking foolish in front of everyone else and he or she can simply have another go, usually after being given additional hints or clues by the computer. The computer can never replace good quality interaction with an effective teacher, but the instant, impartial feedback it offers is something that the teacher is not always able to match.

Research has also shown that with computer-based activities, pupils are more likely to be creative, experiment and take risks, which is precisely what we want them to do, for example when engaging in the creative writing process (see Becta 2003b).

### Benefits of ICT for teachers

So ICT has got a lot to offer for the pupils, but what is in it for you? Well, if your pupils are benefiting in the ways described above then clearly it is going to assist your role as an effective teacher, but there are some additional specific benefits to be aware of. The widespread availability of ICT, particularly the internet, means that you now have easy access to a huge bank of ready-made resources. Why reinvent the wheel when someone else has already created that lesson plan, activity sheet, PowerPoint presentation, instructional text or set of flashcards that you want to use? The government's Standards Site provides an interactive planning tool and a range of resources and support materials which can be used in the teaching of English (http://www.standards.dfes.gov.uk). The materials on the Standards Site represent just a small proportion of what is available on the internet, which offers the potential to save you a great deal of time, effort and head-scratching in trying to come up with stimulating ideas to use in the classroom. If you have not started to make use of the internet in this way then you really do not know what you are missing out on, so why not investigate some of the websites listed at the end of this chapter.

ICT tools, such as wordprocessors, desktop publishing packages and presentation software, make creating your own attractive, stimulating resources a straightforward and satisfying task. You can create professional-looking printed materials as well as visual aids to display on a computer screen or project onto the wall, and because these are stored electronically it means that you can edit and add to them for future use. You can share them with colleagues in your own school, and by encouraging this sort of sharing culture, ultimately everyone benefits. Making use of shared folders on the school's computer network is an excellent way of promoting this way of working. The more that staff put in to it, the more they get out of it, both literally and metaphorically.

In summary then, from the teacher's perspective, ICT enables you to

- access or create stimulating resources
- distribute or display them attractively to individuals, groups and whole classes of pupils
- capture the interest of your pupils and motivate them to want to learn

- address the issue of inclusion by providing all pupils with access to the curriculum
- share your resources with colleagues
- carry out many of your administrative tasks more effectively and efficiently.

There are many things that are done better with ICT than without it and this is demonstrated in the rest of this chapter, which provides you with a range of tips, ideas and advice when using ICT in your English teaching.

## Using ICT in the teaching of English

Having read the previous section, you should be aware of the potential for utilising ICT. The range of possibilities is vast and so it is helpful to think in terms of broad categories of use. We could distinguish between those occasions when it is the teacher who is using the ICT and those when it is the pupils who are using it. Alternatively, we could think in terms of *where* the ICT is being used, and identify activities which take place in the classroom, or in the computer suite, or at home as part of homework tasks. In this chapter, a classification based on the twelve literacy strands identified in the *Primary Framework for Literacy and Mathematics* (DfES 2006b) will be used. These strands are:

1  Speaking
2  Listening and responding
3  Group discussion and interaction
4  Drama
5  Word recognition: decoding (reading) and encoding (spelling)
6  Word structure and spelling
7  Understanding and interpreting texts
8  Engaging and responding to texts
9  Creating and shaping texts
10  Text structure and organisation
11  Sentence structure and punctuation
12  Presentation.

---

**Activity: Investigating the twelve literacy strands**

- If you do not know what the broad objectives contained within each of the twelve strands are, find out by reading the appropriate sections of the *Primary Framework for Literacy and Mathematics* (also available online at http://www.standards.dfes.gov.uk/primary/literacy/).
- For each of the twelve strands, try to identify at least one way in which ICT could be utilised to enhance that aspect of the English curriculum. It could involve you using ICT with the whole class or a group of pupils, or it could be the pupils who are using the ICT, either in the classroom, the computer suite or at home.

When you have done this, compare your ideas with the suggestions presented below.

---

The following suggestions are not intended to be a definitive or complete list of the ways in which ICT can be used in the teaching of English. A complete book could be written on this theme and still it would not cover all of the possibilities. Instead, the suggested activities and approaches are designed to stimulate your thoughts about how to start utilising ICT in your English teaching, and also provide an opportunity to discuss some key issues related to the use of ICT. The suggestions will be presented using the twelve literacy strands, although when the boundaries between the strands are blurred, two or more strands are grouped together to form a single heading.

## 1 Speaking

## 2 Listening and responding

By the time children leave primary school we expect them to be able to 'speak competently and creatively for different purposes and audiences' and 'explain and comment on speakers' use of language' (DfES 2006b: 15). For the vast majority of the time these skills can be developed without the need for ICT resources. However, there is the potential for using radio broadcasts, audio-cassettes and compact discs to model the spoken word for children of all ages. With young children this might be stories, poems and nursery rhymes, whereas with older children this could be extended to include plays. You could make use of television broadcasts, video-cassettes and DVDs which contain a visual as well as an audio dimension. There is the potential for working with the whole class, with a small group or for pupils to work independently of the teacher either individually or in pairs. If only some of the pupils are engaged in these activities, it is important to ensure that the audio is not a distraction to the rest of the class. Headphones are an almost essential resource and you can use a 'splitter' device to allow two or more pairs to be connected to the same source.

You and your pupils could also use audio recording facilities which are available through computers, audio-cassette players and various digital recording devices (for example digital voice recorders as well as many mp3 players). Pupils' speaking activities could be recorded, played back and used as the basis of discussion.

Another category of ICT resources which could be used to enhance these two strands of your English teaching, particularly with children at Foundation Stage and Key Stage 1, is multimedia talking books. These incorporate text, pictures, animations, the spoken word and music in an eye-catching way which will capture the interest of children. They have been available on CD-ROM for a number of years, and are now increasingly available on the internet. Try to be creative in the ways that you use these resources by not thinking solely in terms of individual pupils using them at the computer as a way of filling a few spare moments. Yes, these resources were designed primarily to be used by pupils, but you could also use them with the whole class or a focus group to support speaking, listening and responding activities.

### 3 Group discussion and interaction

As with the first two strands discussed, much of the work here can be done without utilising ICT. However, it does provide an excellent opportunity to make use of the classroom computer which sadly lies redundant for long periods of a typical day. In English, and indeed in many other curriculum areas, there will be occasions when you arrange your pupils into groups and ask them to discuss a particular issue, with one person taking on the role of scribe and another feeding back to the whole class. There are two potential problems with this much-used approach. First, it is difficult for all pupils in the group to read what the scribe is writing because this is being done by hand, and for some members of the group it is upside down. Second, when the written work is submitted, there is the danger of associating the handwritten sheet more with the individual who has produced it than with the group collectively. There is a simple way to overcome both problems: use the computer. The scribe becomes the typist, everyone in the group can see the text clearly on the screen (increase the font size if necessary), and the printed product can be genuinely associated with the group rather than the individual who typed it. If you have only one computer then clearly only one group can work in this way on any given occasion, but in the long term you can ensure that all pupils experience this approach.

### 4 Drama

This strand requires pupils not only to be involved in role-play and the creation of drama, but also to 'share and evaluate ideas and understanding through drama' (DfES 2006b: 16). Television broadcasts, video-cassettes, DVDs and multimedia content on the internet can all be used to model good practice (and bad!) in drama and also provide opportunities for discussion and evaluation. Another way of utilising ICT is to use a video camcorder to record pupils' own performances, with a view to evaluating and improving their own work.

### 5 Word recognition (reading and spelling)

### 6 Word structure and spelling

These two key strands require pupils to be able to read fluently and spell words accurately, and teachers employ a variety of approaches to achieve this. A frequently used approach is to present a text for pupils to read, often working with the whole class. Typically, the text takes the form of a big book, a poster, a photocopied sheet, or the teacher's own handwriting on a blackboard, whiteboard or flipchart. If you have access to an interactive whiteboard (or just a digital projector but without an interactive whiteboard), this opens up a new range of possibilities in presenting electronic texts for pupils to read and discuss. A simple way to get started is to type your text into a wordprocessor or presentation software. This ICT approach offers a number of benefits:

- A handwritten text is usually rubbed out when you have finished with it and so the time spent writing it could be considered as time wasted, particularly since you will have to write it all out again the next time you want to use it. With an electronic text, however, once it has been created it can be used again and again. This may sound obvious, but it will save you a lot of time in the long run.

- Not only are electronic texts available to use again, but also you can edit them before you use them each time. So if you want to change some of the words or phrases in the text in order to emphasise a particular point, you can do this very easily and quickly.
- Electronic texts can be shared with colleagues in school and indeed beyond your own school, via the internet. The most arduous aspect of using electronic texts is creating them in the first place, so why not share the workload. If every member of staff in a typical primary school created four or five electronic texts each term, by the end of the year the school would have built up a resource bank of over one hundred texts which everyone could have access to. The easiest way is to store them in a shared folder on the school's computer network.
- You can interact with electronic texts more effectively than with texts presented in a traditional way. Even if you do not have all the coloured pens and highlighters afforded by an interactive whiteboard, you can use the standard features of most wordprocessors. These will allow you to highlight text, change the text colour of particular words or phrases, insert additional or alternative text, separate a block of text into paragraphs, and so on. The benefit of an interactive whiteboard is that you can do all of these things at the board itself, but even without one you can still interact with the text effectively via the computer keyboard.

An alternative to creating your own texts is to make use of those that have been created by other people and made available on the internet. Some require a live internet connection, whilst others can be downloaded for use later. As with your own electronic texts, make sure you share your internet discoveries with your colleagues so that the school as a whole benefits, not just you. Several websites providing ready-made texts are listed at the end of this chapter.

Another source of texts is the literacy section of the DfES Standards Site. The government has made a number of valuable resource packs available, including electronic texts which can be used to develop pupils' reading skills. One example is *Grammar for Writing* (DfES 2000) which comprises a book and a CD-ROM full of electronic resources. Do not worry if you cannot find the CD-ROM in your school, as its contents and much more besides can be accessed via the Standards Site and also in the *Primary Framework for Literacy and Mathematics* DVD (DfES 2006d).

The use of audio-cassettes, compact discs and multimedia talking books has already been mentioned in relation to the development of pupils' speaking and listening skills. These can also be used to support the development of reading. In the case of audio-cassettes and compact discs, it is essential that the publisher has provided a printed version of the audio book so that pupils can follow the text whilst listening to it. Computer-based multimedia talking books typically display the text on the screen whilst the story or poem is being read by the narrator. A helpful feature of many such talking books is that individual words are highlighted as they are being spoken. The use of these resources is not, on its own, going to teach pupils to read fluently, but they do provide another string to your bow in your attempts to address this key aspect of literacy.

As with reading, the teaching of spelling requires a multipronged approach, and one aspect of this could be the use of computer-based 'drill and practice' software. Rather like junk food, there is a lot of this about and if consumed in large doses it is not good for you or your pupils. But in small doses, as part of a balanced diet of approaches to the teaching of spelling, there is nothing wrong with it. It does offer many of the benefits to individual learners identified earlier in this chapter, but what we do not want is pupils spending lengthy periods of time at the computer using these resources. Typically a word appears on the screen for a set time, possibly accompanied by a visual cue, the word is read out by the computer, then it disappears and the pupil has to type the word he or she has just seen and heard. The word lists are usually fully customisable and there is often a management system which enables the teacher to track the performance of individual pupils (for strategies for learning spellings, see Chapter 12).

Whilst on the theme of spelling, this is an appropriate point to discuss the use of spellcheckers by pupils when they are using a wordprocessor, but before that, there are a couple of questions for you to think about.

---

**Activity: Using a spellchecker**

- To what extent do you use the spellchecker when wordprocessing?
- Do you think that using a spellchecker has had a positive or a negative effect on your ability to spell words accurately? Give reasons for your answer.

---

Spellcheckers are to literacy what electronic calculators are to numeracy: the issues surrounding their use are rather controversial. Some teachers will not allow pupils to touch an electronic calculator until they have developed the ability to recall number facts and have sound mental skills. Similarly, there are teachers who believe that using a spellchecker will make pupils lazy and have an adverse effect on their ability to spell accurately. Some would even talk in terms of banning the use of both calculators and spellcheckers in primary schools. However well intentioned these views might be, these ICT tools are part of our everyday lives and so instead of 'protecting' pupils from them, we should be teaching pupils to make the best possible use of them. Yes, calculators should not be used as a prop for simple arithmetic and similarly spellcheckers should not be seen as a substitute for learning to spell. In fact, you have to be quite good at spelling and reading in order to use a spellchecker effectively. Typically, if you have misspelled a word the spellchecker will offer a list of alternatives. Unless your initial attempt is reasonably close to the correct spelling, you are unlikely to be offered sensible alternatives, and even if you are, you have to be able to make sense of what is on offer. You and your pupils also have to be aware of the limitations of spellcheckers. First, you may correctly spell a word but simply use the wrong one, for example 'After I had eaten my super I went straight to bed.' A spellchecker will not spot that it should be 'supper', not 'super' (did you spot the mistake?). Second, the spellchecker does not recognise some perfectly acceptable words. Two common examples that you may already have come across are 'headteacher' and 'numeracy'. These issues need to be discussed with pupils, otherwise they are not going to make efficient use of a valuable tool (see Chapter 12 for a poem which illustrates the limitations of spellcheckers).

What conclusion did you reach when answering the questions posed above? What effect has using a spellchecker had on your spelling? Many people believe that spell-checkers improve your ability to spell accurately. Sometimes words that used to be spelt incorrectly may now present no problems at all, as a result of being constantly reminded of errors by the spellchecker.

### 7 Understanding and interpreting texts

### 8 Engaging and responding to texts

Earlier in this chapter, we mentioned the use of electronic texts in the teaching of reading. Electronic texts can also be used to address these two strands. There is no need to repeat the points made earlier, so instead this section will be used as an opportunity to consider what we mean by 'texts'.

---

**Activity: Considering texts**

- What do you understand by the term 'texts' as used in the two strands identified above?
- List all the things that could be included in the primary curriculum as constituting 'texts'.

---

Most people consider 'texts' to mean the printed word in the form of books, magazines, newspapers and newsletters, and these media are the ones that pupils in primary schools spend the vast majority of their time working with in literacy lessons and the wider curriculum. However, in our gadget-filled, high-tech world an increasing proportion of the 'texts' we encounter is not in the traditional mould, for example, interactive reference CD-ROMs and DVDs, web pages, email messages and mobile phone text messages. Using a computer-based multimedia encyclopedia is a very different experience from using the traditional paper-based equivalent in the school library. Both reference sources have a part to play in the education of primary school pupils, but their changing patterns of use in our everyday lives is not reflected in the approaches used by most teachers. New 'texts' require new skills and so it is essential that these are integrated into the primary curriculum, otherwise pupils will not be equipped to fully understand and effectively engage with them. When pupils are provided with opportunities to retrieve, select, describe and interpret information from texts, these should include the non-traditional varieties. The same is true when pupils are analysing the content, structure and organisation of texts or commenting on the author's use of language. By incorporating these texts into your English teaching you will provide a more varied and richer experience for your pupils and one that will better equip them for the world in which they live.

**9  Creating and shaping texts**

**10  Text structure and organisation**

**11  Sentence structure and punctuation**

**12  Presentation**

Collectively, these four strands require pupils to be able to write accurately, creatively and coherently for different purposes and audiences. When utilising ICT, the obvious example is pupils using a wordprocessor to create texts. There is a huge potential here, but despite wordprocessors being widely available, many teachers exploit them in only a very limited way. Effective writing comprises several stages such as planning, drafting, evaluating, redrafting and editing, culminating in the production of the finished text. Often, when it comes to creating texts with a wordprocessor, pupils do all but the final stage away from the computer. The planning, drafting and editing are done by hand on paper and then the teacher sends the pupils off to the computer to type neat copies. This is not what wordprocessing is all about. Genuine wordprocessing requires a variety of skills which allow the writer to create a text almost from scratch whilst sitting at the computer. So if all you do is ask your pupils to type up neat copies, do not make the mistake of thinking that you are teaching them how to wordprocess. With computer suites now a common feature in primary schools, there should be plenty of opportunities to provide pupils with sustained periods of time to create texts using ICT, from the planning stage through to final publication or printing, thus enabling pupils to do some genuine wordprocessing. In order to make the best possible use of a wordprocessor, pupils must be taught the necessary skills. Do not assume all pupils will pick up the keyboard skills for themselves. You will need to teach them how to cut, copy and paste text, how to change font types and sizes, how to use tab-stops, how to use the spellchecker, and how to insert tables and graphics, to name just a few. One could argue that teaching wordprocessing skills is as important as, if not more important than, teaching handwriting skills.

When teaching pupils how to use a wordprocessor effectively, ensure that they are using a tool which is suited to their requirements. Typical industry-standard wordprocessing packages such as Microsoft Word may well be suitable for pupils at upper Key Stage 2, but younger children need to be using something which is more child-friendly. There are several widely used packages, for example *Clicker, RM Talking First Word* and *TextEase*. Two common features are built-in word lists and the ability to speak the text that has been typed.

The word lists are usually organised alphabetically, rather like a dictionary, and/or under topic headings such as 'The Romans', 'People who help us', 'The Water Cycle', and so on. Completely new word lists can be created by the teacher and it is usually possible to edit the existing lists. By offering this facility to pupils, we are giving them a greater degree of independence when engaging in the writing process and reducing the amount of time they spend with their hands up, waiting to ask questions such as 'How do you spell . . .?' and 'What's the word that you use when . . .?' Teachers have been giving pupils this sort of independence for years by providing each one with a small exercise book, with a page allocated to each letter of the alphabet, and recording unfamiliar words in the book as they arise during the day. The built-in word lists can be thought of as a modern-day equivalent of the traditional handwritten approach.

How about the digitised speech facility offered by many of these child-friendly wordprocessors? The temptation is to think that it is little more than a gimmick, designed to amuse and interest the pupils, especially when you discover that the first thing that they do is type in all the rude words they know, just so they can hear them being spoken by the computer! This is similar to children looking up rude words when they are given a dictionary to use. We do not prevent pupils using dictionaries, so we should not banish the digitised speech facility on the basis of children's natural curiosity. In fact, it can be of great value if used carefully. First, children will be motivated to write if they know that the computer will read the work back to them. Second, it provides a proofing tool to complement the spell-checker. Earlier, we saw that a spellchecker will not identify a correctly spelt but incorrectly used word, as in the sentence 'After I had eaten my super I went straight to bed.' A child hearing that sentence being read is likely to spot the mistake and therefore be able to correct it before the teacher needs to. Third, if children listen to their writing, rather than just reading it, it will help them to evaluate its content and structure and thus make improvements. Finally, digitised speech helps to reinforce the links between writing, reading, speaking and listening. We are not suggesting that what the pupils hear on the computer should be held up as a good model of how to speak, but it can at least make a contribution to the breaking down of the dividing barriers that sometimes exist between the different aspects of literacy teaching.

Something which teachers do for pupils of all ages is model the writing process, typically by writing on a blackboard or whiteboard. One problem is that you have to spend large amounts of time facing the board rather than your pupils, reducing the potential for effective interaction and increasing the potential for misbehaviour. Another problem is that the editing and revision process which takes place as a result of your discussions with the pupils creates an untidy text which is littered with crossings out and insertions. Both of these issues can be resolved by using a wordprocessor to model the writing process. You can position yourself so that you can use the computer whilst facing the class, with the keyboard on your lap if necessary. Additionally, by using a wireless keyboard, you do not have to be close to the computer, you avoid the hazard of trailing cables, and you can hand the key-board over to a pupil to contribute to the writing of the text. 'Yes,' you are probably saying, 'but isn't it important that we model handwriting as well?' Yes indeed, but handwriting is not the main focus here and there will be many other occasions when it is and when you will choose not to use ICT. 'But isn't it important that pupils see all the crossing out and insertions so that they can appreciate the evolu-tionary stages through which the text has passed?' If that is something that you feel strongly about, then all you have to do is save the text at frequent intervals, using a different name each time. You can then display the text on the screen at any given stage in its development by simply opening the appropriate file.

Earlier in this chapter the issue of what we mean by 'texts' was discussed and that same issue has implications here. Assuming that 'texts' means more than simply paper-based materials, you should be comfortable with the proposal that 'writing' should not be restricted to creating traditional texts. In other words, we should be providing pupils with opportunities to author all of the 'texts' which they experience as end-users. We would not dream of teaching pupils how to read without also teaching them how to write, because each one assists the development of the other. This is equally true of non-traditional texts. So pupils should not only be digesting and interacting with web pages and multimedia presentations, but also be producing such materials themselves. Only by doing this, and having considered issues such as purpose, audience, content and structure, will pupils fully develop an understanding of power and potential of these new channels of communication. Also, because writing these sort of materials requires different skills from those needed to produce a traditional piece of text, you might find that pupils who find writing a challenge or a chore are more likely to be motivated and succeed when given the opportunity to create digital materials.

## The role of ICT in teaching English

Having read this chapter, it is hoped that you will have at least started to appreciate the role that ICT can play in the teaching of English. It can be used by you to support your teaching and by your pupils to enhance their learning across all of the strands in the Primary Framework for Literacy. Within the constraints of a single chapter there is a limit to the issues that can be discussed and the advice that can be offered, but you should be beginning to realise that by embracing ICT you can work more efficiently, more effectively, motivate your pupils, and provide a curriculum which reflects the world in which they will live as adults.

## Key points

- ICT incorporates a wide range of technology, not just computers.
- ICT offers benefits to teachers and pupils in the teaching and learning of English.
- There is much potential for utilising ICT across all twelve literacy strands in the *Primary Framework for Literacy and Mathematics* (DfES 2006b).
- In the teaching of English the term 'texts' must be interpreted as meaning more than simply paper-based materials.
- Electronic texts which might incorporate multimedia can be utilised to enhance the work on speaking, listening, reading and drama.
- The term 'writing' must be interpreted more broadly so that it provides opportunities for pupils to create electronic materials such as web pages and interactive multimedia.
- Computer-based activities can contribute to the development of pupils' spelling skills.
- Sufficient emphasis should be given to the development of wordprocessing skills so as to reflect its importance in everyday life.

## Further reading

DfES (2004d) *The ICT in Schools Survey 2004*. London: DfES. Available at http://partners. becta.org.uk

## Useful websites: general

The literacy section of the Standards Site can be found at http://www.standards.dfes.gov.uk/
   primary/literacy/
The Becta Schools website can be found at http://schools.becta.org.uk/. Click on the
   'Curriculum' link and then on 'English'. Here you will find lots of useful advice on how to
   utilise ICT in your teaching.

## Useful websites: online texts

Big books at the MAPE website – http://www.mape.org.uk/activities/bigbooks/index.htm
Children's storybooks online – http://www.magickeys.com/books/
Giggle poetry – http://www.gigglepoetry.com/
Google book search – http://books.google.co.uk/
Online literature library – http://www.literature.org/
Page by page books – http://www.pagebypagebooks.com/
Project Gutenberg – http://www.gutenberg.org/
Sebastian Swan big books – http://www.sebastianswan.org.uk/
Stories from the web – http://www.storiesfromtheweb.org/

## Useful websites: ICT tools

An example of 'drill and practice' software for spelling is *Starspell*. Further details can be
   found at http://www.fishermarriott.com/
Another example is *Wordshark*, details of which can be found at http://www.wordshark.co.uk/
Information about *Clicker* can be found at http://www.cricksoft.com/
Information about *RM Talking First Word* can be found at http://www.rm.com/
Information about *Textease* can be found at http://www.softease.com/

# 14 Planning for English

## Purpose of this chapter

This chapter aims to:

- Show the place of the planning process in the teaching cycle.
- Describe the core principles in planning for all aspects of English.
- Discuss planning in the Foundation Stage.
- Give an example of creating links across the curriculum using a curriculum map.
- Discuss medium-term planning or schemes of work.
- Describe how to create effective literacy lesson plans.

## The planning process

The planning process is part of a continuous teaching cycle in which observation and assessment feed into the planning of appropriate learning. This process can be summarised in the cycle illustrated in Figure 14.1.

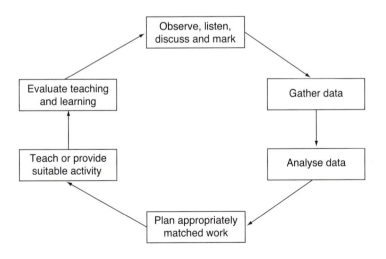

*Figure 14.1* The planning process cycle

## Core principles of teaching English

Planning must be based on a clear understanding of the generic or core business of the teaching of speaking and listening, reading, and writing. The Primary National Strategy (DfES 2004b) cites the core aspects for reading and writing. The principles contained in Table 14.1 have been adapted to incorporate the latest guidance contained in the Primary Framework for Literacy and Mathematics (DfES 2006b). The principles also show the clear interrelationship of speaking and listening, reading, and writing.

---

**Activity: Reviewing the core principles of teaching English**

Review the core aspects in Table 14.1 and with colleagues discuss the interrelationship of each. In particular consider the following:

- When beginning a unit of work on a specific genre what type of activities would you start with?
- To what extent is the core teaching of each aspect discrete?
- To what extent do the different modes of English overlap?

Following consideration of these aspects, review the section on a teaching sequence for shared reading and writing.

---

*Table 14.1* Core aspects of teaching speaking and listening, reading, and writing

| Core teaching of speaking and listening | Core teaching in reading | Core teaching in writing |
|---|---|---|
| • Teach and model the necessary skills to speak and listen for a wide range of purposes in different contexts; provide appropriate activities and opportunities to practise. <br> • Teach pupils active listening and ways of responding to show understanding and recall. <br> • Provide opportunities for interaction in pairs and groups. <br> • Support the development of speaking and listening skills for learning and for a wide range of purposes in different contexts. <br> • Explore ideas and texts through drama to develop and share ideas in varied and creative ways. | • Provide an introduction to the text (establishing a purpose for reading). <br> • Model decoding and practise it (e.g. blending phonemes). <br> • Teach comprehension strategies (e.g. summarising, rereading, having a question or focus to look for). <br> • Teach techniques to navigate texts (e.g. skimming, scanning, paragraphs and topic sentences, page layout). <br> • Provide opportunities to respond to text (e.g. likes, dislikes). <br> • Include specific reading objective(s) (e.g. to identify issues). | • Analyse texts for structural and language features and derive principles of effective writing from these models. <br> • Provide an introduction to writing (gathering content for writing, deciding on purpose, audience and form of writing). <br> • Plan and teach the writing process as appropriate (planning, drafting, revising and editing). |

*A teaching sequence for shared reading and writing*

Understanding the core teaching principles can help planning a coherent sequence for teaching in a unit of work. This is underpinned by speaking and listening skills and considerably enhanced when opportunities for talk are specifically planned for. This sequence is summarised graphically (note how speaking and listening underpin this process):

1   Reading and responding

   - introduction to reading (activating prior learning)
   - during reading, teach reading strategies: decoding and comprehension
   - responses to text
   - specific focus for reading.

2   Analysing texts

   - analysing for structural or language features
   - deriving principles of effective writing from these models.

3   Planning and writing

   - gather or transfer context, stimulate
   - discuss audience, purpose form
   - plan, draft, revise, edit.

## Planning for communication, language and literacy in the Foundation Stage

Planning for learning in the Foundation Stage will need to ensure that a range of experiences are provided that encompass all six areas of learning. Long-term plans provide an overview of the coverage related to different themes across the year. These should ensure that children will not repeat similar activities in a year, provide guidance on the use of the outdoor and indoor environment and suggest a range of stimuli that relate to children's previous experiences. Specific stimulus of visits to areas that will support the children's learning can be very beneficial (such as visiting a garden centre if this is the focus for learning). Also providing first-hand experiences in the setting can bring the learning alive for young children, for example by inviting visitors to talk about specific aspects and to bring a range of resources (such as inviting a fire-fighter with a range of resources, perhaps even a fire engine).

A medium-term plan involves providing an outline of activities and resources linked to the relevant stepping stones and Early Learning Goals from the Curriculum Guidance for the Foundation Stage. The Early Years Foundation Stage (EYFS) (DfES 2007), which is due to be implemented in September 2008, covers progression through areas of learning and development from 0 to 5 years, setting out under 'development matters' the progression of knowledge, skills, understanding and attitudes that children will need to attain the Early Learning Goals by the end of the Foundation Stage. Planning should be informed by ongoing assessments and should be collaborative with colleagues, parents and other agencies as appropriate. Short-term planning is often weekly where practitioners set out 'learning intentions'

Development matters

Look, listen and note

Effective practice

Planning and resourcing

*Figure 14.2* Planning and assessment cycle
Source: DfES 2006f: 15

(QCA 2001: 4) for each activity based on the stepping stones (in EYFS the identified development matters) and Early Learning Goals. The Early Years Foundation Stage emphasises the importance of planning within an ongoing cycle of observation and assessment related to common developmental patterns and planning and resourcing to provide effective learning and teaching (see Figure 14.2).

Short-term plans will set out all six areas of learning (see example in Figure 14.3, adapted from Jolliffe et al. 2005).

## Curriculum maps in Key Stages 1 and 2

Planning for English should not be seen as discrete and clear links should be made across the curriculum. This can be facilitated by creating curriculum maps which can provide an overview of all areas across the curriculum that are being taught over a term. These provide helpful ways of linking subjects to provide meaningful learning experiences for pupils. An example is given in Table 14.2.

## Medium-term plans and schemes of work

The renewed Primary Framework for Literacy and Mathematics (DfES 2006b) provides guidance to show how the specified learning objectives within all twelve literacy strands may be used to plan coherent units of work. Links to a range of resources are provided with suggested timings. Many teachers will find these useful, although there is a danger of over-prescription and the resulting lack of creativity when planning lessons. However, the Primary Framework does indicate the need to be flexible (DfES 2006b) and promotes six key areas with regard to teaching literacy as follows:

# Playing Schools

## Communication, Language and Literacy: *Writing Notices*

**Objectives:**

ELG: to attempt writing for different purposes, using features of different forms such as lists, stories and instructions.

NLS:T 15 to use writing to communicate in a variety of ways, incorporating it into play and everyday classroom life.

**What you need:**

A writing table with an assortment of paper, card and pens. Example notices (see photocopiable xx.) (Later in the week, writing tasks including posters to advertise an event and lists will be introduced.) Alphabet strips. Some high frequency words displayed (e.g. come, play, go, etc.)

**What to do:**

– On the first day during whole class shared work, explain to the children that this area this will be used to write notices for the Playing Schools area and read the sample notices.

– If possible, organise for an adult to work with the children. Ask the adult to model writing a notice for the children.

– Encourage children to independently write their own notices and then to place them in appropriate places around the classroom, making use of the alphabet strips, if required and high frequency words displayed.

## Knowledge and Understanding of the World: *Make a Model*

**Objectives**

ELG Observe, find out about and identify features in the place they live and the natural world.

**What you need:**

Small world play objects consisting of buildings and figures, Clipboards and paper and pens
Copies of photocopiable xxx

**What you do:**

• Ask the children to use the small play objects to reproduce the school and tell the children to discuss with each other why they position objects in certain places.

• Using clipboards and paper and pens, encourage the children to draw their replica school. You could explain this later as a 'map'.

## Mathematical Development: *Problem Solving, Reasoning and Numeracy) Counting dinners*

**Objectives**

ELG: Give children responsibility for counting and checking as part of everyday routines

**What you need:**

Dinner register in the form of a list of names of the whole class (in an enlarged format) on a clipboard
Small board or noticeboard with three headings: School Dinners, Packed Lunches, Home, (provide a fresh sheet for each day), money tin and pretend £1 coins
Numerals 1–30 (or however many in the class) on card, card circles with smiley faces on, Blutack, number lines (1–20).

**What you do:**

• Using the Dinner register prepared, ask the children to ask different children what they are doing for lunch and mark D (for school dinner) P (for packed lunch) or H (for going home) for a selection of children in the class.

• Encourage children to count out money for the school dinners and find out how many pounds they should have in total, when each dinner costs £1 each.

• They then need to count up how many children will be doing each and select the correct number to put on the prepared board.

• To ensure that children develop one-to-one correspondence of counting, provide a number of card circles (with smiley faces on) to match next to the correct number, and ask the children to put a smiley face for each child. (Provide number lines to support.)

## Personal, Social and Emotional Development: *Making Rules*

**Objectives:**

ELG Work as part of a group or class, taking turns and sharing fairly, understanding that there needs to be agreed values and codes of behaviour for groups of people.

• Work with the children to create rule for the playing schools role play area.

## Physical Development: *Over and Under*

**Objectives**

ELG: Travel around, under, over and through balancing and climbing equipment.

**What you need:**

An obstacle course set up using a range of items.

**What you do:**

• Ask an adult to supervise and encourage children to find different ways of travelling around the course, providing support to the less confident.

• When the children have travelled around the course, ask them to help the adult draw the course they took, which the children can help annotate as appropriate, e.g. bridge, road, etc. Make linked to other 'maps' of replica schools.

## Creative Development: *Painting School*

**Objectives**

SS: Make constructions, collages, paintings, drawings and dances.

ELG: Explore colour, texture, shape, form and space in two or three dimensions.

**What you need:**

Painting materials and easels for children to 'paint a school'.
Display photographs of their school as stimulus
Junk modelling materials

**What you do:**

• Encourage the children to look carefully at the photographs and then to paint a picture of the school.

• Follow up with opportunities to use junk modelling materials to make representations of their school

*Figure 14.3* Sample Foundation Stage planning
Source: adapted from Joliffe et al. 2005

*Table 14.2* Example of a curriculum map

## Rearranged curriculum map: Year 4 Term 1

| Week | 1 2 3 4 5 6 7 | | | 8 9 10 11 12 13 14 | | |
|---|---|---|---|---|---|---|
| Geography History | History<br>What was it like for children during the Second World War?<br>*Link narrative reading/writing with making storybooks (D and T) and different audiences (ICT)* | | | Geography<br>How and where do we spend our time?<br>*Link with non-chronological report writing (English) and branching databases/handling data (maths/ICT)* | | |
| Design and technology PSHE Citizenship | Design and technology<br>Storybooks<br>*Link narrative reading/writing with making storybooks (ICT)* | | | PSHE/citizenship<br>Living in a diverse world | | |
| English | Poetry | Instructions | Narrative Second World War stories | Newspapers | Non-chronological reports | Plays |
| Science | Moving and growing | | | Habitats | | |
| Mathematics | Mathematics Framework<br>*Place value, number operations, money, measures, shape* | | | | | |
| Religious education | Celebrations | | | Celebrations – Christmas journeys<br>*Link with play writing and class orchestra (Christmas play)* | | |
| Arts and design | Portraying relationships | | | Journeys | | |
| Information technology | Within other subjects<br>Writing for different audiences<br>*Link with book making (D and T) and writing historical narrative (English)* | | | Branching databases<br>*Link with geography and maths* | | |
| Music | Salt, pepper, vinegar, mustard – exploring singing games<br>*Link with history – Opies' collection of oral playground rhymes* | | | The class orchestra – exploring arrangements<br>*Link with Christmas play, English and PE* | | |
| Physical education | Net/wall games, unit 1<br>Dance activities, unit 4 | | | Net/wall games, unit 1<br>Swimming activities and water safety unit 2: Developing and competence | | |

Source: DfES 2004b: 35

- Improving the teaching of early reading through high-quality systematic phonic work within a rich language curriculum incorporating the four strands (speaking, listening, reading, writing) that support children's vocabulary development.
- Encouraging flexibility through ensuring that teachers match the learning intentions of the lesson with appropriate content and structure, rather than adhere to a rigid lesson structure that inhibits rather than supports the learning objective.
- Structuring learning by provision of guidance for planning sequences of lessons within two-, three- or four-week units of work.
- Raising expectations in areas including for children in Early Years Foundation Stage the importance of the interrelatedness of all areas of learning; provision of key expectations for each year group; clarifying progression in key aspects of literacy and the ability to track backwards and forwards in expectations to support provision for all children; raising expectations for children's acquisition of phonics knowledge; redefining 'pace' to relate to effective learning rather than coverage of objectives.
- Making more effective use of assessment particularly using the Framework objectives and links to National Curriculum levels. Guidance is provided for where to begin specific aspects, and for assessment for learning, during and across a sequence of lessons, through methods such as key questions.
- Broadening and strengthening pedagogy and promoting a range of pedagogic approaches, including direct, inductive, experiential, enquiry and problem-solving and social or relationship approaches.

Units of work are provided for different year groups which the Primary National Strategy suggests can be distributed in different ways across the year, so that schools can make effective links between the literacy units and the rest of the curriculum. The Strategy states that in addition schools will need to decide on a linear teaching and learning progression through all the units for the word skills within reading and writing (word recognition and spelling). The units of work in each block range between two and four weeks in duration with the aim to allow for sufficient time for response in reading, covering speaking and listening objectives, oral composition, writing and constructing multimodal texts. Table 14.3 shows an example provided by the Primary National Strategy as one way of organising the Year 3 units across a school year.

### Example of a scheme of work for English

A medium-term plan or scheme of work will consist of a series of units of work together with a clear outline of teaching of discrete or continuous word-level skills such as phonics, spelling and handwriting. This is particularly important for trainees on teaching practice to ensure a coherent sequence of lessons which fits within the school's overall long-term plan. It should contain the following:

- The context: number of children, specific needs, allocated time per week, previous linked activities.
- Primary Framework for Literacy objectives.
- Outline of teaching activities.

*Table 14.3* Year 3 units of work

| Narrative Block | Unit 1 | Unit 2 | Unit 3 | Unit 4 | Unit 5 |
|---|---|---|---|---|---|
| | Stores with familiar settings (3 weeks) | Dialogue and plays (4 weeks) | Myths, legends, fables, traditional tales (4 weeks) | Adventure and mystery (4 weeks) | Authors and letters (3 weeks) |
| **Non-fiction book** | **Unit 1** | **Unit 2** | **Unit 3** | | |
| | Reports (4 weeks) | Instructions (3–4 weeks) | Information texts (4 weeks) | | |
| **Poetry Block** | **Unit 1** | | | | |
| | (4 weeks, which could be spread out) | | | | |

Source: DfES 2006b

- Resources to be used, including texts.
- Key assessment links.

The box and Table 14.4 are examples of an extract from a medium-term plan for Year 5.

---

**Scheme of work for English**

*Background information*

There are thirty-two pupils in this Year 5 class. The year is divided into sets for English, and this is a middle ability set. I will teach the lessons from Monday to Thursday, the class teacher will teach on Fridays.

*Frequency and duration of lessons*

Mondays – 1.15 to 2.20
Tuesdays to Fridays – 10.50 to 12.00

*Pupils' previous experiences*

The school follows the Primary National Strategy Framework for Literacy. Units that have been completed this term are Poetry, Poetic style, Unit 1 and Stories from other cultures (Unit 3).

*continued on facing page*

*Links to the National Curriculum Programme of Study*

The work this half term will cover the following areas of the National Curriculum:

Reading strategies: 1) a), b), c), d)
Understanding texts: 2) a), b), c), d)
Literature: 4) a), b), c) d), e), f), g), h), i)
Non-fiction and non-literacy texts: 5) a), b), c), d,) e), f), g)
Language structure and variation: 6)
Breadth of study: 7)
Literature: 8) a), c), g)
Non-fiction and non-literary texts: 9) a) , b), c),
Writing composition: 1) a), b), c), d), e)
Planning and drafting: 2) a), b), c), d), e), f)
Punctuation: 3)
Spelling: 4) b), c), d), e), f)
Morphology: 4)  g)
Handwriting and presentation: 5) a), b)
Standard English: 6) a), b)
Language structure: 7) a), b), c), d)
Breadth of study 8), 11), 12)


*Opportunities to use ICT*

The interactive whiteboard will be used in the majority of lessons.


*Cross-curricular links*

Design and technology – instructional texts/recipes.


*Key vocabulary to be introduced*

Dialogue, flashback, complication, resolution, synopsis, concrete poems, verse, stanza, onomatopoeia, alliteration, metaphor, simile.


*Text resources*

Openings from *Matilda, Watership Down, Voyage of the Dawn Treader, The Iron Man, Bill's New Frock, The Fib, Danny the Champion of the World* (book and play-script), *Boy*
Shape poems (W. Magee, G. Douthwaite)
*Gargling with Jelly* (B. Patten)
Instructional texts – various recipes

*continued on next page*

*Assessment*

Assessment will be via teacher observation and marking and informal assessment of the learning objectives.

*Key assessment opportunities*

To assess if pupils can

- analyse a story structure
- makes notes on and use evidence from across a text to explain events or ideas
- write a synopsis of a text
- recognise examples of poetic terms and devices
- reflect on how working in role helps to explore complex issues
- use and explore different question types and different ways words are used, including in formal and informal contexts
- create multilayered texts, including use of hyperlinks and linked web pages.

## Lesson planning

The renewed Framework shows clearly that whilst the literacy hour has provided structure to lessons that 'where these models of planning are followed with undue rigidity, they can act as a constraint on using the most appropriate organisation and structure to promote and develop children's learning (DfES 2006b: 8). The guidance goes on to say that whilst the structure of the three-part lesson has a key part to play, teachers will need to vary the use of this structure. In particular the following key points are made:

- Phases within lessons should introduce, develop and review learning and should support the overall learning intentions of the lesson.
- Children should know what they are learning and why.
- The teacher orchestrates the structure of the learning, but allows children opportunities to explore and question to build their learning.
- Timings of parts of lessons will meet the needs of the lesson.
- Planning across a period of time will be needed but should be adapted to meet children's needs.
- Teacher should ensure that learning in the Early Years Foundation Stage is built on.

The following also need to be borne in mind when planning lessons:

- Links to the Primary Framework for Literacy and Mathematics should be given.
- Detail given for the teaching content of the whole-class work with key questions or teaching points.
- Specific planning for a guided session if included, showing the introduction, focus and follow-up (mini plenary) as well as the focus for assessment and monitoring.

*Table 14.4* Sample English medium-term plan Year 5, term 1: overview 2nd half term

| Class: Top set | Year group(s) 5 | Term 1 | Year 5 | Teacher: |

**Continuous objectives**

Spell words containing unstressed vowels, group and classify words according to their spelling patterns and meanings, punctuate sentences accurately including using speech marks and apostrophes.

**Overview of units**

| Unit | Strands/Objectives Narrative/Non/Fiction/ Poetry | Text(s) | Suggested outcome(s) and activities | Cross-curricular links |
| --- | --- | --- | --- | --- |
| 1 Weeks: 4 | Fiction – significant children's authors | *Matilda, Danny the Champion of the World, Boy,* R. Dahl | 1 Collection of story openings for class resource book<br>2 Synopsis of known text<br>3 Character sketches<br>4 Class dictionary of idiomatic phrases | |
| 3 Weeks 2 | Poetic Style: Concrete Poetry | **Shape Poems,** W. Magee *Gargling with Jelly,* B. Patten | 1 Evaluate a favourite poem<br>2 Read aloud poems<br>3 Annotate poetic techniques | Art |
| 6 Weeks 2 | Non-fiction: instructional texts TL 22, 25 | Various recipes, rules | 1 Write instructions<br>2 Use ICT to create multilayered texts and include hyperlinks | D & T |

*continued on next page*

*Table 14.4* continued

Details of units and activities Week 1

| | Unit | Text | Text(s) | Suggested outcome(s) and activities | Cross-curricular links (where appropriate) |
|---|---|---|---|---|---|
| 1 | Fiction – significant children's authors 1. Story Openings | **Reading: To analyse the features of story openings and compare a number of story openings:** to know the features of story openings; to know that different types of stories begin in different ways. **Reading: To experiment with alternative ways of opening a story using e.g. description, action or dialogue:** to know that different story openings have different effects on the reader. Speaking and Listening • to be able to identify and respond to the effects of sounds and images in texts; | *Matilda* (Description), *The Voyage of the Dawn Treader, Watership Down* (Setting), *The Snowman,* (Dialogue), *Iron Man, Bill's New Frock* (Action). | Through shared reading, discuss the features of a good beginning. Highlight using an OHP or photocopies the 'who, what, where, when' using openings. Compare openings and in shared writing make a grid of types of openings and comment on the effects on the reader. Pupils analyse different story openings using various class texts. Pupils also match different story openings (photocopied) to respective texts. Make a collection of different types of story openings e.g. using dialogue, flashback, immediate action and evaluate the effect on the reader. Group them according to predetermined criteria. Compile into a class resource book. Listening and responding – identify the main effects of sounds and images, identify contribution of each element to overall effect. | |

- Independent work clearly outlined with notes for any additional adults.
- Plenary sessions should identify the focus, showing questions to consolidate learning and build links and provide a range of opportunities for children to review their learning, clarify their understanding and discuss what they have been taught.

### Learning objectives

The first step to planning an effective lesson is to decide on a focused objective. Objectives are those things which you expect the children to achieve during the lesson. They are usually set out under phrases like 'the children will be able to', 'the children will understand' and 'the children will know that' and might include such things as:

The children will be able to:

- Write a poem which includes rhyming couplets.

Objectives for a single lesson should be limited and achievable and they should be made clear to the children at the beginning of the lesson in child-friendly language.

---

**Activity: Analysing learning objectives**

Look at the objectives below and decide with colleagues which are achievable objectives with a clear focus.

Try also putting those that you feel are achievable in child-friendly language.

| *Objectives* | *Comments* |
|---|---|
| • To be able to use drama techniques to explore issues in a story. | |
| • To be able to write a haiku poem. | |
| • To be able to use commas in lists. | |
| • To know that instructions need to be written in a clear sequence. | |
| • To understand how to use conjunctions to join sentences. | |
| • To know strategies for spelling new words. | |

---

### Timing lessons

Particularly for the less experienced teacher or trainee, it is important to decide on clear timings for the following:

- the introduction which sets out the learning objective and how children will achieve it through clear success criteria

- whole-class work (ensuring this is interactive, lively and allows clear modelling of particular aspects)
- guided or independent work with sufficient time allowed for the children to be able to achieve something of worth
- the plenary sessions to review the work with the children, where appropriate help them to self-assess their work and to reiterate teaching points.

Lessons should be lively with a smooth transition from one aspect to another. However, it is also important that sufficient time is allocated for children to carry out particular activities.

## Differentiation

All classes will demonstrate a range of abilities and strengths in different areas. Assessment for learning is therefore the key to effective differentiation as it provides the vital information needed. Differentiation may involve planning a separate pro-gramme of work for one child or a small number of children, as well as preparing different activities or variations on activities for others. This is differentiation by task. Differentiation can also be achieved by support (i.e. with the help of an adult or more able peer) or by outcome where the different levels are shown by the completed piece of work. The key is to provide appropriate support that fits the specific task. The renewed Primary Framework's progression of objectives across year groups will help tracking back and forwards in order to provide appropriate objectives for children who are working significantly above or below age-related expectations.

## Plenary sessions

Plenary sessions have become widespread practice across the curriculum as a result of the introduction of the National Literacy Strategy in 1998. However, the quality of many plenary sessions has been questioned, for example by Ofsted. One of the common reasons for this is the lack of time allocated for the plenary at the end of the lesson. However, it is crucial for effective learning that pupils review what they have learned and that teachers can not only assess what children have achieved, but also reiterate key teaching points. This part of the lesson therefore needs to be planned carefully and should not simply consist of children clearing away or showing their work to others. The *Literacy Coordinator's Handbook* (DfES 2002a) pro-vides some useful guidance on the planning of plenary sessions. Guidance is also provided through the electronic Framework.

### Before the lesson

- Take account of the plenary and provide a range of opportunities for children to review their learning, clarify their new understanding, and discuss what they have been taught.
- Identify questions that will help the children to consolidate and extend their literacy and mathematics skills and recognise the progress they have made towards meeting the lesson's objectives and any targets that have been set.
- Build links between the plenary and other elements of the lesson.

*During the plenary*

- Challenge children to justify and refine their ideas and findings.
- Provide feedback which aims to clarify, refine and extend children's thinking, reasoning and communication skills.
- Assess the learning against the lesson objectives and log this information to inform future plans.

*After the plenary*

- Review the success of the plenary and record briefly information gathered on particular children.
- Use the information to inform future plans.

---

**Activity: Analysing effective lesson planning**

Review the following prompts for effective lesson planning below and apply to a lesson you are planning to teach.

*Objectives*

- Is it assessable or achievable in this lesson?
- Is it written in child-friendly language?
- Does it also have linked success criteria?
- Are links provided to the Primary Framework for Literacy?

*Introduction*

- How will the lesson be introduced?
- How will the children's interest be gained and sustained?

*Whole-class teaching*

- How will links be made to prior learning?
- What visual aids or multi-sensory teaching will be incorporated?
- What resources will be used?
- In what ways will the learning be modelled?
- What specific questions will be asked?
- How will the lesson be interactive?
- What opportunities for talk among pupils will be provided?

*continued on next page*

***Guided or independent work***

- How will the task be explained?
- How will the task be structured?
- What support will be provided?
- How will the learning be monitored?

***Plenary session***

- What activities will be included to demonstrate pupils' learning?
- What key questions will be asked?
- Which teaching points will be reinforced?

## Talking, reading and writing

Planning for English is undoubtedly complex but at the heart is a clear understanding of the cycle of planning and assessment. It is also crucial that practitioners have a clear grasp of the core aspects of teaching speaking, listening, reading and writing. Whilst key skills will require a discrete progression of teaching, many aspects are interrelated. It is also important to bear in mind that talk underpins the learning process and that effective writing should follow plenty of opportunities to plan and talk through the content first. Writing should also be based on having explored good models through reading. One might summarise the process thus:

Good writers talk a lot, read a lot and write a little (but effectively).

Trainee teachers and less experienced teachers will need to plan in far greater detail for individual lessons, where more experienced teachers can rely on annotations on unit plans devised by the school or from the Primary National Strategy. Whatever the detail, careful consideration needs to be given to all aspects of the lesson.

## Key points

- Understanding the learning process is the key to planning, which must be clearly linked to assessment for learning.
- The core aspects of teaching speaking, listening, reading and writing are fundamental to planning effectively.
- Planning in the Foundation Stage links the six areas of learning and should provide first-hand experiences with a balance of teacher-led and child-directed activities.
- Planning for Key Stages 1 and 2 should begin with looking at links across the curriculum through a curriculum map.
- Long-term plans will ensure coverage of all areas and where schools work on a two-yearly cycle that repetition is avoided.
- Medium-term plans consist of coherent units of work which can be drawn and adapted from the Primary National Strategy materials.
- Short-term planning requires the teacher to consider clear focussed objectives, timing and key aspects of the three main parts of the lesson.

## Further reading

Boys, R. (2003) *PCGE Professional Workbook: Primary English*. Exeter: Learning Matters.

DfES (2006b) *Primary National Strategy: Primary framework for literacy and mathematics*. Ref: 02011-2006BOK-EN. London: DfES. Available at http://www.standards.dfes.gov.uk/primaryframeworks/

Jolliffe, W., Waugh, D. and Taylor, K. (2005) *All New 100 Literacy Hours, Year R*. Leamington Spa, UK: Scholastic.

# 15 Assessment for learning of English

## Purpose of this chapter

This chapter aims to:

- Describe the forms of assessment related to English.
- Discuss the characteristics of assessment for learning.
- Give examples of involving pupils in the assessment process.
- Discuss the assessment of speaking and listening.
- Discuss how to build assessment into curriculum planning.
- Discuss the assessment of reading and writing.

## Forms of assessment

Assessment of all subjects can be divided into two main types:

- Assessment *of* learning (AoL) or summative assessment.
  This is a summary of what pupils have learnt at a specific point in time. It is a 'snapshot' of what has been learned or achieved.
- Assessment *for* learning (AfL) or formative assessment.
  This is a process of obtaining information to decide on what point learners are in their learning, where next and how to get there (Assessment Reform Group, 1999, 2002a, 2002b).

As stated in the Primary National Strategy guidance:

> AfL is any assessment activity which **informs** the next steps to learning. The key message is that AfL depends crucially on actually **using** the information gained.
>
> (DfES 2004b: 10)

The following sections discuss the role of each type of assessment, in relation to English. However, the major consideration will be given to the role of AfL to support the effective teaching of English.

## Summative assessment or assessment of learning

Summative assessment (or AoL) can be divided into statutory assessment (Standard Attainment Tests) and non-statutory school-based types of assessment. Both of these are carried out usually at the end of a school year or at other key points to provide information that monitors pupils' overall progress. Statutory assessment at Foundation Stage, Key Stages 1 and 2 consists of the following.

### Foundation Stage Profile

This provides a description of a child's development and progress in relation to the 'stepping stones' and the Early Learning Goals contained in the Curriculum Guidance for the Foundation Stage (replaced in 2008 by the Early Years Foundation Stage). There are thirteen assessment scales, each with nine points; the following relate to communication, language and literacy:

- language for communication and thinking
- linking sounds and letters
- reading
- writing.

The key point to bear in mind with regard to this type of assessment that is based on observations made by practitioners throughout the Reception year and assessments are done in the context of normal activities.

### National Curriculum levels

Teachers are required to report children's attainment against National Curriculum levels of attainment and use level descriptors to decide which level a child has achieved. These are broad statements which enable a decision to be made as to a 'best fit' to describe a child's achievement. In English teachers often meet to moderate judgements about a 'best fit' for each child particularly with respect to writing. At the end of Key Stage 1, a child is expected to achieve level 2, and the expectation at the end of Key Stage 2 is level 4. These levels are further subdivided into three subdivisions within each level (a, b and c, with a denoting the highest) to support teachers' finer judgements. The Qualifications and Curriculum Authority and the DfES have supplied 'P-scales' (DfES 2002b), which provide statements of achievement for children with special educational needs who are working below level 1.

### Standard Attainment Tests (SATs)

Children are required to take SATs at the end of Year 2 and Year 6, in English, Maths and Science. At Key Stage 1, Year 2, teachers mark these, but at Key Stage 2 they are externally set and marked. Tests are conducted in reading and writing, and speaking and listening are assessed by teacher judgement. Whilst these tests provide some information at a specific point of a child's achievement, there are many limitations in relying on them as a means of understanding a child's progress, strengths and weaknesses. The running record conducted at Key Stage 1 is, however, one example of a test that does provide some important diagnostic information about a child's reading skills. Many schools also carry out QCA optional tests in Maths and English every year in Key Stage 2, to provide year-on-year information on a child's progress.

### Diagnostic assessment

Diagnostic assessment is a form of test or assessment which provides information about specific difficulties a child may be having. The running record or miscue analysis in reading is one example. Another example is provided by the Primary National Strategy in the form of diagnostic marking guidelines for writing (DfES 2001a) as an aid to a systematic analysis of children's writing.

### Formative assessment or assessment for learning

A considerable amount of research, combined with effective classroom practice, has fused into what is known as assessment for learning (AfL), which has been shown to make a significant difference to children's learning. Paul Black and Dylan Wiliam's research found that:

> There is a body of firm evidence that formative assessment is an essential feature of classroom work and development of it can raise standards. We know of no other way of raising standards for which such a strong prima facie case can be made on the basis of evidence of such large learning gains.
>
> (Black and Wiliam 1998: 148)

This research has had a direct impact on government policy and in 2003, with the introduction of the Primary National Strategy, emphasis was placed on the use of formative assessment by providing guidance on AfL and comprehensive professional development materials have been produced (DfES 2004b).

## Characteristics of assessment for learning

The following principles underpin AfL:

- The active involvement of children in their own learning.
- The provision of effective feedback to children.
- A recognition of the profound influence that assessment has on motivation and self-esteem of children, both of which are crucial influences on learning.
- The need for children to assess themselves and understand how to improve.
- The adjustment of teaching to take account of the results of assessment.

In order for these principles to be put into practice, the following characteristics of AfL are needed:

- effective questioning (providing wait time, framing questions, and follow up)
- using marking and feedback strategies
- sharing learning goals
- peer and self-assessment.

The key change that AfL supports is the active involvement of children in under-standing their own learning and how to improve. One effective strategy is to share learning objectives with children in child-friendly language and also to share the criteria by which they can judge success. Success criteria summarise the key points that children need to understand as steps to success in achieving the learning objective. Ideally, children are involved in creating the success criteria with their teachers. The following is an example of success criteria from *Assessment for Learning* (DfES 2004b: 33) for Year 2:

> *Activity: To be able to write instructions*
> Success criteria:
>
> • Use imperatives ('Take jelly out of the packet').
> • Make sure the instructions are in the correct order ('Pour boiling water on the jelly. Then stir until the jelly melts').
> • Use bullet points, numbers or first, second, to support layout.

Other strategies that are successful are to use the acronyms WALT, WILF and WINK to involve children in their learning.

| | |
|---|---|
| WALT: | **Wh**at **a**re we **l**earning **t**oday? |
| WILF: | **Wh**at am **I** (the teacher) **l**ooking **f**or? |
| WINK: | **Wh**at **I n**ow **k**now |

Figures 15.1 and 15.2 provide some examples related to writing.

*Figure 15.1*

WALT: **Wh**at **a**re we **l**earning **t**oday?

*We are learning to write 'Super Sentences'.*

*Figure 15.2*

WILF:  **W**hat am **I** (the teacher) **l**ooking **f**or?

*The teacher is looking for interesting and exciting words.*

## Involving pupils in the assessment process

Schools have developed a range of methods for involving children in assessing their own learning, particularly in plenary sessions, such as 'three stars and a wish', where children share three things they have done well and one thing they would like to improve on. Another example is the use of traffic lights to show how confident children feel about an aspect of their learning (see Figure 15.3). These can be used in the form of cards that pupils hold up to indicate their level of understanding.

Red – don't understand

Amber – not sure

Green – got it!

*Figure 15.3*

The above aspects are fundamental to effective learning and teaching and will be explored more fully in relation to each aspect of English.

## Activity: Understanding fitness for purpose

To ensure understanding of the range of types of assessment, look at the range of assessments below and decide the purpose of each. (There are some suggested answers on page 274.)

| Assessment activity | Purpose | Summative or formative |
|---|---|---|
| • Standardised reading test | | |
| • Differentiated questioning | | |
| • Phoneme–grapheme correspondence test | | |
| • Moderated sample of child's writing | | |
| • Running record or miscue analysis of reading | | |
| • Guided writing feedback | | |

## Assessment of speaking and listening

Speaking and listening have always been an area that can be difficult to assess. This is because of the fluid nature of talk and the difficulty of using accurate criteria. One key point is to ensure that in making any summative judgments of National Curriculum levels, then a range of observations contribute to an overall level given to provide a 'best fit'.

It is important to link assessment to teaching objectives and to be clear about the nature of the speaking and listening being assessed, to apply agreed criteria, and to find efficient ways of recording achievements. Evidence should be collected system-atically in the following situations:

- Activities have been specifically set up to teach speaking and listening skills and the criteria for success clearly shared with children.
- Planned activities include substantial oral or group work, which may be related to other aspects of English or other curriculum areas.
- A particular contribution of a child is significant.

### *Developing an overall plan for assessing speaking and listening*

Developing a plan for assessing speaking and listening should be part of a whole-school policy, which takes the following into account:

- encouraging self and peer assessment
- collecting evidence systematically
- summarising achievement in order to plan for progression
- standardising assessments through moderation.

### *Making and recording assessments*

Collecting evidence can take different forms: what is important is to be systematic and to find an approach that is manageable and supports future teaching:

- notes made by the teacher or other adults
- notes made by the children, e.g. talk logs
- taped work
- succinct and accessible records that inform future teaching
- loose-leaf systems with a separate sheet for each child.

## Building assessment into curriculum planning

Building assessment into the planning can help ensure that this takes place systematically:

- Focus on two or three children each week.
- Decide on key objectives for whole-class monitoring and then record them using a traffic light system, with coloured dots or ticks (i.e. green for achieved, orange for needs reinforcement, and red for not achieved). An example for Year 2 is provided in Table 15.1.
- Integrate Speaking and Listening with other English records.
- Make termly checks on children's progress.
- Provide an annual review of progress.

### *Assessing against National Curriculum level descriptions*

The summary of National Curriculum level descriptions (Table 15.2) from Grugeon et al. (2005) can be helpful when it is necessary to find a level that best describes a child's level of achievement. It is important that this judgement is made over a range of activities and over a period of time, so that it accurately summarises their achievement.

### *Children's self-assessment*

Involving children in assessment is a key part of AfL. It can have profound effects on the learning through giving the children active involvement in their own learning and understanding the means by which they may improve. One example of this is using talk diaries (see Chapter 6).

*Table 15.1* Key objectives recording grid

| Pupil's name | Objective 1<br>Speak with clarity and use intonation when reading and reciting texts | Objective 2<br>Tell real and imagined stories using the conventions of familiar story language | Objective 3<br>Explain ideas and processes using language and gestures appropriately |
|---|---|---|---|
|  |  |  |  |
|  |  |  |  |
|  |  |  |  |
|  |  |  |  |
|  |  |  |  |
|  |  |  |  |

*Table 15.2* Summary of National Curriculum level descriptions for speaking and listening

|  | Listening | Talk clarity | Vocabulary |
|---|---|---|---|
| **Level 1** | Listens to others<br>Usually responds appropriately | Audible | Simple |
| **Level 2** | Listens carefully<br>Responds appropriately | Clear | Increasing |
| **Level 3** | Listens confidently in more contexts | Confident | More varied |
| **Level 4** | Listens carefully in discussions | Confident in more contexts | Developing |
| **Level 5** | Can speak and listen in more formal contexts | Clear in a wide range of contexts | Varied vocabulary and expression |
| **Level 6** | Adapts to the demands of different situations | Fluent | Shows variety and fluency |

*continued on next page*

*Table 15.2* continued

|  | **Discussion** | **Explanation** | **Further clarification** |
|---|---|---|---|
| **Level 1** | Conveys meaning | Provides some detail | Beginning to extend ideas |
| **Level 2** | Shows awareness of others | Includes some relevant detail | Starts to adapt vocabulary and tone to context |
| **Level 3** | Shows understanding of main points | Begins to adapt talk to the needs of the listener | Some awareness of Standard English. Can explain and communicate ideas |
| **Level 4** | Asks questions and responds to the views of others | Talk is adapted to the purpose | Some use of Standard English. Develops ideas thoughtfully and conveys opinions clearly |
| **Level 5** | Pays close attention, asks questions, and takes account of others | Engages the interest of the listener by inclusion of detail | Beginning to use Standard English appropriately. Responsiveness to ideas |
| **Level 6** | Takes an active part, shows understanding and sensitivity | Increasingly interesting through variety of expression | Usually fluent in Standard English in formal situations. Increasingly confident |

Source: Grugeon et al. 2005: 488

## Assessment of reading

The two main purposes of assessment in reading are first to assess the child's ability to decode the words and second to assess the child's level of comprehension. One of the most effective ways of assessing a child's reading is through the informal process of listening to a child read, looking closely for a child's strengths and weaknesses and any pattern of errors. The running record or miscue analysis is a systematic way of doing this and notes the types of errors such as substitution, self-correction, non-response, omission, insertion, hesitation, repetition, as well as reading strategies used to decode words. The resulting analysis can result in effective remediation and focused teaching.

### Miscue analysis

To carry out a miscue analysis with a child you will need to have a copy of the text the child is reading and then mark it for any errors using symbols. As a result of the renewed Primary Framework for Literacy, and the latest guidance about substituting the 'Searchlights' model of reading, the way in which this is recorded has changed. Typical symbols used in miscue analysis are now:

M   meaning (use of context)
S   structure (use of grammatical knowledge)
V   visual (use of word recognition and graphic knowledge
P   phonic (use of sound–letter correspondences).

The following may also be recorded:

/   for each word read correctly
H   for hesitation
T   for a word which the teacher tells the child
O   a circle around a word omitted.

It is important to spend some time with a child carrying out the following procedure before asking him/her to read, in order to make it a non-threatening process:

• Discuss illustrations, cover, author, content etc.
• Read a short section to the child first.
• Ask the child to read from one copy as you record miscues on another.

When analysing a child's reading, for each miscued word ask the following questions:

• Did the miscue look like the text (e.g. *tiring* for *trying*)?
• Did the miscue sound like the text (e.g. *sledge* for *sleigh*)?
• Did the word make sense in context (e.g. *happy* for *merry*)?
• Is the sentence grammatically acceptable (e.g. *I haven't got a name for him yet* for *I haven't thought of a name for him yet*)?
• Did the child self-correct (e.g. *would* read as *want* and then corrected)?
• Was the miscue due to the child being unfamiliar with the idiom used (e.g. *Last year I received . . .* may be an unfamiliar phrasing for the child)?

### Reading conferences

Reading conferences or interviews are more lengthy one-to-one teaching methods. An example of a reading conference prompt sheet is provided in the box. Conferences are demanding on teachers' time, but conducted periodically (e.g. termly) can be informative particularly about the child's attitude to reading and provide a much fuller picture of strengths and weaknesses and the range and genre of texts read. Colin Harrison (2004) comments that a reading interview can be a much more informative type of assessment than testing, due to the in-depth understanding of the child's attitude and breadth of skills.

---

**Reading Conference**

*Name:*                                               *Date:*

*Self-assessment*

Do you enjoy reading?
Do you think you are a good reader?
Is there any particular type of reading you would like to improve at?

*Range of reading*

What makes you choose a book?
What is your favourite kind of reading (fiction, non-fiction or on-screen texts)?
Do you have a favourite author?
When do you like reading best?
What have you enjoyed reading recently?

*Skills*

What do you do when you don't know a word?
If you want to find out about something interesting what do you do?
How do you use information books to answer a question?

*Current reading*

What are you reading now?
What do you like about it?
What do you want to read next?

---

### Guided reading

Guided reading provides an effective way for a teacher to use his/her time to work with a group with matched reading ability on a particular aspect of reading, with the group having copies of the same text. Sessions are planned in three parts to introduce the text and particular vocabulary, etc. and then pupils are given a particular focus or question to look for as they read independently the prescribed section or pages, with younger children reading aloud to enable the teacher to listen for errors. Finally a period of review of what has been read takes place and the discussion considerably helps comprehension of the text. Guided reading also provides an ideal opportunity for the teacher to make detailed ongoing assessment of the child's reading ability.

When listening to children read individually it is important to note strategies they are using and what strategies might support the next steps in their developing reading skills. An example of an individual reading comment sheet is provided in Table 15.3.

*Table 15.3* Example of an individual reading comment sheet

| READING RECORD | Name: |
|---|---|
| **Date:** | |
| **Book:** | |
| **Known/Unknown text**<br>**Author/Genre/Contents**<br>**Prediction of content** | |
| **Strategies observed when**<br>**reading aloud**<br>use of phonics including blending phonemes<br>semantic cues (knowledge of content)<br>syntactic (grammatical knowledge)<br>self-correcting<br>use of pictures | |
| **Child's response**<br>Relevant comments on:<br>The book as a whole, main ideas; main events;<br>characters; new information; way book is written<br><br>**Overall impression**<br>e.g. overall independence; accuracy; fluency;<br>sense of meaning; awareness of punctuation;<br>confidence; involvement<br><br>**Experience and support needed** | |

## Comprehension skills

The assessment of children's comprehension has in the past been undertaken through comprehension tests or exercises. However, many of these exercises are very limited in demonstrating children's comprehension skills and often are merely exercised in manipulating the syntax of the sentence. For example: 'The glop was nopping the plax.' 'Who was nopping the plax?' A meaningless sentence, but one which nevertheless can be answered correctly ('The glop'). It is important to bear in mind the different levels of response to text. These consist of:

- *Literal:* that is being able to understand the words actually on the page.
- *Inferential:* requiring reading between the lines to ascertain information that is not specifically stated. One example is: 'Peter sheltered beneath his umbrella until the bus came. When he got home his mother hit the roof.' We could make two inferences from this, first, that the weather was wet, and second, why his mother was cross (possibly because he was late).

- *Evaluative:* reading beyond the lines to reflect on aspects such as motive, consequences etc.
- *Appreciative:* requiring a personal critical response to text.

The Core Position Papers underpinning the renewal of guidance for teaching literacy and mathematics (DfES 2006c) provide some detailed discussion of developing comprehension and the important role of inferences in understanding text. Two types of inferences are identified: coherence inferences and elaborative inferences. *Coherence inferences* range from use of pronouns instead of names in texts to varying vocabulary (such as vessel for ship), both of which improve the style and interest in a text. *Elaborative inferences* enrich the text where the reader can gain a clear mental image in some cases by limited but carefully chosen words.

Five specific strategies that have been shown to be particularly effective in developing comprehension skills are prediction, questioning and clarifying, imaging and summarisation (Brown and Palinscar 1985) and are often termed reciprocal reading. Underpinning this is the need for opportunities for meaningful discussion of text through paired, group or guided work.

Another effective means of teaching and improving comprehension skills is through Directed Activities Related to Texts (DARTs). These consist broadly of two types: *text analysis*, requiring the reader to locate and organise material, and *text reconstruction*, requiring the reader to sequence text or predict events. These activities are also best carried out when children are organised to work with a partner or in a group, as the resulting discussion requires the children to clarify, expand and explain their ideas.

Formal or summative assessments of reading are carried out throughout a child's schooling, beginning with the Early Learning Goals at the end of Foundation Stage and then with Key Stage 1 and Key Stage 2 statutory assessments (SATs). Foundation Stage assessments are made through teacher observation; at the end of Key Stage 1, children carry out a running record which is related to a score and National Curriculum level. They also complete a comprehension booklet based on a short text. At the end of Key Stage 2, assessment is through a reading booklet with a series of different genres and types of questions which aim to test literal, inferential and evaluative comprehension. SATs provide standardised scores which can be used to compare a child's progress over a period of time and are used alongside a teacher assessment of a child's ability.

## Assessment of writing

One of the most important methods of assessment of children's writing is carried out orally during the process of writing when the teacher spends time with a child or a group of children and offers advice. This can be done effectively during guided writing sessions which have a particular focus and group children of a similar ability. Writing conferences can also be carried out on a one-to-one basis, periodically, particularly when a child's lack of progress is causing concern. Here the important features are to note the child's ability to tackle a piece of writing before commencing, through planning orally or in note form, their response during the writing and any particular difficulties encountered, and then afterwards with the completed piece of work to review progress.

Opportunities for assessing progress in writing occur in dedicated literacy teaching time and also across the curriculum where children have the opportunity to practise and apply the skills they have been taught. These opportunities are at times informal as well as formal. They engage children in peer and self-assessment as well as teacher-led assessment.

## Involving children

Children can be involved in the assessment process through the sharing of learning objectives and success criteria using, for example WALT, WILF and WINK (see page 261). Another method is to have children work in pairs and to ask them at strategic points during their writing to stop and discuss with a partner. This of course needs careful guidance with clear criteria agreed:

*A response partner is someone who*

- helps me with my work
- tells the truth about my work
- helps me to make my work better.

Using a few prompt questions to guide children is helpful (see pages 261–2).

## Marking writing

One of the most common ways in which teachers assess writing is through marking, but research has shown that this can be ineffective unless it is focused on a specific objective or target. Rather than mark everything that needs correcting, one possible way, recommended as part of AfL, is to identify three successes and one improvement. Alternatively, a system that identifies one specific positive comment about the work, one specific point about improving that relates to the individual child and one that relates to the class target for improving writing.

The Primary National Strategy has produced guidance for marking writing with an overall writing analysis sheet particularly aimed at helping children progress from National Curriculum level 3 to level 4. Such an analysis can be helpful in providing an overall picture of specific strengths and weaknesses and where to target future teaching (see Table 15.4). It is also important to share with children particular strengths and to enable them to understand how to improve.

## Diagnostic assessment

Where a child is causing concern with regard to progress in writing, it may be useful to conduct a writing miscue analysis which looks at the process of writing as well as the result. It covers

- writing behaviour
- the writing process
- the purpose for writing
- the intended audience

*Table 15.4* Writing analysis sheet

| Grammar | Judgement of effective use | | |
|---|---|---|---|
| Significant features at word and sentence level | **Yes** | **No** | **Partial** |
| **Sentence structure**<br>simple sentences<br>complex sentences<br>variation within sentences<br>co-ordination<br>subordination<br><br>**Word choice**<br>noun groups<br>verb choice<br>tense<br>adjectives<br>adverbs<br>pronouns<br><br>**Punctuation used to demarcate**<br>sentences<br>clauses<br>phrases<br>words in lists<br>direct speech | | | |
| **Organisation and effect**<br>Significant whole text features | | | |
| appeal to reader<br>development of topic, content, theme<br>openings and closings<br>organisation and length of paragraphs<br>presentation and layout | | | |

Source: DfES 2001a

- form or format
- text construction
- vocabulary choice
- spelling
- punctuation.

Table 15.5 is an example of recording this process, which will need to be adapted so that it is appropriate to the age of the child.

The renewed Primary Framework for Literacy provides the following guidance with regard to assessing children's writing:

- Writing is a complex, unitary skill, so these elements are interactive and interdependent even though they can each be analysed.
- The different facets of writing develop together: when teaching specific points it is important to show how they relate to writing as a whole.
- Children need to learn how to orchestrate skills at word, sentence and text level in order to be able to write independently.

*Table 15.5* Writing miscue analysis record

| | |
|---|---|
| **Name:** | **Date:** |
| **1   Writing behaviour** (willingness to commence, motivation and engagement with task) | |
| **2   Writing process: (methods used)**<br>• Planning<br>• Editing<br>• Independence | |
| **3   Purpose/intention** (understanding of reason for writing)<br>• Awareness shown | |
| **4   Audience** (signs of identifying audience for writing)<br>*Awareness of reader*<br><br>• Accessibility/clarity<br>• Register/tone used | |
| **5   Structure/form** (suits purpose and audience)<br>*Choice of structure*<br><br>• Consistency of form<br>• Sequence of ideas | |
| **6   Technical features** (significant aspects)<br>• Spelling specific errors or types of errors<br>• Vocabulary – range<br>• Punctuation – accuracy<br>• Syntax: sentence structure<br>• Other featues, e.g. conjunctions | |

Source: adapted from Bearne 2002: 498

- When assessing it is always important to look at the parts in relation to text as a whole, e.g. how individual sentences contribute to overall effect.

Target statements for writing are also provided by the Primary National Strategy which provided guidance to schools in the following areas:

- to audit writing achievement in each year group
- to set curricular targets for year groups and learning targets for children
- as a steer for teachers' planning
- to help focus teaching on key elements of writing
- as criteria for monitoring teaching and learning.

The assessment of writing also needs to be summative at specific points to record a child's progress. This requires teachers to give pieces of work a National Curriculum level which can be problematic. One effective way of assisting teachers is through moderation of writing with colleagues, where the same piece of work is analysed by different teachers and the results compared. Any such assessments of children should support future teaching and learning.

## Key points

- Summative assessment or assessment of learning (AoL) provides information about a child's progress at specific points.
- Assessment for learning (AfL) provides valuable information to support the teaching process.
- Involving children in understanding their own learning through sharing learning objectives and success criteria is a powerful strategy to support learning.
- Diagnostic assessment particularly with regard to reading and writing can support children with specific difficulties.
- The importance of developing a systematic and manageable process for assessing and recording all aspects of English.

---

### Answers for the activity on understanding fitness for purpose on page 263

| Assessment activity | Purpose | Summative or formative |
|---|---|---|
| • Standardised reading test | To provide a standardised reading score as a snapshot of a child's reading ability at that time. | Summative |
| • Differentiated questioning | To provide information during teaching about a child or several children's understanding. | Formative |
| • Phoneme–grapheme correspondence test | To check children's knowledge at a given point in time. | Formative – usually diagnostic and informs future teaching |
| • Moderated sample of child's writing | To provide information of a child's achievement usually denoted by NC levels. | Summative |
| • Running record or miscue analysis of reading | To provide information about a child's decoding and overall reading skills. | Formative – diagnostic |
| • Guided writing feedback | To provide feedback at the point of writing during guided sessions. | Formative |

# Further reading

Black, P., Harrison, C., Lee, C., Marshall, B. and Wiliam, D. (2002) *Working Inside the Black Box: Assessment for learning in the classroom*. London: King's College Department of Education and Professional Studies. Available at http://www.kcl.ac.uk/depsta/education/publications/blackbox.html

Clarke, S. (1998) *Targeting Assessment in the Primary Classroom: Strategies for planning, assessment, pupil feedback and target setting*. London: Hodder and Stoughton.

DfES (2001d) *Supporting the Target Setting Process: Guidelines for effective target setting for pupils with Special Educational Needs*. Ref: 0065/2001. Nottingham: DfES Publications.

For more information on AfL, in particular the ten principles, see http://www.qca.org.uk/ca/5–14/afl.

For target statements for writing, see http://www.standards.dfes.gov.uk/primary/literacy/publications/

# Conclusions

This book has explored a range of key issues related to teaching English to children from 3 to 11. While it is not possible to explore every topic in depth within one book, we hope that *English 3–11* will provide readers with an overview of English teaching and strong insights into key areas. The book should be seen as a starting point for further reading, as well as for reflection and discussion with fellow professionals.

As we discussed in the Introduction, the curriculum for English and the strategies recommended for teaching and learning are in an almost constant state of change. As we write, the renewed Primary Framework for Literacy (DfES 2006b) and new Early Years Foundation Stage (DfES 2007a, 2007b) materials have become available, and will require that schools study them carefully before determining how they will affect their ways of working. Indeed, some of the key principles for the effective teaching of English are challenged by the Rose Report (DfES 2006a), which recommends that phonics should play a central role in teaching and learning early reading and writing.

Some of the key themes of the Primary National Strategy include creativity and effective pedagogy, and the importance of talking to learn. There seems to be a recognition that some important elements of English were being neglected by schools as they strove for improved literacy standards through the literacy hour. We hope that *English 3–11* will help readers to seek opportunities to be creative in their teaching and to consider innovative ways of working.

Underpinning everything we do as teachers will be an understanding of how to manage children effectively and how to create an environment which enables them to learn and to enjoy doing so. The way that we plan and our ability to assess accurately and to let this inform our planning will also be crucial, as will an awareness of new approaches to planning, assessment and class management.

Developments in technology continue to challenge teachers, many of whom began their careers before computers became a feature of most classrooms and when interactive whiteboards were beyond our conception. Not only do we have to understand how we can maximise our use of the technology which is available now, but also we need to be prepared to learn how to use those of which we cannot yet conceive! For it is quite certain that the next few years will continue to see more innovations reaching our schools. If we are to use these discerningly, we will need to develop not only the facility to make the equipment work, but also the ability to decide which might benefit our pupils, and which would add little to the quality of teaching and learning in our classrooms.

All of which illustrates the size of the task which faces teachers in the twenty-first century. The modern teacher needs to have a broad perspective and a receptivity to change, if he or she is to respond to change effectively. Without this, change can be both threatening and unsettling, and teachers' understanding of how they can modify their practice will be limited.

So what can you do, now that you have read this book, to further your development as a teacher of English from 3 to 11? We suggest the following:

- Keep up to date on changes to the curriculum and new ideas for teaching by looking regularly at some or even all of the following: *The Times Educational Supplement* (TES), the *Guardian* weekly educational supplement, the DfES Standards Site (http://www.standards.dfes.gov.uk), professional journals, academic journals, and at details of the latest publications about English in primary schools.
- Make use of the references in this book to engage in further reading and to gain a different perspective from ours.
- Discuss some of the classroom activities and practices described in this book with fellow professionals, and adapt them to meet the needs of the children you teach.
- Build portfolios of poetry and children's stories which you can draw upon throughout your career.
- Continually look for examples of varied and interesting non-fiction texts to include in your 'literate' classroom.
- Analyse your classroom, asking yourself if it is language-friendly: a good environment for developing speaking and listening and reading and writing.
- Consider how you cater for children of different abilities and their individual needs.
- Think about how your assessment of pupils' progress impacts upon your planning.
- Reflect regularly upon your own teaching, and look for opportunities to observe that of others, so that you can develop as a teacher of English.

A teacher who does all of the above will be ideally placed to engage with and embrace change, while being able to consider its value and relevance to the children he or she teaches, and will, therefore, be a professional. We hope that this book will help you to achieve this.

# References

Adams, M. J. (1990) *Beginning to Read: Thinking and learning about print*. Cambridge, MA: MIT Press.

Adams, M. J. and Bruck, M. (1993) 'Word recognition: the interface of educational policies and scientific research', *Reading and Writing: An interdisciplinary journal*, 5: 113–39.

Airs, J., Wright, J., Williams, L. and Adkins, R. (2004) 'The performing arts', in R. Jones and D. Wyse (eds) *Creativity in the Primary Curriculum*. London: David Fulton.

Alexander, R. (2000) *Culture and Pedagogy: International comparisons in primary education*. Oxford: Blackwell.

Alexander, R. (2004) *Towards Dialogic Teaching*. Cambridge: Dialogos.

Arizpe, E. and Styles, M. (2002) *Children Reading Pictures: Interpreting visual texts*. London: RoutledgeFalmer.

Assessment Reform Group (1999) *Assessment for Learning: Beyond the black box*. Cambridge: University of Cambridge Faculty of Education. Available at http://www.assessment-reform-group.org.uk/

Assessment Reform Group (2002a) *Assessment for Learning: Ten principles*. Cambridge: University of Cambridge Faculty of Education. Available at http://www.assessment-reform-group.org.uk/

Assessment Reform Group (2002b) *Testing, Motivation and Learning*. Cambridge: University of Cambridge Faculty of Education.

Bandura, A. (1977) *Social Learning Theory*. Englewood Cliffs, NJ: Prentice Hall.

Barnes, D. and Todd, F. (1977) *Communicating and Learning in Small Groups*. London: Routledge & Kegan Paul.

Barnes, D., Britton, J. and Rosen, H. (1969) *Language, the Learner and the School*. Harmondsworth: Penguin.

Barnes, E. (1997) 'Punctuation signs, symbols and spaces', *The Primary English Magazine*, 2(3).

Barrs, M. (2000) 'The reader in the writer', *Reading Literacy and Language*, 34(2): 54–60.

Bawden, N. (1974) *Carrie's War*. London: Puffin.

Beard, R. F. (2000) 'Long overdue? Another look at the National Literacy Strategy', *Journal of Research in Reading*, 23(34): 245–55.

Bearne, E. (2002) *Making Progress in Writing*. London: RoutledgeFalmer.

Bearne, E., Grainer, T. and Wolstencroft, H. (2004) *Raising Boys' Achievements in Writing*, Joint Research Project, United Kingdom Literacy Association and the Primary National Strategy. Baldock: United Kingdom Literacy Association.

Becta (2003a) *What the Research Says about ICT and Motivation*. Coventry: Becta. Available at http://partners.becta.org.uk/

Becta (2003b) *What the Research Says about Using ICT in English*. Coventry: Becta. Available at http://partners.becta.org.uk/

Bereiter, C. and Scardamalia, M. (1987) *The Psychology of Written Composition*. Hillsdale, NJ: Lawrence Erlbaum.

Black, P. and Wiliam, D. (1998) *Inside the Black Box: Raising standards through classroom assessment*. London: King's College School of Education. Available from Slough, UK: National Foundation for Educational Research/Nelson.

Black, P., Harrison, C., Lee, C., Marshall, B. and Wiliam, D. (2002) *Working Inside the Black Box: Assessment for learning in the classroom*. London: King's College London, Department of Education and Professional Studies. Available at http://www.kcl.ac.uk/depsta/education/publications/blackbox.html

Blackledge, A. (1994) *Teaching Bilingual Children*. Stoke-on-Trent, UK: Trentham Books.

Blatchford, P. (1991) 'Children's handwriting at 7 years: associations with handwriting on school entry and pre-school factors', *British Journal of Educational Psychology*, 61: 73–84.

Blatchford, P. and Plewis, I. (1990) 'Pre-school reading-related skills and later reading achievement: further evidence', *British Educational Research Journal*, 16(4): 425–8.

Blatchford, P., Burke, J., Farquhar, C., Plewis, I. and Tizard, B. (1987) 'Associations between pre-school reading related skills and later reading achievement', *British Educational Research Journal*, 13(1): 15–23.

Bloom, B. S. (1956) *Taxonomy of Educational Objectives: The classification of educational goals. Handbook 1: Cognitive Domain*. New York: Longmans, Green.

Blyton, E. (1968) *The Three Golliwogs*. London: Dean & Son.

Bourdieu, P. (1977) *Outline of a Theory of Practice*. Cambridge: Cambridge University Press.

Bouttell, J. (1986) Article in *Guardian*, 12 August 1986, cited in D. Crystal (1990) *The English Language*. Harmondsworth: Penguin.

Boys, R. (2003) *PGCE Professional Workbook: Primary English*. Exeter: Learning Matters.

Bradley, L. and Bryant, P. (1983) 'Categorising sounds and learning to read: a causal connection', *Nature*, 301: 419–21.

Branford, H. (1997) *Fire, Bed and Bone*. London: Walker.

Brent Language Service (2002) *Enriching Literacy: Text, talk and tales in today's schools*. Stoke-on-Trent, UK: Trentham Books.

British Film Institute (BFI) (2003) *Look Again!* Available at http://www.bfi.org.uk/education/teaching/lookagain/

Bromley, H. (2000) 'Never be without a *Beano*: comics, children and literacy', in A. Andersen and M. Styles (eds) *Teaching through Texts*. London: Routledge.

Brooks, G. (1998) 'Trends in standards of literacy in the United Kingdom, 1948–1996', *Topic*, 19: 1–10.

Brooks, G., Pugh, A. K. and Schagen, I. (1996) *Reading Performance at Nine*. Slough, UK: National Foundation for Educational Research.

Brown, A. and Palinscar, A. (1985) *Reciprocal Teaching of Comprehension Strategies: A natural program for enhancing learning*. Urbana-Champaign, IL: University of Illinois.

Browne, A. (1996) Interview. Available at http://www.education.wisc.edu/ccbc/authors/experts/browne.asp

Browne, A. (2001) *Developing Language and Literacy 3–8* (2nd edn). London: Paul Chapman.

Bruner, J. S. (1962) Cited by R. Nickerson, 'Enhancing creativity', in R. J. Sternberg (ed.) (1999) *Handbook of Creativity*. Cambridge: Cambridge University Press.

Bruner, J. S. (1985) 'Vygotsky: a historical and conceptual perspective', in J. Wertsch (ed.) *Culture, Communication and Cognition: Vygotskian Perspectives*. Cambridge: Cambridge University Press.

Bruner, J. S. (1986) *Actual Minds, Possible Worlds*. Cambridge, MA: Harvard University Press.

Bruner, J. S. (1996) *The Culture of Education*. Cambridge, MA: Harvard University Press.

Bryant, P. (1993) 'Phonological aspects of learning to read', in R. Beard (ed.) *Teaching Literacy: Balancing perspectives*. London: Hodder & Stoughton.

Bryant, P. E. and Bradley, L. (1985) *Children's Reading Problems*. Oxford: Blackwell.

Bryson, B. (1990) *Mother Tongue: The English Language*. Harmondsworth: Penguin.

Buckley, B. (2003) *Children's Communication Skills: From birth to five years*. London: Routledge.

Bunting, R. (1997) *Teaching about Language in the Primary Years*. London: David Fulton.

Burkard, T. (1999) *The End of Illiteracy? The discovery of the Holy Grail at Clackmannanshire*. London: Centre for Policy Studies.

Burnett, C. and Myers, J. (2004) *Teaching English 3–11*. London: Continuum.

Byars, B. (1981) *The Midnight Fox*. London: Puffin.

Campbell, R. (1999) *Literacy from Home to School: Reading with Alice*. Stoke-on-Trent, UK: Trentham Books.

Carless, S. (1989) 'Spelling in the primary school curriculum',in P. Pinsent (ed.) *Spotlight on Spelling*. Bicester, UK: A B Academic.

Carter, D. (2000) *Teaching Fiction in the Primary School*. London: David Fulton.

Cato, V., Fernandes, C., Gorman, T., Kispal, A. with White, J. (1992) *The Teaching of Initial Literacy: How do teachers do it?* Slough, UK: National Foundation for Educational Research.

Central Advisory Council for Education (1967) *Children and their Primary Schools* (Plowden Report). London: HMSO.

Center, Y. (2005) *Beginning Reading: A balanced approach to teaching literacy during the first three years at school*. London: Continuum.

Chall, J. S. (1983) *Learning to Read: The great debate* (updated edn). New York: McGraw-Hill.

Chomsky, N. (1957) *Syntactic Structures*. The Hague: Mouton.

Chomsky, N. (1965) *Aspects of Theory of Syntax*. Cambridge, MA: MIT Press.

Clarke, S. (1998) *Targeting Assessment in the Primary Classroom: Strategies for planning, assessment, pupil feedback and target setting*. London: Hodder & Stoughton.

Clay, M. M. (1979) *The Early Detection of Reading Difficulties: A diagnostic survey with reading recovery procedures* (2nd edn). London: Heinemann.

Clay, M. M. (1993) *Reading Recovery: A guidebook for teachers in training*. London: Heinemann.

Clay, M. M. and Tuck, B. (1991) *A Study of Reading Recovery Subgroups: Including outcomes for children who did not satisfy discontinuing criteria*. Auckland, NZ: University of Auckland.

Comber, B. (1999) *IT's Got Power in It: Critical literacies and information technologies in primary schools*. Adelaide, SA: University of South Australia, Language and Literacy Research Centre.

Conteh, J. (2003) *Succeeding in Diversity: Culture, language and learning in primary classrooms*. Stoke-on-Trent, UK: Trentham Books.

Cookson, P. (ed.) (2000) *The Works*. London: Pan Macmillan.

Cooper, H. (1993) *The Bear Under the Stairs*. London: Picture Corgi Books.

Corden, R. (2000) *Literacy and Learning through Talk: Strategies for the primary classroom*. Buckingham: Open University Press.

Corden, R. (2004) 'Group work, learning through talk', in T. Grainer (ed.) *The RoutledgeFalmer Reader in Language and Literacy*. London: RoutledgeFalmer.

Corson, D. (1988) *Oral Language across the Curriculum*. Clevedon, OH: Multilingual Matters.

Cowley, S. (2004) *Getting the Buggers to Behave*. London: Continuum.

Craft, A. (2000) *Creativity across the Primary Curriculum: Framing and developing practice*. London: RoutledgeFalmer.

Craft, A. (2002) *Creativity and Early Years Education: A lifewide foundation*. London: Continuum.

Cripps, C. C. (1988) *A Hand for Spelling*. Wisbech, UK: Learning Development Aids.

Cripps, C. C. (1998) *A Hand for Spelling* (revised edn). Wisbech, UK: Learning Development Aids.

Cropley, A. J. (2001) *Creativity in Education and Learning: A guide for teachers and educators*. London: Kogan Page.

Crystal, D. (1987) *The Cambridge Encyclopedia of Language*. Cambridge: Cambridge University Press.

Crystal, D. (1990) *The English Language*. London: Penguin.

Csikszentmihalyi, M. (1992) *Flow: The psychology of human happiness*. London: Rider.

Csikszentmihalyi, M. (1996) *Creativity*. New York: HarperCollins.

Cummins, J. (1996) *Negotiating Identities: Education for empowerment in a diverse society*. Ontario, CA: California Association for Bilingual Education.

Dahl, R. (1977) *Danny the Champion of the World*. London: Puffin.

Dahl, R. (1989) *Matilda*. London: Puffin.

Dahl, R. (2001) *Revolting Rhymes*. London: Puffin.

Davies, A. and Ritchie, D. (1998) *THRASS Teacher's Manual*. Chester: THRASS (UK). Available at http://www.thrass.co.uk

Davies, D., Howe, A., Fasciato, M. and Rogers, M. (2004) 'How do trainee primary teachers understand creativity?' Unpublished conference paper, British Educational Research Association.

Daw, P., Smith, J. and Wilkinson, S. (1997) 'Factors associated with high standards of spelling in Years R–4', *English in Education*, 31(1): 36–47.

Dawes, L. (2001) 'Interthinking – the power of productive talk', in P. Goodwin (ed.) *The Articulate Classroom: Talking and learning in the primary school*. London: David Fulton.

Dawes, L. and Sams, C. (2004) *Talk Box: Speaking and listening activities for learning at Key Stage 1*. London: David Fulton.

DES (1975) *A Language for Life* (Bullock Report). London: HMSO. [00]

DES (1990) *English in the National Curriculum*. London: HMSO.

DES/WO (1989) *Discipline in Schools* (Elton Report). London: HMSO.

Devereux, J. and Miller, L. (2003) *Working with Children in the Early Years*. London: David Fulton.

DfEE (1998a) *National Literacy Strategy: Framework for Teaching*. London: DfEE.

DfEE (1998b) *Reading and Writing for Information*. Oxford: Oxford University Press.

DfEE (1999) *English in the National Curriculum*. London: HMSO.

DfEE/QCA (1999) *The National Curriculum: Handbook for primary teachers in England*. London: HMSO.

DfES (2000) *National Literacy Strategy: Grammar for Writing*. London: DfES. Available at http://www.standards.dfes.gov.uk/primary/publications/literacy/63317/

DfES (2001a) *Marking Guidelines for Writing*. Available at http://www.standards.dfes.gov.uk/primary/publications/literacy/63341/nlsmarkingguidelines0501.pdf

DfES (2001b) *National Literacy Strategy: Developing Early Writing*. London: DfES.

DfES (2001c) *Strategies to Enhance Children's Understanding of Texts*. Nottingham: DfES Publications.

DfES (2001d) *Supporting the Target Setting Process: Guidelines for effective target setting for pupils with Special Educational Needs*. Ref: 0065/2001. Nottingham: DfES Publications.

DfES (2002a) *Literacy Coordinator's Handbook*. Nottingham: DfES Publications.

DfES (2002b) *Towards the National Curriculum for English: Examples of what pupils with special educational needs should be able to do at each P level*. Ref: 0517/2002. Nottingham: DfES Publications.

DfES (2003a) *Excellence and Enjoyment: A strategy for primary schools*. Nottingham: DfES Publications.

DfES (2003b) *Involving Parents, Raising Achievement*. Ref: PICE/IPRA. Nottingham: DfES Publications.

DfES (2003c) *Speaking, Listening, Learning: Working with children in Key Stages 1 and 2*. Ref: 0626/2003 G. Nottingham: DfES Publications.

DfES (2003d) *The Impact of Parental Involvement on Children's Education*. Ref: LEA/0339/2003. Nottingham: DfES Publications.

DfES (2004a) *Behaviour in the Classroom: A course for newly qualified teachers*. Ref: 0030/2004. Nottingham: DfES Publications.

DfES (2004b) *Excellence and Enjoyment: Learning and teaching in the primary years. Professional development materials*. Nottingham: DfES Publications.

DfES (2004c) *Excellence and Enjoyment: Learning to learn. Progression in key aspects of learning.* Nottingham: DfES Publications.

DfES (2004d) *The ICT in Schools Survey 2004.* London: DfES. Available at http://partners.becta.org.uk/

DfES (2005a) *Communicating Matters: The strands of communication and language.* Ref: 1770/2005DOC-EN. Nottingham: DfES Publications.

DfES (2005b) *Excellence and Enjoyment: Social and emotional aspects of learning.* Ref: 1319/2005. Available at http://www.standards.dfes.gov.uk/

DfES (2006a) *Independent Review of the Teaching of Early Reading* (Final Report by Jim Rose). Ref: 0201/2006DOC-EN. Nottingham: DfES Publications.

DfES (2006b) *Primary National Strategy: Primary Framework for Literacy and Mathematics.* Ref: 02011/2006BOK-EN. London: DfES. Available at http://www.standards.dfes.gov.uk/primaryframeworks/

DfES (2006c) *Primary National Strategy: Primary Framework for Literacy and Mathematics: Core Position Papers underpinning the renewal of guidance for teaching literacy and mathematics.* Ref: 03855/2006BKT-EN. Nottingham: DfES Publications.

DfES (2006d) *Primary National Strategy: Primary Framework for Literacy and Mathematics* DVD-ROM. Ref: 02014/2006DVD-EN. London: DfES Publications. Also available at: http://www.standards.dfes.gov.uk/primaryframeworks/

DfES (2006e) *Primary National Strategy: The new conceptual framework for teaching reading. The Simple View of Reading: overview for literacy leaders and managers in schools and early years settings.* London: DfES.

DfES (2006f) *The Early Years Foundation Stage* (consultation document). Nottingham: DfES Publications.

DfES (2007a) *Early Years Foundation Stage: Principles into Practice Card 2.2.* Ref: 00012/2007PCK-EN. Nottingham: DfES Publications.

DfES (2007b) *Practice Guidance for the Early Years Foundation Stage.* Ref: 00013/2007BKT-EN. Nottingham: DfES Publications.

Dyson, A. H. (2000) 'On reframing children's words: the perils, promises and pleasures of writing children', *Research in the Teaching of English*, 34: 352–67.

Dyson, A. H. (2001) 'Where are the childhoods in childhood literacy? An exploration in outer (school) space', *Journal of Early Childhood Literacy*, 1(1): 9–39.

Education Department of Western Australia (1994) *Oral Language: Developmental continuum.* Melbourne, Vic.: Longman.

Edwards, V. (1998) *The Power of Babel: Teaching and learning in multilingual classrooms.* Stoke-on-Trent, UK: Trentham Books.

Ehri, L. C. (1987) 'Learning to read and spell words', *Journal of Reading Behavior*, 19: 5–31.

Ehri, L. C. (2003) 'Systematic phonics instruction: findings of the National Reading Panel'. Paper presented at the seminar on phonics convened by the DfES, March.

Ehri, L. C., Nunes, S. R., Stahl, A. S. and Willows, D. (2001) 'Systematic phonics instruction helps students learn to read: evidence from the National Reading Panel's meta-analysis', *Review of Educational Research*, 71: 393–4.

Essex Writing Project (2003) *Visually Speaking: Using multimedia texts to improve boys' writing.* Chelmsford, UK: The English Team, Essex Advisory and Inspection Service.

Ferreiro, E. and Teberosky, A. (1982) *Literacy before Schooling.* London: Heinemann.

Film Education Working Group (FEWG) (1999) *Making Movies Matter: Report of the Film Education Working Group.* London: British Film Institute.

Fine, A. (1992) *Bill's New Frock.* London: Longman.

Fisher, R. (2002) 'Creative minds: building communities of learning for the creative age'. Paper presented at Teaching Qualities Initiative Conference, Hong Kong Baptist University. Available at http://www.pantaneto.co.uk/issue25/fisher.htm.

Fisher, R. (2004) 'What is creativity', in R. Fisher and M. Williams (eds) *Unlocking Creativity: Teaching across the curriculum*. London: David Fulton.

Fisher, R. and Williams, M. (eds) (2004) *Unlocking Creativity: Teaching across the curriculum*. London: David Fulton.

Fitzpatrick, F. (1996) Unpublished notes. Department of Teaching Studies, Bradford and Ilkley Community College.

Fox, R. (2005) *Teaching and Learning: Lessons from psychology*. Oxford: Blackwell.

Frith, U. (ed.) (1980) *Cognitive Processes in Spelling*. London: Academic Press.

Frith, U. (1985) 'Developmental dyslexia', in K. E. Patterson, J. C. Marshall and M. Coltheart (eds) *Surface Dyslexia*. Hove, UK: Lawrence Erlbaum.

Galton, M., Simon, B. and Croll, P. (1980) *Inside the Primary Classroom*. London: Routledge.

Galton, M., Hargreaves, L., Comber, C., Wall, D. and Pell, A. (1999) *Inside the Primary Classroom 20 Years on*. London: Routledge.

Gamble, N. and Yates, S. (2002) *Exploring Children's Literature*. London: Paul Chapman.

Gardner, H. (1997) *Extraordinary Minds*. New York: HarperCollins.

Geekie, P., Cambourne, B. and Fitzsimmons, P. (1999) *Understanding Literacy Development*. Stoke-on-Trent, UK: Trentham Books.

Gentry, J. R. (1987) *Spel . . . is a Four-Letter Word*. Leamington Spa, UK: Scholastic.

Goodman, K. S. (1967) 'Reading: a psycholinguistic guessing game', *Journal of the Reading Specialist*, 4: 126–35.

Goodman, K. S. (1973) 'Psycholinguistic universals in the reading process', in F. Smith (ed.) *Psycholinguistics and Reading*. New York: Holt, Rinehart & Winston.

Goodman, K. S. (1998) *In Defence of Good Teaching: What teachers need to know about reading wars*. York, MA: Stenhouse.

Goodman, Y. (1984) 'The development of initial literacy', in H. Goelman, G. Oberg and F. Smith (eds) *Awakening to Literacy*. Portsmouth, NH: Heinemann.

Goodwin, P. (ed.) (2002) *The Articulate Classroom: Talking and learning in the primary classroom*. London: David Fulton.

Goswami, U. (1995) 'Phonological development and reading by analogy: what is analogy and what is not', *Journal of Research in Reading*, 18(2): 139–45.

Goswami, U. and Bryant, P. (1990) *Phonological Skills and Learning to Read*. Hove, UK: Lawrence Erlbaum.

Gough, P. B. and Tunmer, W. E. (1986) 'Decoding, reading and reading disability', *Remedial and Special Education*, 7: 6–10.

Graddol, D., Leith, D. and Swann, J. (1996) *English History, Diversity and Change*. London: Routledge with the Open University.

Grainger, T. (1997) *Traditional Storytelling in the Primary Classroom*. Leamington Spa, UK: Scholastic.

Grainger, T. (ed.) (2004) *The RoutledgeFalmer Reader in Language and Literacy*. London: RoutledgeFalmer.

Gravelle, M. (2000) *Planning for Bilingual Learners: An inclusive curriculum*. Stoke-on-Trent, UK: Trentham Books.

Gregory, E. (1997) *Making Sense of a New World*. London: Paul Chapman.

Grugeon, E., Dawes, L., Smith, C. and Hubbard, L. (2005) *Teaching Speaking and Listening in the Primary School* (3rd edn). London: David Fulton.

Hall, K. (2003) *Listening to Stephen Read: Multiple perspectives on literacy*. Buckingham: Open University Press.

Hall, N. and Robinson, A. (2003) *Exploring Writing and Play in the Early Years*. London: David Fulton.

Halliday, M. A. K., McIntosh, A. and Strevens, P. (1964) *The Linguistic Sciences and Language Teaching*. London: Longman.

Hannon, P. (2000) *Reflecting on Literacy in Education*. London: RoutledgeFalmer.

Harrison, C. (2004) *Understanding Reading Development*. London: Sage.

Harrison, C. and Coles, M. (2001) *The Reading for Real Handbook*. London: RoutledgeFalmer.

Hatcher, P. J., Hulme, C. and Snowling, M. J. (2004) 'Explicit phoneme training combined with phonic reading instruction helps young children at risk of reading failure', *Journal of Child Psychology and Psychiatry*, 45: 338–58.

Hayes, D. (2000) *The Handbook for Newly Qualified Teachers*. London: David Fulton.

Hayes, D. (2003) *Planning, Teaching and Class Management in Primary Schools* (2nd edn). London: David Fulton.

Head, C. and Waugh, D. (2007) *50 Shared Non-fiction Texts for Year 1*. Leamington Spa, UK: Scholastic.

Heath, S. B. (1983) *Ways with Words*. Cambridge: Cambridge University Press.

Her Majesty's Inspectorate (HMI) (1989) *Aspects of Primary Education: The education of children under five*. London: HMSO.

Hetherington, E. M., Parke, R. D. and Locke, V. O. (1999) *Child Psychology: A contemporary viewpoint* (5th edn). Boston, MA: McGraw-Hill.

Holdaway, D. (1979) *The Foundations of Literacy*. Sydney: Ashton Scholastic Research.

Holdaway, D. (1982) 'Shared book experience: teaching reading using favourite books', *Theory into Practice*, 21(4): 293–300.

House of Commons (Education and Skills Committee) (2005) *Teaching Children to Read*. Norwich: The Stationery Office.

Hughes, T. (1968) *Five Autumn Songs for Children's Voices*. Crediton, UK: Richard Gilbertson.

Hutt, S. J., Tyler, C., Hutt, C. and Christopherson, H. (1989) *Play, Exploration and Learning*. London: Routledge.

Ireson, J., Blatchford, P. and Joscelyne, T. (1995) 'What do teachers do? Classroom activities in the initial teaching of reading', *Educational Psychology*, 15(3): 245–56.

Johnson, D. W. and Johnson, R. T. (1999) *Learning Together and Alone: Cooperation, competitive and individualistic learning* (5th edn). Boston, MA: Allyn & Bacon.

Johnson, D. W., Johnson, R. T. and Holoubec, E. (1988) *Circles of Learning: Cooperation in the classroom* (revised edn). Edina, MN: Interaction Book Company.

Johnson, D. W., Johnson, F. P. and Stanne, M. (2001) *Cooperative Learning Methods: A meta-analysis*. Available at http://www.clcrc.com/pages/cl-methods.html

Johnston, R. and Watson, J. (2005) *The Effects of Synthetic Phonics Teaching on Reading and Spelling Attainment: A seven year longitudinal study*. Edinburgh: Scottish Executive.

Jolliffe, W. (2006a) *Phonics: A complete synthetic programme*. Leamington Spa, UK: Scholastic.

Jolliffe, W. (2006b) 'The National Literacy Strategy: missing a crucial link? A comparative study of the National Literacy Strategy and Success for All', *Education 3–13*, 34(1): 37–48.

Jolliffe, W. (2007) *Cooperative Learning in the Classroom: Putting it into practice*. London: Paul Chapman.

Jolliffe, W., Head, C. and Waugh, D. (2004) *50 Shared Texts for Year 1*. Leamington Spa, UK: Scholastic.

Jolliffe, W., Waugh, D. and Taylor, K. (2005) *All New 100 Literacy Hours, Year R*. Leamington Spa, UK: Scholastic.

Jones, R. and Wyse, D. (eds) (2004) *Creativity in the Primary Curriculum*. London: David Fulton.

Kagan, S. (1994) *Cooperative Learning*. San Juan Capistrano, CA: Kagan Cooperative Learning.

Kenner, C. (2000) *Home Pages: Literacy links for bilingual children*. Stoke-on-Trent, UK: Trentham Books.

Kenner, C. (2004) *Becoming Biliterate: Young children learning different writing systems*. Stoke-on-Trent, UK: Trentham Books.

Kerr, J. (1968) *The Tiger Who Came to Tea*. London: Collins.

Kress, G. (1982) *Learning to Write*. London: Routledge & Kegan Paul.

Kress, G. (1997) *Before Writing: Rethinking the paths to literacy*. London: Routledge.

Kyriacou, C. (1991) *Essential Teaching Skills*. Cheltenham: Stanley Thornes.

Lambirth, A. (2005) *Primary English Reflective Reader*. Exeter: Learning Matters.

Lewis, C. S. (1950) *The Lion, the Witch and the Wardrobe*. Harmondsworth: Penguin.

Littlefair, A. (1991) *Reading All Types of Writing*. Milton Keynes: Open University Press.

Livingstone, S. and Bovill, M. (1999) *Young People, New Media*. London: London School of Economics.

Lloyd, S. (1998) *The Phonics Handbook*. Chigwell, UK: Jolly Learning.

Lofting, H. (1968) *Doctor Doolittle Stories*. London: Cape.

Loughrey, D. (1989) 'Once upon a time ', *Education 3–13*, 17(3): 45–50.

Lucas, B. (2001) 'Creative teaching, teaching creativity and creative learning', in A. Craft, B. Jeffrey and M. Leibling (eds) *Creativity in Education*. London: Continuum.

Luke, C. and Roe, K. (1993) 'Introduction to special issues: media and popular cultural studies in the classroom', *Australian Journal of Education*, 37(2): 115–18.

McIver, A. (no date) *The New First Aid in English*. Glasgow: Robert Gibson.

McKee, D. (1980) *Not Now, Bernard*. London: Red Fox.

McNamara, D. and Waugh, D. (1993) 'Classroom organisation', *School Organization*, 13(1): 41–50.

McWilliam, N. (1998) *What's in a Word? Vocabulary development in multilingual classrooms*. Stoke-on-Trent, UK: Trentham Books.

Mackay, D., Thompson, B. and Schaub, P. (1970) *Breakthrough to Literacy*. London: Longman.

Mackey, M. (1999) 'Popular culture and sophisticated reading: "Men in black"', *English in Education*, 33(1): 47–57.

Magorian, M. (1998) *Goodnight Mr Tom*. Harmondsworth: Penguin.

Malaguzzi, L. (1998) *The Hundred Languages of Children* (2nd edn). Greenwich, CT: Ablex.

Marsh, J. and Hallett, E. (1999) *Desirable Literacies*. London: Sage.

Marsh, J. and Millard, E. (2000) *Literacy and Popular Culture: Using children's culture in the classroom*. London: Paul Chapman.

Medwell, J. and Wray, D., with Moore, G. and Griffiths, V. (2001) *Primary English: Knowledge and understanding*. Exeter: Learning Matters.

Medwell, J., Wray, D., Poulson, L. and Fox, R. (1998) *The Effective Teachers of Literacy Project* (Report of a Research Project commissioned by the Teacher Training Agency). Exeter: University of Exeter.

Medwell, J., Wray, D. and Minns, H. (2001) *Primary English: Teaching theory and practice*. Exeter: Learning Matters.

Mercer, N. (1995) *The Guided Construction of Knowledge: Talk amongst teachers and learners*. Clevedon, UK: Multilingual Matters.

Mercer, N. (2000) *Words and Minds: How we use language to think together*. London: Routledge.

Merchant, G. and Thomas, H. (eds) (1999) *Picture Books for the Literacy Hour: Activities for the primary teacher*. London: David Fulton.

Millard, E. and Marsh, J. (2000) 'Sending Minnie the Minx home: comics and reading choice'. Paper presented at the Education for Social Democracies Conference, Institute of Education, London, July.

Mo, T. (1982) *Sour Sweet*. London: Deutsch.

Montgomery, D. (1997) *Spelling: Remedial Strategies*. London: Cassell.

Morpurgo, M. (1999) *Kensuke's Kingdom*. London: Egmont.

Morris, R. (2001) 'Better teaching fosters better classroom control', *Education*, 107(2): 135–8.

Morris, S. and Collins, J. (2002) *Supporting Pupils for whom English is an Additional Language in the Literacy Hour*. Birmingham: Sandwell Literacy Centre.

Moses, B. and Corbett, P. (2002) *Works 2: Poems for Every Subject and Occasion*. London: Pan Macmillan.

Mosley, J. (1996) *Quality Circle Time*. Wisbech, UK: Learning Development Aids.

Mudd, N. (1994) *Effective Spelling: A practical guide for teachers*. London: Hodder & Stoughton.

Murphy, J. (1974) *The Worst Witch*. London: Young Puffin.

National Reading Panel (2000) *Report of the National Reading Panel. Teaching Children to Read: An evidence-based assessment of the scientific research literature on reading and its implications for reading instruction*. NIH Publication no. 00-4769. Washington, DC: National Institute for Child Health and Human Development.

National Writing Project (1989a) *Responding to and Assessing Writing*. Walton-on-Thames, UK: Nelson.

National Writing Project (1989b) *Responding to Written Work*. Walton-on-Thames, UK: Nelson.

National Writing Project (1990) *Children's Perceptions of Writing*. Walton-on-Thames, UK: Nelson.

Ofsted (1999) *Raising the Attainment of Minority Ethnic Pupils*. London: Ofsted.

Ofsted (2002) *The National Literacy Strategy: The first four years, 1998–2002* (HMI 555). London: Ofsted.

Ogle, L., Sen, A., Pahlke, E., Jocelyn, L., Kastberg, D., Roey, S. and Williams, T. (2003) *International Comparisons in Fourth-Grade Reading Literacy: Findings from the Progress in International Reading Literacy Study (PIRLS) of 2001* (US Department of Education, NCES 2003-073). Washington, DC: US Government Printing Office.

Palinscar, A. S. and Brown, A. L. (1984) 'Reciprocal teaching of comprehension monitoring activities', *Cognition and Instruction*, 1: 117–75.

Peters, M. L. (1970) *Success in Spelling*. Cambridge: Cambridge Institute of Education.

Peters, M. L. (1975) 'Spelling – further thoughts', *Education 3–13*, 3(1).

Peters, M. L. (1985) *Spelling: Caught or Taught? (A New Look)*. London: Routledge & Kegan Paul.

Piaget, J. (1954) *The Construction of Reality in the Child*. New York: Free Press.

Pohan, C. (2003) 'Creating caring and democratic communities in our classrooms and schools', *Childhood Education*, 79(6): 369–73.

Pollard, A. (2002) *Reflective Teaching: Effective and evidence informed professional practice*. London: Continuum.

Pugh, G. (1999) 'Young children and their families', in L. Abbott and H. Moylett (eds) *Early Education Transformed*. London: Falmer Press.

Pullman, P. (1995) *The Firework-maker's Daughter*. London: Doubleday.

Qualifications and Curriculum Authority (QCA) (2001) *Planning for Learning in the Foundation Stage*. Ref: QCA 01/799. London: QCA Publications.

Qualifications and Curriculum Authority (QCA)/Department for Education and Skills (DfES) (2003) *Speaking, Listening, Learning: Working with children in Key Stages 1 and 2*. London: HMSO.

Robinson, K. (2001) *Out of our Minds: Learning to be creative*. Oxford: Capstone.

Robinson, M. (1997) *Children Reading Print and Television*. London: Falmer Press.

Rosenblatt, L. (1978) *The Reader, the Text, the Poem: The transactional theory of literacy work*. Carbondale, IL: South Illinois University Press.

Rosenblatt, L. (1989) 'Writing and reading: the transactional theory', in J. Mason (ed.) *Reading and Writing Connections*. Boston, MA: Allyn & Bacon.

Ross, A. (1992) *Inspirations for Speaking and Listening*. Leamington Spa, UK: Scholastic.

Rowling, J. K. (1997) *Harry Potter and the Philosopher's Stone*. London: Bloomsbury.

Rumelhart, D. E. and Mcclelland, J. L. (eds) (1986) *Parallel Distributed Processing, Vol. 1: Foundations*. Cambridge, MA: MIT Press.

Schonell, F. J. (1957) *Essentials in Teaching and Testing Spelling*. London: Macmillan.

Seidenberg, M. S. and McClelland, J. L. (1989) 'A distributed, developmental model of word recognition and naming', *Psychological Review*, 96: 523–68.

Sendak, M. (1970) *Where the Wild Things Are*. Harmondsworth: Penguin.

Sharan, S. (1990) *Cooperative Learning: Theory and research*. Westport, CT: Praeger.

Shaw, B. (1916) *Pygmalion*. New York: Brentano. Available at http://www.bartleby.com/138

Siraj-Blatchford, I. (1994) *The Early Years: Laying the foundations for racial equality*. Stoke-on-Trent, UK: Trentham Books.

Skinner, B. F. (1957) *Verbal Behavior*. New York: Prentice Hall.

Slavin, R. E. (1983) *Cooperative Learning*. New York: Longman.

Slavin, R. E. (1995) *Cooperative Learning: Theory, research, and practice*. Boston, MA: Allyn & Bacon.

Slavin, R. E. and Madden, N. A. (2005) *Fast Track Phonics, Volumes 1–3*. Nottingham: Success for All-UK.

Smith, F. (1971) *Understanding Reading: A psycholinguistic analysis of reading and learning to read*. New York: Holt, Rinehart & Winston.

Smith, F., Hardman, F., Wall, K. and Mroz, M. (2004) 'Interactive whole class teaching in the National Literacy and Numeracy Strategies', *British Educational Research Journal*, 30: 395–411.

Snow, C. E., Burns, S. and Griffin, P. (1998) *Preventing Reading Difficulties in Young Children*. Washington, DC: National Academy Press. Available at http://www.nap.edu/readingroom/books/prdyc/execsumm.html.

Storr, C. (1967) *Clever Polly and the Stupid Wolf*. London: Puffin.

Sutcliff, R. (2004) *The Eagle of the Ninth*. Oxford: Oxford University Press.

Sweeney, J. (1999) *50 Fantastic Poems with Wonderful Writing Prompts*. New York: Scholastic Professional Books.

Sylva, K., Melhuish, E., Sammons, P., Siraj-Blatchford, I. and Taggart, B. (2004) *Effective Pre School and Primary Education*. London: DfES/Sure Start. Available at http://www.ioe.ac.uk/projects/eppe/

Tann, S. (1991) *Developing Language in the Primary Classroom*. London: Cassell.

Teacher Training Agency (TTA) (2000) *Raising the Attainment of Minority Ethnic Pupils: Guidance and resource material for providers of initial teacher training*. London: TTA.

Thomas, W. and Collier, V. (1997) *School Effectiveness and Language Minority Students*. Washington, DC: National Clearing House for Bilingual Education.

Tizard, B. and Hughes, M. (1984) *Young Children Learning: Talking and thinking at home and at school*. London: Fontana.

Todd, J. (1982) *Learning to Spell*. Oxford: Blackwell.

Topping, K. (2001) *Thinking Reading Writing*. London: Continuum.

United Kingdom Literacy Association and Primary National Strategy (UKLA/PNS) (2004) *Raising Boys' Achievements in Writing*. Royston, UK: UKLA.

Vygotsky, L. S. (1962) *Thought and Language*. Cambridge, MA: MIT Press.

Vygotsky, L. S. (1978) *Mind in Society: The development of higher psychological processes*. Cambridge, MA: Harvard University Press.

Vygotsky, L. S. (1986) *Thought and Language* (translated, revised and edited by A. Kozulin). Cambridge, MA: MIT Press.

Waugh, D. (1996) *Curriculum Bank Writing at Key Stage 1*. Leamington Spa, UK: Scholastic.

Waugh, D. (1998) 'Practical approaches to teaching punctuation in the primary school', *Reading*, 32(2): 14–17.

Waugh, D. (2000a) *Further Curriculum Bank Writing at Key Stage 1*. Leamington Spa, UK: Scholastic.

Waugh, D. (2000b) *Further Curriculum Bank Writing at Key Stage 2*. Leamington Spa, UK: Scholastic.

Waugh, D. (2005) *All New 100 Literacy Hours: Year 2*. Leamington Spa, UK: Scholastic.

Waugh, D. with McGuinn, N. (1996) *Curriculum Bank Writing at Key Stage 2*. Leamington Spa, UK: Scholastic.

Waugh, D., Jolliffe, W. and Taylor, K. (1999) *100 Literacy Hours for Year 2*. Leamington Spa, UK: Scholastic.

Wells, G. (1986) *The Meaning Makers*. London: Heinemann Educational.

Wells, G., Chang, G. and Maher, A. (1990) 'The literate potential of collaborative talk', in M. Maclure, T. Phillips and A. Wilkinson (eds) *Oracy Matters*. Milton Keynes: Open University Press.

Welsh Language Board (1999) *Two Languages: Twice the choice* (pamphlet). Cardiff: Welsh Language Board.

Whitehead, M. (2002) 'Dylan's routes to literacy: the first three years with picture books', *Journal of Early Childhood Literacy*, 2(3): 269–89.

Whitehead, M. (2004) *Language and Literacy in the Early Years* (3rd edn). London: Sage.

Wilkinson, A. (1965) *Spoken English* (*Educational Review* occasional publications, no. 2). Birmingham: University of Birmingham.

Williams, R. (1965) *The Long Revolution*. Harmondsworth: Penguin.

Wilson, A. (2005) *Language Knowledge for Primary Teachers*. London: David Fulton.

Wood, D. (1986) 'Aspects of teaching and learning', in M. Richards and P. Light (eds) *Children of Social Worlds*. Cambridge: Polity Press.

Wood, D. (1988) *How Children Think and Learn*. Oxford: Blackwell.

Wragg, E. C. (1993) *Class Management*. London: Routledge.

Wragg, E. C. (1997) *The Cubic Curriculum*. London: Routledge.

Wragg, E. C., Wragg, C. M., Haynes, G. S. and Chamberlain, R. P. (1998) *Improving Literacy in the Primary School*. London: Routledge.

Wray, D. (1995) *English 7–11*. London: Routledge.

Wray, D. (2004) *Teaching Literacy: Using texts to enhance learning*. London: David Fulton.

Wray, D. (2006) *Teaching Literacy across the Primary Curriculum*. Exeter: Learning Matters.

Zar, J. (1992) 'Candidate for a pullet surprise' (spelling checker poem). Available at http://www.bios.niu.edu/zar/poem.pdf

# Index

## DATE DUE